Strategy for Survival

An Exploration of the Limits to Further Population and Industrial Growth

Arthur S. Boughey
University of California at Irvine

W.A. Benjamin, Inc.
Menlo Park, California • Reading, Massachusetts • London
Amsterdam • Don Mills, Ontario • Sydney

Acknowledgment is gratefully made to the authors and publishers who permitted us to reproduce the following illustrations:

Figures 3-17, 5-5, 5-10, 6-2, 6-7, 6-8, 6-9, 6-10, 7-8, 7-9, 8-1, 8-2, 8-3, and 8-4. From THE LIMITS TO GROWTH: *A report for THE CLUB OF ROME's Project on the Predicament of Mankind,* by Donella H. Meadows, Jørgen Randers, William W. Behrens III. A Potomac Associates book published by Universe Books, New York, 1972. Graphics by Potomac Associates.

Figures 3-4, 3-5, 5-11, 6-3, 6-4, 6-5, and 6-6. From *THINKING ABOUT THE FUTURE,* by H.S.D. Cole, Christopher Freeman, Marie Jahoda, and K.L.R. Pavitt (Eds.), Sussex University Press. THINKING ABOUT THE FUTURE was published in the United States under the title, MODELS OF DOOM, *A Critique of the Limits to Growth,* Universe Books, New York, 1973.

Figures 9-8, 9-9A, 9-9B, 9-10, 9-11, 9-12, 9-13, 9-14, and 9-15. From *Mankind at the Turning Point* by Mihajlo Mesarovic and Eduard Pestel. Copyright © 1974 by Mihajlo Mesarovic and Eduard Pestel. Reprinted by permission of the publisher, E.P. Dutton & Co., Inc.

ISBN 0-8053-1095-9
ABCDEFGHIJ -AL-79876

W.A. Benjamin, Inc.
2725 Sand Hill Road
Menlo Park, California 94025

Preface

This book has been prepared as a basic account of the development of social systems simulation models, and their implications as to the possible limits to growth, in both size and activities, of our global human populations.

Since their appearance at the beginning of the decade, the Forrester-Meadows world models have provided the central theme for a number of college courses on the limits to growth in our global social systems. This was the case with a lower division, nonmajor course which I developed and offered over the past four years at the University of California at Irvine. Because of the encouragement I received in presenting the course, and because the current world dilemma involves each and every one of us, I compiled and organized this present text. The assembled material provides a setting into which we can insert the fast-moving scenarios of current national and international events, and I believe every college student should be exposed to such an anlysis of the sequence of cause and effect in both domestic and world affairs.

This work has been extensively illustrated with both original and already published material. Much of the present information on global-systems modeling is contained in exhaustively detailed publications. Critical extracts from these have, with the tolerant cooperation of their authors and publishers, been assembled here in one text.

Biographical source material, including the aforementioned works as well as others on a suitable level, is listed at the end of each chapter. In order to avoid repetition, each reference is listed only in the chapter in which it is first mentioned, although reference to it may occur in later chapters; the sources of the brief quotations from various authorities that reinforce the argument in the main text are treated similarly.

Chapter 1 traces the explosive expansion of both population and industry since the onset of the Industrial Revolution and shows how this has led the world to its present growth dilemma. Chapter 2 describes the nature of exponential growth, while Chapter 3 describes the possible limits to exponential growth, especially in terms of population and resources. It examines limits to food and industrial production, as well as considering energy and mineral reserves, and accumulating pollution.

The basic features of systems models are described and illustrated by reference to familiar situations in Chapter 4. Chapter 5 describes the modeling of our global systems — in particular the Forrester-Meadows World 1 and World 2 models — and describes the criticisms leveled against them. Chapter 6 explores the possibility of continuous growth in this world system by the development and introduction of various technological innovations. The effects that a modification of population policies would have on the world system are discussed and modeled in Chapter 7, and Chapter 8 considers the technological and population control policies necessary to bring the world system into equilibrium.

Regional systems, as opposed to global systems, are examined in Chapter 9, and reference is made to the Mesarovic-Pestel model and its several scenarios. Finally, Chapter 10 explores human society even more deeply, on a national rather than a regional or global basis. It discusses the prospects for the development of a stable egalitarian world and the strategies that appear, from various modeling exercises, to offer the most realistic prospects for the achievement of such a utopia.

Because the uniqueness of our human species resides in our ability to achieve, transmit, and adapt to cultural advances rapidly, we have the extraordinary ability to cope with change in our physical environment. This has, of late, begun to prove somewhat of a mixed blessing. While it has undoubtedly permitted our most advanced societies extensively to exploit the natural resources of this planet, and enormously to increase both their material productivity and their leisure periods, it has also caused ecological degradation on such a scale as to have brought our total global system close to the brink of environmental disaster.

In its material evolution, the cultural history of humankind is a still-unfolding account of the continuous fashioning of ever more effective new tools. Our conceptual progress likewise has been concurrent with the development of increasingly powerful analytical instruments. From the first simple microscopes that enabled us to perceive the cellular structure of tissues, to the linear accelerators that permit us to theorize the ultimate physical particle, each new instrument devised by science has revealed a smaller cosmos within what we, for a time, believed to be the ultimate microcosm.

Thirty-five years ago a revolutionary new instrument, the electronic computer, was developed. It has enabled us to reverse this earlier concentration upon the search for the ultimate microcosm and directed attention instead toward the quest for the ultimate *macrocosm*. It has enabled us to approach, for the first time, the total *function* of our universe, rather than its minute ultimate structure. Initially computer technology was exploited primarily for processes of information retrieval and statistical calculation, and its immense potential in the systems analysis of social behavior remained largely unrealized. Only in the past ten years have various independent applications of computer technology begun to direct attention to its immense potential for solving a wide range of social problems. It was high time for such innovation; it has been apparent for more than a decade that our global human population has entered an entirely new behavioral mode, very different from the one that had prevailed since the industrial revolution first began approximately two centuries ago.

Already, in its developing application to this new field of social systems modeling, computer technology has had both its greatest and its most controversial success. At first, social models were expressed in words or graphic symbols. Later it became evident that they were more clearly stated in mathematical equations. The most recent attempts at the preparation of social systems models in these terms merely reveal a multiplicity of nonlinear processes. Before these can be integrated into a simulation model, they must be cycled sequentially through a series of iterative steps, a process far beyond our computational ability without the aid of computers. Many social problems are now being approached by following a computer modeling technology, and modeling processes different from the original systems dynamics procedure are developing separate techniques and languages, as well as simulating various human environmental interactions.

A.S. Boughey
October 1976

Contents

Introduction

It is difficult for citizens in the industrialized societies of modern developed nations to appreciate that we are in the midst of the greatest social revolution that our world has ever known. Our own problems in these societies are largely economic. We wait, more or less patiently according to our temperament and our circumstances, for an end to the ever present threats of recession and a return to the status quo of privileged elitism. We hope that interest rates and unemployment will go down again, that the Stock Exchange and car sales will continue to rise, and that construction and development will recommence as before. We trust that the Organization of Petroleum Exporting Countries (OPEC) will eventually be broken and oil prices lowered. It is just a question of finding the right stimulus to restart the economy, or so traditional economic paradigms and political leaders of all parties would have us believe. Radical revolutionaries have for many years been predicting a very different kind of outcome from such recessional periods, but they have usually been dismissed as misguided subversives and ignored along with garbage, pollution, poverty, crime, and other distressing features of modern industrialized urban life. The urgent question that we must all now ask ourselves is: Into what kind of world will we finally emerge? What is it like for those unfortunates still on the other side of affluence? Can they too make it into this comfortable elitist world? Perhaps an even more basic question is: Do they wish to do so?

A few better-educated members of the nation-states that constitute the underdeveloped world have long been very much aware of how things actually stand, but they were rarely the political leaders. At first, when their nations continued to cooperate economically with their previous colonial masters, or former preferred trading partners, their voices were rarely heard outside their own countries. Only student protesters were sufficiently vocal and visible enough to attract momentary international attention. Now, suddenly, the industrialized nations have been forced to pay full attention to such messages. One member of the Western club has been blackballed by the General Assembly of the United Nations, and another may receive the same treatment. Indeed, the United Nations may not be the toothless tiger that Garrett Hardin maintains its originators intended it to be. Inspired by OPEC, other cartels are rapidly forming with the avowed intent of advancing astronomically the price of commodities essential to industrialized national economies. The whole relationship of buyer and seller in the international market has been reversed. Originally, the industrialized societies, most of whom to a certain degree soon exhausted their domestic reserves of at least some of the nonrenewable resources vital to industrial production, adjusted to these shortages by annexing further supplies in a series of colonial or neocolonial adventures. In their trade relationships with these annexed and dependent territories, the metropolitan industrial powers fixed the market price for the raw materials that were traded for their manufactured products. The price was right so long as the junior partners were willing to continue in an essentially agrarian societal stage.

> On the assumption that Americans do not pursue even more environmentally destructive activities in the future, an increase of 75 million Americans would be equivalent to adding 3.7 billion Indians to the world population. From the standpoint of consumption of scarce fuel and mineral resources, 75 million additional Americans are the equivalent of 2 billion Colombians, 10 billion Nigerians, or 22 billion Indonesians.
>
> D. N. Thompson, 1973

Once, however, an agrarian society developed aspirations of becoming an industrialized society, with the same living standards as its former master, the inequity of the previous trading arrangements became all too apparent. The same realization came to the workers within industrialized societies, who eventually perceived that the material rewards for their labor could be raised substantially by utilizing their own particular forms of cartel and embargo — the union and the strike. Two passages from the agreed resolutions emerging from the 1974 World Population Conference in Bucharest epitomize these changed relationships between developed and underdeveloped nations and between rich and poor. They read:

> Recognizing that per capita use of world resources is much higher in the more developed countries, the developed countries are urged to adopt appropriate policies in population, consumption, and investment, bearing in mind the need for fundamental improvement in international equity. . . .

> It is imperative that all countries, and within them all social sectors, should adapt themselves to more rational utilization of natural resources, without excess, so that some are not deprived of what others waste.

The socioeconomic systems of the urbanized world have gradually evolved from our earliest settlements, first established some fifteen thousand or so years ago, and are thus for the first time universally and very seriously threatened from both within and without. Some of the industrialized nations, such as Italy and Britain, show every sign of imminent monetary collapse. Agrarian nations like Bangladesh, Chad, and Ruanda equally appear at risk of biological failure, due to the neo-Malthusian factors of famine and pestilence. Portugal and Ethiopia show obvious signs of political instability. Such dire threats of imminent disaster from one cause or another have provoked an increasing number of exercises intended to explore the nature of constraints limiting continuing socioeconomic growth, and to estimate the reality of the prospects of possible system failures. Most of these exercises proceed additionally to examine the necessary steps that must be taken to avoid eventual system collapse — the knockout or KO, as the Europeans have chosen to describe it.

This rather sudden emergence of a holistic and ecological approach to human systems came as no surprise to ecologists, who have long been concerned with stability in the natural systems they investigate. It required a greater effort of accommodation on the part of social scientists, long nurtured upon the more comfortable assurance of the growth ethic. The Forrester-Meadows models described in this text pioneered this new study of the equilibrium state in social systems, utilizing the innovative systems dynamics computer modeling technique. The successful construction of such simulation and predictive social models for all familiar human situations will represent the greatest progress we have yet achieved in our quest for the power that will enable us ultimately fully to control our own destiny.

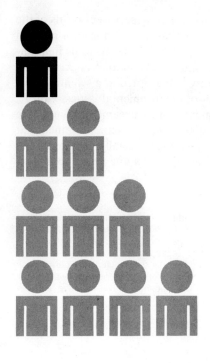

Chapter One

The Human
Predicament

In June 1974 the U.S. House of Representatives rejected by a vote of 201 to 204 a Land-Use Planning Act. This bill had been prepared in an attempt to introduce greater coherence to regional land-use decisions. It made available grants enabling individual states to institute a statewide land-use planning process, and eventually a state land-use program. It would have required the compilation of a state inventory of natural resources as the basis on which to decide the future course of development. Environmental values, energy, and recreational and economic considerations would have received special emphasis.

Such evaluations are particularly pertinent at this time, because whereas less than 200,000 of the 3.6 million square miles of the United States are presently included in urban areas, the Commission on Population Growth and the American Future estimates that in another twenty-five years approximately half a million square miles will be so covered. The Land-Use Planning Act would have guided this 150 percent expansion of the nation's urban area by providing the essential information base from which to develop plans to minimize further environmental degradation.

Bedroom versus Boardroom Issues

The schismatic nature of the vote in the House on the Land-Use Planning Act reflected a deeply divisive opinion in the country at large, one that indeed still persists. This is well evidenced by the American newspaper editorials of the time, which accentuate this general divisiveness that has been such a marked characteristic of the nation in the present decade. Its basis seems to lie in a fundamental ignorance as to the real nature and effects of our concern over resource utilization. In 1972, this same disunity had erupted in a scientific controversy between two well-known promoters of environmental issues, Paul R. Ehrlich and Barry Commoner. Their argument, which became known as the *bedroom versus boardroom conflict,* developed because Ehrlich maintained that the present deterioration of the environment is due especially to the human population explosion, while Commoner insisted that it is due rather to uncontrolled industrial expansion.

> Nowadays, more than ever before, man tends toward continual, often accelerated, growth — of population, land occupancy, production, consumption, waste, etc. — blindly assuming that his environment will permit such expansion, that other groups will yield, or that science and technology will remove the obstacles.

Executive Committee of the Club of Rome, 1972 (commentary in The Limits to Growth*)*

Although these two distinguished scientists soon agreed upon a truce in order to battle the common enemy — environmental degradation — the issue reappeared, this time on an international scale, at the United Nations conference in Bucharest in 1974 that was called to examine the question of world population growth. The thirty-one nations presently judged to constitute the industrialized world were apparently somewhat disturbed to find that their suggestions to the remainder of the world as regards the immediate implementation of rigorous population control measures were roundly countered by accusations that the real issue was not continuing population growth, but the unabashed industrial expansion to which each one of these industrialized nations was enthusiastically committed.

Early Environmental Warnings

The first warnings that such international controversies might eventually arise came in the form of now classical writings from several perceptive authors. Thomas Malthus is commonly recognized as the first such worker to warn, in the late eighteenth century, that populations were outrunning their food supplies. Earlier, Adam Smith had observed that economic growth was the product of capital accumulation and technical invention. He conceded that a stationary economic growth would ultimately develop, but did not forecast the inevitable disasters that Malthus predicted would arise from the circumstance that population increase was of a geometric form, while food production increase was of arithmetic form. A third classical economist, David Ricardo, was, like Malthus, more pessimistic in his views on the future prospects facing mankind. He predicted that continuing economic growth would result in higher wages, reducing returns on agricultural investments and raising the price of agricultural goods. It was not, however, until 1968, when Paul Ehrlich produced his popular work, *The Population Bomb,* that such classical views of growth were once more brought dramatically to our attention.

> Thus far, we have met each new piece of bad news with disbelief and sometimes outrage. There has been a lot of talk about "who is to blame," and some groups have taken the position that they have been singled out for unfair treatment. . . . charges and counter charges fill the air, clog the media, and do nothing at all to hasten an adjustment to new ways of life.
>
> *P. R. Ehrlich and A. H. Ehrlich, 1974*

The earliest warnings of environmental deterioration were sounded by Rachel Carson in her *Silent Spring,* published in 1962. Her work addressed more especially the perils of unrestricted use of persistent broad-spectrum pesticides. Barry Commoner, in 1972, in *The Closing Circle,* examined the whole question of industrial pollution and its environmental effects. The assumption that the global environment was a universal sink into which anyone had a perfect right to empty unwanted wastes was elegantly portrayed in 1968 by Garrett Hardin in his paper "The Tragedy of the Commons."

These early twentieth-century warnings as to the consequences of unrestricted population growth and the associated environmental degradation were followed after an interval of a few years by the construction of several models whose purpose was to test the validity of the various doomsday prophecies inherent in these several warnings. The first and most famous of these models, which has received the greatest publicity, is the Forrester-Meadows series of world models outlined in *The Limits to Growth* in 1972, and discussed in more detail in *Toward Global Equilibrium,* published the year after, and in several later works. These Forrester-Meadows models, as already mentioned, were produced by a group of scientists working initially from the Sloan School of Management at the Massachusetts Institute of Technology, under the sponsorship of a private research promoting group, the Club of Rome. The models were constructed upon the principle of *system dynamics.* The concept of system dynamics computer models as applied to social systems had been developed several years earlier at M.I.T. by J. W. Forrester, who described it in its more complete forms in his *Urban Dynamics,* published in 1969, and *World Dynamics,* published in 1971.

System Dynamics Computer Models

System dynamics is a methodology that requires the construction of a mental or written plan of a system incorporating the feedback loops that determine the various rate variables. When the several cybernetic interactions in the plan are translated into mathematical expressions that are then incorporated into a computer program, what results is known as a *system dynamics computer model.* A system dynamics computer model of any social system is at this present stage an admittedly imperfect simulation of a real-world social system. Nevertheless, such models can be tested and further refined in terms of the validity of their simulative capacity. The veracity of each component mathematical expression can be checked and, if necessary, modified or amplified. At any stage of development of a system dynamics computer model, its predictive potentiality can be utilized. In all ways, it therefore has to be both more comprehensive and more accurate than the mental models that have until now provided the sole basis for individual and governmental decisions.

As J. W. Forrester — the acknowledged founder of the application of system dynamics to social systems — remarks, we have in the past tended to use computers in the wrong way. Computers do very well some things that the human brain cannot so effectively do (such as mass computations), and perform rather badly some of the operations (like decision making) that the human brain does rather well. Despite these obvious limitations, we have in the past tended to use computers for what we ourselves do well, and neglected to employ them for the activities that we ourselves perform somewhat ineffectively. Using computer models in system dynamics, a model can be reconstructed and improved repeatedly until it faithfully combines and traces the sequences of interactions that result from the statements of behavior incorporated within it. Such a model, while it is constructed from mathematical assumptions, incorporates the multiple feedback loops of real systems, and reflects their linear or nonlinear relationships. A mental model considers only one-on-one linear processes in the form of partial regressions. It cannot cope with multiple interactions or nonlinear relationships. This difference between system dynamics computer models and the intuitive mental models that they supersede explains why the paradigms we have until now used to explain the functions of our social systems are beginning frequently to prove ineffective. The systems dynamics approach emphasizes the inflexibility of these earlier paradigms, and underscores the fact that their sometimes faulty premises cannot be corrected simply by the collection and input of additional information.

If further proof of this circumstance is needed, it is provided by recent writings in history and economics. These two classical disciplines once provided the social paradigms on which it was possible to arrive at some understanding of the manner in which human societies function, or at least how they functioned in the past. The failure of mental models to provide any rational forecasting capability is well illustrated by two representative recent works, by

Gerhard Hirschfeld in history, and by R. L. Heilbroner in economics. While excellent within the classical context of their respective disciplines, both of these works, and others like them, were published well after the fact. They merely confirm subjectively and intuitively the futuristic conclusions already deduced, presented, and objectively substantiated by the construction of system dynamics computer models.

Several other groups about the world had been simultaneously pursuing such futuristic issues, originally without the use of system dynamics computer models. Sometimes their reactions were especially strong, not so much to the use of such models as to the particular conclusions drawn from the global model of the Meadows group. This was the case with the Sussex group, a consortium of specialists working at the University of Sussex in the United Kingdom, whose specific criticisms, together with those of others, will be considered later. Interestingly, one group of futurologists, what may be termed the Ehrlich establishment, has recently published dire doomsday scenarios without any consideration of, or reference to, system dynamics computer models. Perhaps at least partly because of this omission, these scenarios appear presently to have gained little credence.

The modeling of social systems by the system dynamics approach can usually be based on present constructs of particular interactions and on already available data. It does not necessarily entail the acquisition of new data. When the available statistics are entered as data in the computer model and run for an appropriate time, the results are, however, frequently unexpected and contrary to intuitive mental models of the system. Thus, these computer models provide for more flexible conceptual responses in a rapidly changing world than is within the capacity of a mental model.

Urban Models

Forrester first developed the system dynamics approach to industrial models in the 1950s and described it in *Industrial Dynamics*. He then applied this technique, the simulation of dynamic computer models, to fundamental urban processes and described it in *Urban Dynamics* in 1968. He tested these models against common traditional programs for improving depressed areas in the inner city. Traditional urban renewal practices included such procedures as increasing the number of jobs, devising training programs to increase skills, offering financial aid to the depressed area, and providing for the construction of low-cost housing. Forrester's urban systems model revealed that the effects of these four traditional procedures on the depressed area to which they were being applied ranged from neutral to detrimental. He attributed this to the fact that the basic circumstance that results in the development of depressed areas in the inner city is an *excess* of low-income housing, rather than a housing shortage in this category. Tax and legal practices usually combine to encourage the

retention of old buildings in such areas. As these buildings age, they are occupied by progressively lower income groups, who, in order to afford such ac-
commodations, are compelled to occupy them at high-population densities.
The neighborhood population rises on this account, but the number of industrial jobs does not; it becomes more difficult to find work. Thus a social trap
is created. High-density populations are attracted by the low-cost housing, but
this in-migration movement swamps the available employment opportunities.
Eventually, the lack of job activity curtails further in-migration to the area and
leaves some of the aging housing empty, abandoned, and in disrepair. Nevertheless the buildings that are occupied are crowded, while the abandoned housing stands vacant and in unsound condition. If the job market is improved by
resorting to one device or another, the abandoned buildings tend to be reoc-
cupied, but again at high density.

This apparently inexorable process of development and decay had long
been explained on a basis of what is known as the *Burgess zonal hypothesis,* a
dynamic written model developed over forty years ago. According to this zonal
hypothesis, urban activities could be grouped on a basis of their arrangement in
successive concentric zones, which from the center outward are:

1. A central business district
2. Wholesale commerce
3. Slum dwellings
4. Middle-income industrial workers' residences
5. Upper-income single-family residences
6. Upper-income suburban commuter residences

Because the Burgess model was of a dynamic, not static form, it is the
zonal *sequence* that is fixed, not the static position of each zone. As the city
grows, each zone encroaches on its outward neighbor, creating a *transition
zone.*

The Forrester system dynamics computer model of such an urban situation demonstrates that improvement in the deteriorated neighborhoods of the
inner city — that is, Burgess zone 3 — can be attained only by *decreasing,* not
increasing, the amount of high-density housing available. By so limiting the
amount of high-density housing, the job market is improved, because fewer
people can live in the area and a scarcity of available labor is created. The job
market cannot be swamped by in-migration because no vacant accommoda-
tions are available, and people are unable to move in and take up residence in
the area. Moreover, the unused housing units that have been condemned can be
demolished to make way for industrial facilities that can offer still more
employment.

In fact, urban system dynamics models demonstrate than an increase in
the population of a city crowds housing, overloads job opportunities, creates
congestion, increases pollution and crime, and generally reduces the quality of

urban life. The Forrester models also demonstrate that an equilibrium is approached when this quality of life is so lowered that the attractive features of the area are neutralized, and there is no remaining inducement for further inmigration. Before this equilibrium point is reached, however, the social trap will have closed on a large mass of unfortunates who remain entangled in the system, unable to escape.

> . . . system dynamics computer models . . . are strikingly similar to mental models. They are derived from the same sources. They may be discussed in the same terms. But computer models differ from mental models in important ways. The computer models are stated explicitly. The "mathematical" notation used for describing the model is unambiguous. It is a language that is clearer, simpler, and more precise than such spoken languages as English and French. . . . The language of a computer model can be understood by almost anyone.
>
> *J. W. Forrester, 1973*

The Forrester-Meadows Global Models

The application of system dynamics to the study of the *global* socioeconomic system was first described at an international conference on world problems in 1970. At this conference, J. W. Forrester presented a dynamic model of the interactions between global population, industrialization, depletion of natural resources, agriculture, and pollution. This model, often referred to as World 2, was described in a book published by Forrester a year later and entitled *World Dynamics*.

This first global model was then expanded and developed by a group of Forrester's associates working initially at M.I.T., now at Dartmouth College, and including D. H. Meadows and D. L. Meadows. This second model is often known as World 3; it was initially described in summary in *The Limits to Growth*. This publication aroused much interest and provoked further controversy of the kind that had greeted the presentation of World 2.

As recently and somewhat inadequately outlined by Peter Roberts, these Forrester-Meadows models stimulated various efforts around the world to emulate and improve upon the World 2 and World 3 models, and even to challenge their conclusions. The motivation of these several groups appears to vary somewhat, but the publication of their results, anticipated over the next few years, should provide interesting commentaries on the current modeling work described in this text.

Concern over rising crime rates, decline in the environment, changing family structure and relationships have all contributed to a general feeling of unease. It is as if society was on the verge of, or perhaps even in the first phase of, some kind of vast social or cultural revolution whose exact nature has not yet been understood but of which people see premonitions all around them.

H. G. Simmons, 1973

Specific Resource Models

The global resource computer models prepared by the Forrester-Meadows group on a system dynamics basis represent, as it were, a second stage of the environmental alerts sounded in the first place in the several non-modeling works listed earlier. The Forrester-Meadows models will be considered at some length later in this text. A third stage of environmental alerts is represented by models relating to specific resource items or to specific regional areas. Indeed, the Forrester-Meadows global models themselves required the prior construction of models that followed individual resource items. For example, as described in *Toward Global Equilibrium*, the fate of DDT in the global environment was modeled in this manner, as will be discussed in Chapter 3.

One way of looking at pollution such as occurs from DDT persistence is to regard it as a constraint on population size. This general concept was modeled by G. R. Ultsch several years ago (Fig. 1−1). He considers that environmental deterioration results from an overloading of the natural pathways for decomposition of waste, and failure to establish effective alternate pathways for artificial decomposition to handle various human wastes. The pollution model that Ultsch developed provides for a balancing of human production against natural and artificial decomposition so that pollution does not occur.

Regional Models

Of the earlier regional models that have been produced, perhaps *Blue Print for Survival*, which described the steps that Great Britain would have to take in order that its population could live within its small island areas, provoked the most controversy. The most recent global attempt to model the whole world by regions will be examined when the Mesarovic-Pestel models are presented. The regional type of model that has now begun increasingly to appear can be illustrated by a recent study of Kern County, California. This model demonstrates the critical role that water plays in Kern and the other rich agricultural counties of the lower basin of the San Joaquin Valley of California.

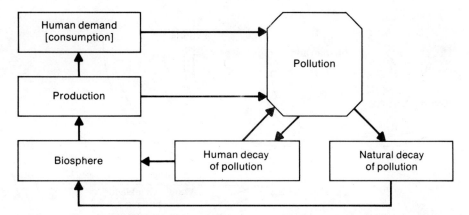

Figure 1—1 Population and pollution. A simple feedback model illustrating how accumulating wastes operate to control population increase. If the pollution generated by human activities is not disposed of by natural processes of decay, it must be handled by human-generated processes; otherwise, it will accumulate in the biosphere and inhibit further natural and industrial production. From G. R. Ultsch, 1973.

A Regional Water Model
for Kern County

Kern County is the most productive of the five adjoining counties comprising the lower basin of the San Joaquin Valley in California, the others being Kings, Tulare, Fresno, and Merced counties, which between them produce 80 percent of the agricultural products of the state. Apart from a declining petroleum extraction industry, the most significant economic activity in Kern County is agriculture, or agriculture-related industry. Rainfall is very light, rarely exceeding more than 4—5 inches a year; and this agricultural industry is entirely dependent on irrigation water, supplied by the Kern River, by subsurface pumping, and by canals supplying imported water. The relationship between these several variable inputs is shown in the system dynamics process model in Figure 1—2. By further definition of the several variables, this socioeconomic system can be represented by the flow chart shown in Figure 1—3. From this flow chart, a computer program can be prepared permitting the model to be run with various inputs. Table 1—1 shows the result of running the Kern model for one hundred years with these variable inputs as indicated. Table 1—2 summarizes Table 1—1, comparing the output with population projections for the area.

It is clear from this modeling investigation that unless some change in the socioeconomic structure of the Kern County region is soon implemented, it will become a depressed region, or one from which considerable net out-migration

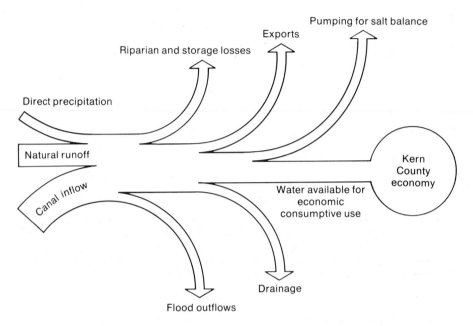

Figure 1−2   A model depicting the elements involved in water and salt balance in Kern County, California.   This process model shows how the various inputs and outputs of water in the Kern County economy can be related diagrammatically to one another. It was developed by Don C. Wilkin.

will occur. Possible changes that would prevent the realization of this system dynamic computer model prediction are an immediate and drastic curtailment of population growth, the provision of a substantial further input of water from outside sources, extensive modification of irrigation practices, or the establishment of nonpolluting, nonwater-using industries. For the moment, none of these four events appear imminent, although a limited amount of "drip" irrigation is now being introduced and plans for construction of a "peripheral canal" further north to bring in more irrigation water have been under discussion for some time. This peripheral canal would arc across the drainage basin of the Sacramento and San Joaquin rivers in Northern California, and remove up to two thirds of their fresh water flow, which otherwise passes into San Francisco Bay (Fig. 1−4). Hardly surprisingly, plans for the construction of the peripheral canal are strongly opposed by the environmental groups that are vigorously engaged in conserving what remains of San Francisco Bay.

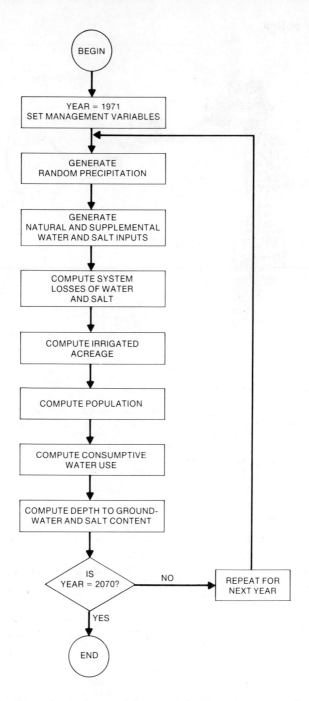

Figure 1−3 Flow chart of a model to analyze Kern County, California, water requirements. This model, developed by Don C. Wilkin, relates water use in Kern County to the human carrying capacity as dictated by water supply. The various iterations in the computer program are indicated as sequential operations in this flow chart. After D. C. Wilkin, unpublished work.

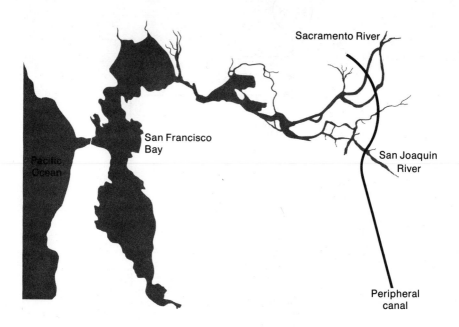

Table 1−1   Output from the Kern County water model. These data are systems variables obtained from the model shown in Figures 1−2 and 1−3, which follows water use in Kern County, California. They show the human carrying capacity in terms of various irrigation procedures and several projected further water sources.

Model Projections for Year 2070		East Side Canal Peripheral Canal	East Side Canal	Peripheral Canal	Neither
Salt balanced by pumping average groundwater	Population	406,270	391,450	345,462	333,621
	Irrigated acres	690,551	651,699	531,117	500,084
	Conductance	810	774	1,035	1,023
	Depth	248	252	249	251
Salt balanced by pumping only groundwater over 2,000 micromhos	Population	453,601	451,588	382,964	375,523
	Irrigated acres	814,637	809,344	629,414	609,941
	Conductance	843	876	871	883
	Depth	256	255	250	248
No salt balance	Population	465,223	461,791	380,749	377,613
	Irrigated acres	845,092	836,109	623,610	615,405
	Conductance	11,499	13,681	10,666	12,900
	Depth	253	248	253	248

1970 Population = 324,618
1970 Conductance = 892 micromhos
1970 Irrigated acres = 799,178
1970 Depth to well water = 206 feet

◄ **Figure 1−4   Map showing the situation of the proposed peripheral canal which would draw still further water supplies from Northern California and direct them to agricultural and domestic use in the Central Valley and Southern California.** Something like two-thirds of the fresh water which currently flows into San Francisco Bay would be diverted by this projected canal.

Table 1−2   The estimated carrying capacity of Kern County and the projected population. In this table, carrying capacity limits calculated from the water model data shown in Table 1−1 are set against the estimated population projections. It can be seen that even with a continuation of out-migration at its present levels, and the immediate achievement of zero population growth, Kern County in one hundred years' time will have exceeded its carrying capacity. If present fertility rates continue and there is no migration movement out of the county, and water and salt balance are maintained, then the population will reach nearly three times what the present agricultural economy of the county can support.

	2070 Population Size, Kern County			
	Estimated Carrying Capacity		Projection Estimate	
	Without Peripheral Canal	With Peripheral Canal	Present Fertility, No Out-migration	Zero Population Growth, Out-migration
Water balance Salt balance (1,000 micromhos)	334,000	345,000		
			828,000	412,000
Water balance No salt balance (10,000 micromhos)	378,000	380,000		

The Mesarovic-Pestel Regional Models

The Meadows models indicate the need for immediate realization of replacement fertility values in all populations. A very similar exercise also sponsored by the Club of Rome has, as already mentioned, been carried out by two workers, Mihajlo Mesarovic and Eduard Pestel, but on a regional basis, not a global one, and recognizing that the world can be divided roughly into ten regions. The Mesarovic-Pestel models predict that a 10-year delay before this condition of replacement fertility rates is achieved will by the end of the millennium have produced in the underdeveloped countries an additional 1.7 billion people. A 20-year delay would produce an additional 3.7 billion persons in the underdeveloped nations, approximately the present world population. The Malthusian processes of famine, pestilence, and war would then kill about the same number of people, the models estimate, as would have been prevented from being born by the immediate achievement of replacement fertility. In other words, the underdeveloped nations are now at their maximum carrying capacity under present technology; any excess population growth beyond that is simply not at this time sustainable without major socioeconomic changes.

The Mesarovic-Pestel models were used to examine the effects of the worldwide energy crisis and, in particular, the results of manipulating the price and supply of petroleum. The results are shown in Table 1−3, which presents five different scenarios. It is apparent that the Middle East members of OPEC, the oil producers' cartel, can greatly advance their level of prosperity by increasing the price of crude oil. However, they already have pushed it beyond the optimal price indicated by the model. Oil embargos will slow this OPEC-nation economic advancement, but cannot halt further improvement of the already favorable situation of developed nations. Retaliation for high oil prices in the

Table 1−3 The effect of oil prices and embargos on further industrial development. The Mesarovic-Pestel regional system dynamics computer models were used to present five scenarios, each supposing different economic relationships between the oil-exporting Middle East nations and the oil-importing industrialized nations. It appears that the Middle East nations can increase their prosperity by raising oil prices, as indeed they did in the years immediately before 1973, but they have to beware of retaliatory measures. An oil squeeze would lower the rate of economic growth in the industrialized nations, but not halt it.

Scenario	Gross Regional Product Achieved by A.D. 2025 (in billions of U.S. dollars)	
	Developed Nations	Middle East Nations
1. Low-price oil	5,500	300
2. Oil squeeze (as in 1973 embargo)	7,000	1,800
3. Optimum-price oil (already exceeded)	8,000	2,500
4. Retaliation (raising cost food and products)	8,000	1,500
5. Cooperation (optimum price oil, food, and products)	8,200	1,800

form of higher charges for food and industrial product exports will scarcely hurt the developed nations, but will significantly slow the economic advancement of the Middle East cartel nations. Meanwhile, the underdeveloped non-cartel nations (sometimes now known collectively as the Fourth World) have been left in the various versions of the models to their own devices and to international charity. Perhaps, in the real world, neither of these possible forms of assistance will prove very effective in forestalling otherwise inevitable Malthusian holocausts.

Ecological Models

Because of their dramatic conclusions, the Forrester-Meadows series of models have been the main focus of both argument and attention. These models were, however, not the only dynamic models under construction at the time, nor was this M.I.T. group of workers the only group engaged in such research. Under the title first of *community ecologists,* then of *systems ecologists,* several workers in the 1960 decade had already begun to study the bioenergetics of natural systems, as has been described by ecologists such as K. E. F. Watt, D. W. Goodall, G. M. Van Dyne, and C. S. Holling, some of whose work is discussed later. This new systems approach to ecosystems was reviewed by B. C. Patten in 1971. Such work received a great impetus in the United States when some aspects of it were generously funded under the IBP (International Biological Program) biome studies project, although to date this project has made disappointing progress toward the realization of its declared primary modeling objectives. Just as Forrester was doing independently, one of these ecologists, H. T. Odum, also applied these ecological modeling techniques to socioeconomic problems, publishing his often revolutionary ideas initially in monograph form.

Urban Models

Urban ecosystems are commonly described by ecologists as *detritus ecosystems.* That is, they do not contain their own sources of either energy or materials, but must obtain these from some portion of the extraurban satellite area which they dominate. In this respect, urban ecosystems can be compared with natural detritus ecosystems such as a coral reef, or on a much smaller scale, a ball of dung. These derive their energy and materials in the first case from detritus particles carried passively by ocean currents, and in the second case by ejected biological wastes. The primary limits to urban growth are thus the amount of energy and material resources extracted from the exploited satellite area and transported to the city.

For a time such an urban system can grow without impediment. The heat generated by the utilization of the energy and the wastes produced as a by-product of the material consumption can be released into the common urban environment. Unfortunately, the capacity of this environment to process the wastes and absorb the heat eventually reaches its threshold. Growth beyond this limiting point then produces system dysfunction in one or more components.

> Funds spent on urban ecosystem research and design and on huge data banks alone will yield little relevant information on solutions to urban system problems. Applied research on urban systems lacks a unified basis of principles and is now inefficient.
>
> *F. W. Stearns and Tom Montag, 1974*

A number of system simulation models have appeared for urban ecosystems. Some are theoretical; others are based on actual case studies. Various schools have developed urban models. Two of the best known are the School of Landscape Architecture in the University of Pennsylvania at Philadelphia, founded by Ian McHarg; and the School of Urban and Regional Planning in the University of Waterloo, Ontario, Canada, organized by Robert Dorney. Both have applied their conceptual models to actual sites; Woodlands, on the outskirts of Houston, Texas, designed by the McHarg school, is the first community in the world to be constructed on an ecological equilibrium basis.

Urban simulation models of necessity are more specifically problem-oriented than conceptual in nature. They are usually designed to provide concise answers to precisely stated problems. Econometric models of this more limited scope have long been provided by urban architects and have furnished the urban design for many city developments. The broadening of the scope of such endeavors began with the publication of McHarg's *Design with Nature.* Recent presentations, by P. D. Leslie and M. A. Ulrich for Vancouver, British Columbia, and W. J. Parton, of an urban-rural model illustrate the directions which modeling of urban systems is now taking.

Odum did not provide a popular title such as *system dynamics* to his new technique for the study of human socioeconomic systems, and some consider that his basic procedure differs little from that of the Forrester approach. Figure 1−5 provides an example of a typical Odum model system, showing how he linked system interactions and input variables in a model designed primarily to follow energy relationships. In his initial analysis, Odum addresses himself to working socioeconomic systems, that is, socioeconomic systems presently *in equilibrium.* He does not emphasize, as the Forrester-Meadows group does, the level of input values that are required to prevent the system from reaching disequilibrium at some particular level or after some particular time interval.

> When human societies first evolved as a significant part of the systems of nature, man had to adapt to the food and fuel energy flows

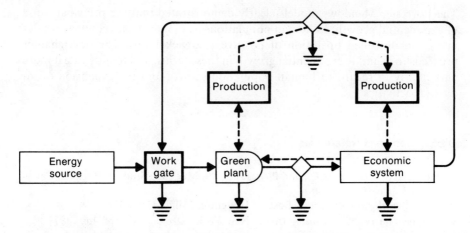

Figure 1–5 Energy-currency diagram of an economic system. This flow diagram, prepared in the first instance by H. T. Odum, shows how energy enters an economic system and flows (continuous line) in one direction, while money circulates in the system (broken line) in a contrary direction. The triangular lines represent energy sinks where energy exits from the system modeled; the diamonds are interaction points in the system.

available to him, developing the now familiar patterns of human culture. Ethics, folkways, mores, religious teachings, and social psychology guided the individual in his participation in the group and provided means for using energy sources effectively.

H. T. Odum, 1971

Exponential Growth and Resources Limits

All the types of system simulation models described in this introductory chapter, whether global or regional, have provoked argument. Because they were addressed in the main to the global socioeconomic system, and because they predicted imminent collapse if the *status quo* were allowed to continue, the computer models presented by the Meadows group stimulated the greatest controversy, much of which still continues. These models were subsequently found to contain minor errors; but as several other research institutes and various other groups of researchers confirmed, the general conclusions still remain unchallengeable. The most fundamental of these is that *exponential growth in the human population, and in its industrial base, cannot continue indefinitely in a world of finite resources.* This is the issue with which this chapter opened; it is clear that the implications of this circumstance are as yet far from agreed upon.

The Forrester-Meadows models clearly demonstrated that the principal cause of exponential growth, in human populations as in industrial activities, resides in the uncontrolled operation of positive feedback loops. The next chapter proceeds to examine exponential growth in these terms, and to illustrate it more particularly in regard to human population growth and the expansion of industrial activities.

Bibliography and References

Boughey, A. S.; Wilkin, D. C.; and Pick, J. B.   "A Modeling Study of Regional Carrying Capacity" (in prep.).

Carson, Rachel.   *Silent Spring*. Boston: Houghton Mifflin Co., 1962.

Commoner, Barry.   *The Closing Circle*. New York: Alfred A. Knopf, Inc., 1971.

Commoner, Barry.   "Review: The Closing Circle." *Environment* **14**(3):25, 40−52 (1972).

Ehrlich, P. R.   *The Population Bomb*. San Francisco: Ballantine Books, Inc., 1968.

Ehrlich, P. R., and Ehrlich, A. H.   *The End of Affluence*. New York: Random House, Inc., 1974.

Ehrlich, P. R., and Holdren, J. P.   "Review: The Closing Circle." *Environment* **14**(3):24, 26, 31−39 (1972).

Forrester, J. W.   "Counterintuitive Behavior of Social Systems." In *Toward Global Equilibrium*, edited by D. L. Meadows and D. H. Meadows, pp. 3−30. Cambridge, Mass.: Wright-Allen Press, 1973.

Forrester, J. W.   *Industrial Dynamics*. Cambridge: M.I.T. Press, 1961.

Forrester, J. W.   *Urban Dynamics*. Cambridge: M.I.T. Press, 1969.

Forrester, J. W.   *World Dynamics*. Cambridge: Wright-Allen Press, 1971.

Goldsmith, Edward.   *Blue Print for Survival*. New York: Houghton Mifflin, 1972.

Hardin, Garrett.   "The Tragedy of the Commons." *Science* **162**:1243−46 (1968).

Heilbroner, R. L.   *An Inquiry into the Human Prospect*. New York: W. W. Norton & Co., Inc., 1974.

Hirschfeld, Gerhard.   *The People, Growth and Survival*. Chicago: Aldine Publishing Co., 1973.

Malthus, Thomas.   *Essay on the Principle of Population*. 7th ed. London: J. M. Dent and Sons Ltd., 1816.

Meadows, D. H., et al.   *The Limits to Growth*. New York: Universe Books, 1972 (second edition, 1975). In the second edition only the graphic model output is altered, not the text.

Meadows, D. L., and Meadows, D. H. (Eds.).   *Toward Global Equilibrium: Collected Papers*. Cambridge: Wright-Allen Press, 1973.

Mesarovic, Mihajlo, and Pestel, Eduard.   *Mankind at the Turning Point*. New York: E. P. Dutton & Co., Inc., 1974.

Odum, H. T.   *Environment, Power, and Society*. New York: John Wiley & Sons, Inc.−Interscience, 1971.

Patten, B. C.   *Systems Analysis and Simulation in Ecology*, Vol. I. New York: Academic Press, 1971.

Ricardo, David.   *The Principle of Political Economy and Taxation*. London: J. M. Dent and Sons Ltd., 1911.

Ridker, R. G.   "To Grow or Not to Grow: That's Not the Relevant Question."
    Science **182**:1315−1318 (1973).

Roberts, Peter.   "The World Can Yet Be Saved." *New Scientist* **65**(933):200−201
    (1975).

Sills, D. L. "The Environmental Movement and Its Critics." *Human Ecology* **3**(1):1−41
    (1975).

Simmons, H. G.   "System Dynamics and Technocracy." In *Thinking about the Future,*
    edited by H. S. D. Cole et al., pp. 192−208. London: Chatto and Windus, 1973.

Smith, Adam.   *The Wealth of Nations,* Vol. 1. London: J. M. Dent and Sons Ltd.,
    1910.

Thompson, D. N.   *The Economics of Environmental Protection.* Cambridge, Mass:
    Winthrop Publishing, Inc., 1973.

Ultsch, G. R.   "Man in Balance with the Environment: Pollution and the Optimal
    Population Size." *BioScience* **23**(11):642−643 (1973).

Van Dyne, G. M.   "Ecosystems, Systems Ecology, and Systems Ecologists." *Oak
    Ridge National Laboratory Report 3957* (1966), pp. 1−31.

Watt, K. E. F.   *Ecology and Resource Management.* New York: McGraw-Hill Book
    Co., Inc., 1968.

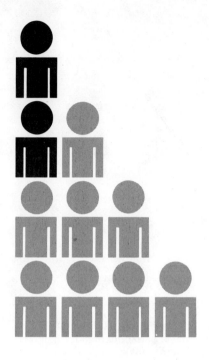

Chapter Two

The Nature of Exponential Growth

Although we may be unfamiliar with the theoretical concept of exponential growth under that name, in actuality it is something to which we are all frequently exposed, consciously or unconsciously, in one form or another in our everyday lives. Stated very simply, exponential growth is a form of increase that occurs when to an initial starting amount or number are continuously added increments resulting from growth in the initial sum.

Incremental Growth Increase

This kind of incremental growth increase is readily comprehended with the aid of a diagram such as that illustrated in Figure 2–1. Here the initial amount is expressed in the form of a given number of dollars, to which is added interest each year at the rate of 10 percent. If the annual 10 percent increments were not taken into account when calculating each annual interest increment, but were set aside to accumulate, in 10 years the original sum of dollars would be equaled in amount by the accumulated ten annual increments. This doubling of the original sum in 10 years could be represented by a straight-line graph, illustrating a form of increase that is usually known as *arithmetical growth* (Fig. 2–2).

However, if each year the annual increment is added to the original sum before calculating the next annual increment — that is, if interest is compounded annually — interest is calculated on the accumulation of previous in-

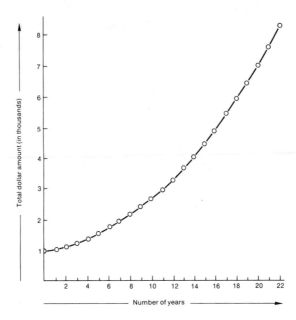

Figure 2−1 Exponential increase. The annual growth of a sum of $1,000 invested at 10 percent interest compounded annually is of *exponential* form. Initially, the annual growth is slow, because the annual increment is small relative to the original sum invested. Later, annual growth is very rapid, because in time the accumulated increments have far exceeded in amount the original investment. This form of growth is also known as logarithmic or geometric growth.

crements as well as on the original sum. Thus, whereas in the second year the interest on the increment is small, as this represents only a tenth of the original sum, by the time we reach the end of the tenth year, interest on the total of increments is substantial. Even if we only summed the ten 10 percent increments, they alone virtually equal the original sum; but in point of fact, over the years interest has successively been calculated upon interest. In the final year, this accumulating interest on interest will therefore considerably exceed the sum of the ten annual 10 percent increments on the original amount that is obtained by arithmetical increase.

If we now chart a graph plotting the rate of growth of our money, instead of the arithmetical increase in Figure 2−2, we get the exponential curve of Figure 2−1. This curve initially starts to rise slowly, because — as we have just seen — the increments of interest are at first small relative to the original sum. However, toward the end of the period, when the total of interest accrued has considerably exceeded the original sum, the growth curve charting the increase in the total amount of dollars has become very steep. It is for this reason that most American states have enacted laws against usury, protecting naive borrowers from building up immense debts far exceeding in amount the original sum borrowed.

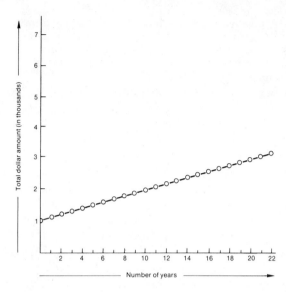

Figure 2-2   Arithmetic increase.   The annual growth of a sum of $1,000 invested at 10 percent *simple* interest is of *arithmetic* form. Initially, the annual growth rate is slow, although not substantially less than that for exponential increase shown in Figure 2-1. Because the annual increments are accumulated but not included in the interest calculation, the annual increment continues to be based on the original investment. The slow initial annual growth rate thus continues indefinitely.

In fact, whatever the rate of incremental addition we have, that is, whatever the interest rate, and whatever the period that elapses before this is compounded, the curve of total growth will always end by rising very steeply. Exponential increase or exponential growth is thus maintained by a positive feedback loop that is continually adding to the initial sum and augmenting the total that is obtained when all the previous increments are added. This positive feedback loop may be represented very simply, as in Figure 2-3.

Exponential growth, as expressed in these last few paragraphs, can be used to hypothecate all kinds of ultimately ridiculous situations. It has, for example, been used to illustrate how quickly the universe can be filled with people, with elephants, and with bacteria, or to present the farcical consequences of exponential increases in many of the common items that are a feature of our everyday lives. Charles Darwin calculated over a century ago that if a pair of male and female elephants began to produce single offspring when they reached 31 years of age, and continued until they died at 100, there would be six surviving young. Assuming the persistence of these same vital statistics of elephant demography, the living descendents of a single pair after a 750-year interval would total nearly 19 million elephants. Although Darwin did not proceed to this further calculation, such an elephant multitude would totally consume the world's present annual cereal grain production every week.

Figure 2−3   The positive feedback loop in exponential growth.   In this very simple diagram the current state of a financial investment is represented by the ▶ letter S. This amount is continuously increased by the operation of a positive feedback loop, which represents the rate of compounded interest paid on the ever-increasing investment.

The absurdity of extrapolating exponential growth in bacterial populations was exemplified some years ago by R. H. MacArthur and J. H. Connell. They estimated that when a bacteria species reproduces by fission — that is, by dividing into two — every 20 minutes, exponential growth commencing with one bacterium would in 36 hours produce a layer of bacteria one foot deep over the entire earth. An hour after this, the bacterial layer would be over our heads. Within a few thousand years, it would weigh as much as the visible universe and be expanding outward at the speed of light. So indeed would any other living thing which continued reproducing for such an interval of time in an exponential growth phase.

Partly because of the fanciful results of such projections as these, it is difficult to comprehend the real dimensions of exponential growth. More usually, a simple rule of thumb is utilized to convert the exponential rate of growth to the *doubling time*, that is, the period which will elapse before the original sum is doubled. It is possible to derive this doubling time by utilizing differential calculus; but when the growth rate does not exceed 10 percent, a close approximation to the real value is obtained by taking the constant 70 and dividing this by the percentage rate of increase. For example, if we have $1,000 in a certificate of deposit at 10 percent annual interest compounded annually, it will take seven years to double this sum to $2,000. If we have a population of one million people increasing at an annual rate of 3.5 percent, it will take twenty years to double this population to number two million people.

One can have an economy doubling every 30 years or 200 years, and after 20 or 30 doublings has reached *half* of its element size, but one more doubling carries it the rest of the way. And so one of the reasons we are surprised, psychologically surprised, by what is going on now is, that we have the feeling that because there was no problem for 200 years, that there should not be anything that can happen very suddenly in the future. But the other *half* of the economic doubling occurs in one doubling time, occurs in one 30 or 40 year period.

J. W. Forrester, 1975

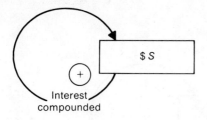

Population Growth

In the case of financial growth, unless our banker or broker insists on deducting expenses, the positive feedback loop is the only control mechanism operating on our simple growth system, at least until we pay tax on our gains. The same is true of a living population formed by organisms such as bacteria or amoebae, where reproduction is by binary fission. In these biological examples, theoretically no organism ever dies; it disappears because it splits into two further individuals. However, in the majority of organisms, adults generate offspring and themselves either die in the process, or die at some later stage following reproduction. Thus, while there is a positive feedback of offspring into the population, there is also a *negative* feedback comprising the numbers of adults who die and thereby *reduce* the size of the population.

The simple model for this circumstance is expressed as in Figure 2–4. Provided the positive feedback — that is, the incremental addition of offspring to the population — exceeds the negative feedback — that is, the totality of births is greater than the deaths in the population — there will be exponential growth in the system. However, should this negative feedback loop exceed in quantity the positive feedback loop — that is, should the total number of deaths exceed the total number of births — the total population size will diminish, and the population will decline. If this process continues, the population is at risk of extinction.

> . . . all species have an inherent capability for continuous geometric (exponential) growth in an unlimited environment. Species populations are potential "positive feedback" systems in which an increase in the population will result in even greater future increase.
>
> *F. W. Stearns and Tom Montag, 1974*

Theoretical Expressions of Exponential Growth

In a biological model the amount of change (Δ) in a population size (N) over a time interval (Δt) is conventionally represented by the expression:

$$\frac{\Delta N}{\Delta t} = B - D$$

where B is the number of births in time t and D is the number of deaths. Births

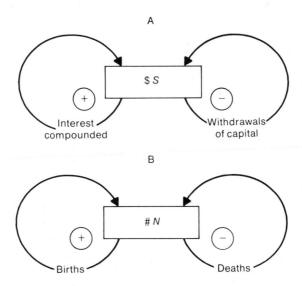

Figure 2-4 Feedback loops. The very simple system modeled in Figure 2-3 had only a single feedback loop. While some real systems do have a positive feedback loop only, most have a counteracting negative feedback loop, as in the systems modeled here. In example A, withdrawals of money will decrease the size of the capital sum. If the withdrawals remain less than the interest increments, the sum invested will continue to increase exponentially. When withdrawals exceed interest increments, the sum will decline. This is what has occurred recently in the case of many fixed incomes derived from mutual funds, whose dividends have tended to decline along with a decline in their market value. In example B, *births* represent a positive, *deaths* a negative feedback loop regulating population size (*N*) by an essentially similar fundamental process.

provide the positive feedback loop in Figure 2-4A, deaths the negative feedback loop. The expression assumes that the population, *N*, is a closed system, and there is no movement into or out of the population other than by birth or death. Figure 2-4B shows how this very simple dynamic model can indicate increments and withdrawals when a sum of money is concerned.

In the above expression, *B* and *D* are *levels* — that is, actual amounts — but these values can also be written as rates: the *birth rate* (*b*) and *death rate* (*d*). The amount of change (△*N*) then becomes the *rate* of change (*dN*), and the time interval (△*t*) becomes instantaneous (*dt*). The actual rate of change in the population (*dN*) at any moment of time (*dt*) can be calculated from the rate of births (*b*) and of deaths (*d*). The first expression can then be written alternatively as:

$$\frac{dN}{dt} = bN - dN$$

or:

$$\frac{dN}{dt} = (b - d)N$$

(Care should be taken not to confuse the d's on each side of this expression, as they represent very different things.) More usually, this expression is set down in the form of a differential equation as:

$$\frac{dN}{dt} = rN$$

This is one of the basic equations in population biology. The constant r is known as the *intrinsic rate of natural increase* of the population. It is the equivalent of what bankers term the *rate of compound interest,* and what social scientists describe as the *natural increase.* In popular language, when applied to a human population, it is known as the *population growth rate,* and is expressed as an annual percentage figure usually lying somewhere between 0.0 and 5.0 percent. The intrinsic rate of natural increase is a constant, also usually varying between 0.0 and 5.0. Figure 2–5 shows a graph plotting exponential growth resulting from such a theoretical value of r.

The mathematical expression for the rate of natural increase can be adjusted to provide not just the rate of change in population size, but what numerical effect this has on the total population. The expression becomes:

$$N = N_O e^{rt}$$

This expression for exponential size increase can be obtained mathematically by using differential calculus to solve the rate-of-increase equation. Or it can be taken on trust by the nonmathematician who merely needs to know the following:

- Expression N_O is the number of individuals in the starting population.
- Expression e is the constant 2.71828 (raising e to the power e^{rt} must be looked up in a standard handbook of mathematic tables after the numerical values for r and t have been entered).
- Expression r is the intrinsic rate of natural increase.
- Expression t is the amount of time that elapses before the next calculation of population size is to be made.

The total population after a given lapse of time with any particular exponential growth rate and a stated initial size can then be estimated directly.

Spurious Forms of Exponential Growth

There are several forms of population growth which, when they are expressed graphically, take the form of an exponential curve, but which do not ac-

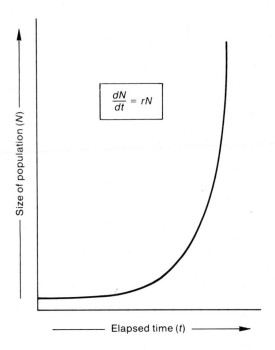

Figure 2−5 The intrinsic rate of natural increase. In this graph, theoretical values are inserted for an initial population size (*N*), the time interval (*t*), and the rate of increase (*r*). The resulting curve is of identical form with that for capital growth with compound interest (Fig. 2−1); both illustrate exponential growth. Because of its shape, this type of growth is sometimes said to produce a J-shaped curve. In technical language, the intrinsic rate of natural increase, *r*, has a logarithmic form when expressed over time.

tually represent this type of growth. Figure 2−6 shows the population growth in Orange County, California, from 1790 to 1970. This graph would appear to illustrate very well the operation on population size of a feedback loop in which births have exceeded deaths for nearly two centuries. That this is not exactly true is illustrated in Figure 2−7, where it can be seen that in the last two decades the enormous increase in the population of Orange County has been due not so much to an excess of births over deaths as to *in-migration*. When examining apparent examples of exponential growth in human populations, we therefore have to be sure in the first place that we really have intrinsic population growth, and that this is not modified by in- or out-migration from the population in question. We must be sure we are dealing with a *closed*, not an *open* population.

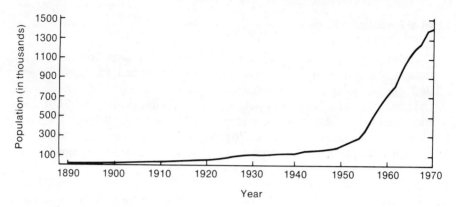

Figure 2−6 Population growth in Orange County, California.   This graph of the increase in size of the human population in Orange County from 1790 to 1970, originally prepared by Robert Wong, appears to show growth of an exponential form. Figure 2−7 shows that while growth from natural increase was indeed once of exponential form, the rate of increase due to the excess of births over deaths has not been as high as is apparently indicated by this graph. After R. Wong, unpublished work.

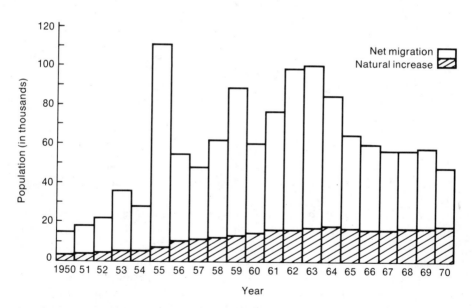

Figure 2−7 Migration and natural increase in Orange County, California.   Splitting the two components of population growth into natural increase and net migration, as done originally by Robert Wong, shows that the apparently extreme rate of exponential growth in Figure 2−6 is actually the result of a very high in-migration rate. After R. Wong, unpublished work.

Level of Feedback Values

Another point to remember about exponential growth is that it is in-dependent of the *level* of the positive and negative feedback mechanisms, and related only to the *difference* between them.

In the case of a human population, a very high death rate (*HD*) does not necessarily mean a declining population or one increasing slowly. The birth rate can be at an equally high level (*HB*) and actually still can exceed the death rate. Such *HB:HD* situations are presently very common in certain African countries, and in some Latin American ones. Despite this *HB:HD* ratio, these countries can still achieve a rate of increase of 2.5 percent, which gives them a doubling time of about 28 years. In the same way, there may be some low-death-rate (*LD*) nations which, despite the low mortality, do not have a very high rate of natural increase, because they also have a low value for their positive feedback loop — that is, their birth rates (*LB*). The thirty or so in-dustrialized nations of the world are in this *LB:LD* category. Their rate of natural increase is mostly below unitary value — that is, below 1.0 percent, and their doubling time is therefore at least 70 years. Some even have a presently declining population.

Industrial Growth

Using the same simple feedback model constructed for exponential growth in a population, industrial growth can likewise be shown to be of an ex-ponential nature. To make this conversion, instead of total population we write *industrial capital;* instead of a positive feedback loop from added births, we write *new investment;* instead of a negative feedback loop arising from deaths, we write *depreciation of capital.* We then have a model, as in Figure 2−8, of es-sentially the same structure as the population model in Figure 2−4A. The only difference is that the *industrial output,* which is more usually known on a national scale as the gross national product, is an auxiliary addition to the feed-back mechanism.

As might therefore be expected, there is an abundance of charts featuring graphs for industrial growth, all of which are of exponential form (Fig. 2−9). Every economist, and therefore every politician, has traditionally believed that industrial growth is infinite and will go on forever. In the United States, it has been customary to define a business recession as a period of at least three successive quarters in which the gross national product fails to increase. Every effort is then made to restart the upward trend. As we shall see later, economet-ric models suppose that the economic growth of individual nations reflects the amount of investment capital which is available to them, and all that is necessary to initiate the economic expansion of a country is to initiate capital investment. Indeed, this is the essential present function of the World Bank, which provides low-interest, no-collateral loans to underdeveloped countries.

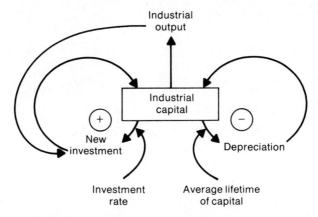

Figure 2–8   The capital feedback loop system.   This model is essentially the same as that shown in Figure 2–4A for capital and in Figure 2–4B for population. Instead of a negative feedback loop, for withdrawal of capital in the first case, or for deaths in the second case, depreciation of capital is entered here. Instead of births, as in Figure 2–4B, new investment is substituted. The main difference between the two models in Figure 2–4A and here is that industrial output is shown as a product of the total capital investment.

> One might speculate that the U.S. industrial machine now dictates its own needs, requiring man to satisfy its ever-increasing appetite for energy, materials and human labor. . . . If resource supplies and economic growth rates should decline, we may find urban conditions worsening.
>
> *F. W. Stearns and Tom Montag, 1974*

In the publication *The Limits to Growth,* the Meadows group illustrates this expected exponential industrial growth by extrapolating the curves based on observed values to the year 2100. Table 2–1 illustrates the estimated per capita GNP on this basis for a number of selected countries. The Meadows group combines exponential growth in population with that in the growth of GNP, and produces a combined figure that illustrates the average annual growth rate of the GNP. This is illustrated in Table 2–2. It is important to bear these figures in mind in Chapter 3, when limitations on exponential growth are considered.

**Other Forms of Exponential
Growth**

The Meadows group provides other examples of exponential increase not only in population and industrial production, but also in pollution and in the exploitation of nonrenewable resources. It is possible to think of examples of

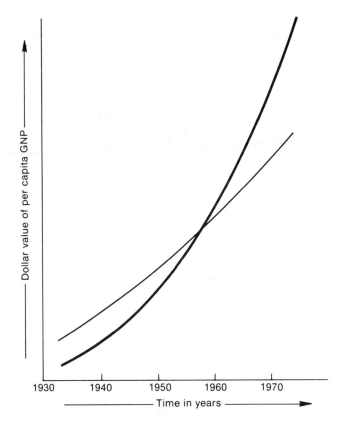

Figure 2–9   Increase in per capita Gross National Product.   Since the Great Depression the dollar value of the GNP of the United States has shown exponential growth (heavy line). Much of this increase is an artifact, the result of inflation, as revealed when the GNP is adjusted to 1958 dollar values (thin line). The chart in Figure 3–3 suggests the possibility that further actual increases of per capita GNP in rich countries like the United States may not be so considerable in the future.

many other types. There is, for instance, an exponential increase in the amount of energy being used in the world, in the amount of water being used, in the number of cars being produced, and in the number of passenger-miles flown in commercial aircraft — and even, unfortunately, at times in the rate of unemployment. There is also observable an exponential increase in the maximum speed of transportation, productivity of labor, the number of books published, and the amount of information stored in computer data banks.

It seems very doubtful, although incredible, that organizations, whether governmental or private, even pause to consider that exponential growth eventually has to come to an end. Most prosperous middle-class citizens are continually inundated with literature from stockbrokers that emphasizes the circumstance that the stock market, despite some admitted perturbations, over the years has shown a continuous and exponential increase in the value of

Table 2-1   Recent gross national product. These actual figures for 1968, expressed in American dollars on a per capita basis, reflect the economic production of eight selected countries. The four industrialized nations at the top of the table had both a higher per capita GNP and a higher growth rate in this statistic than the four underdeveloped nations listed. In 1968, this feature was a diagnostic of all industrialized nations when compared with underdeveloped ones; the situation has since changed somewhat. Also, Sweden has now assumed the lead, with Switzerland second and the United States dropping to third place (see also Figure 3-3).

	Annual GNP per Capita	Percent Annual Growth in GNP
United States	3,980	3.4
West Germany	1,970	3.4
Japan	1,190	9.9
Soviet Union	1,100	5.8
Brazil	250	1.6
Indonesia	100	0.8
India	100	1.0
China (People's Republic)	90	0.3

Table 2-2   Future gross national product. The 1968 figures for GNP shown in Table 2-1 have been projected forward to A.D. 2000 by the Meadows group in *The Limits to Growth* on a basis of current national population growth. When this is done, there are minor repositionings of the eight countries shown in Table 2-1, but the four industrialized nations still head the table. Moreover, and more importantly, their per capita GNP is now proportionately very much higher than that of the underdeveloped countries than it was in 1968, after little more than three decades. Some economic developments in the early 1970s have partially modified the sharp contrasts expressed in this table, as is discussed in the text.

	Annual GNP per Capita Projected to 2000
Japan	23,200
United States	11,000
Soviet Union	6,330
West Germany	5,850
Brazil	440
India	140
Indonesia	130
China (People's Republic)	100

shares. Each new nation, as it develops, insists on its own national airline without apparent reference to the number of passenger-miles in the world already being accommodated by existing facilities. Speculators in real estate, silver, postage stamps, or coinage assume an exponential rate of increase in the demand for these commodities, which will eventually create such a pressure as to inflate their value. Commercial life, it seems, is often envisaged as a chain-letter exercise in which a continuing franchise expansion provides for an almost immediate and certain gain for an unlimited number of participants.

Social Needs

It is not difficult to identify the individual items of our current array of socioeconomic systems that planners and economists are liable to project into exponential increase to provide for population and industrial growth. As social organisms, we have material needs; we also have certain psychological needs. With these last this text is unavoidably not greatly concerned; our knowledge of this important area is as yet too inadequate to permit the synthesis of a general overview at this level. As to material needs, we clearly have to provide ourselves with industrial products to satisfy these needs; but simultaneously, our technology must devise methods of eliminating the inevitable waste products. As shown by the Ultsch model described in Chapter 1, negative production such as this need to avoid waste pollution could place an early limit on population growth if its exponential increase were permitted. Indeed, exponential increase in pollution is one of the major features entered into the system models to be considered in later chapters. Pollution, in the sense it is used here, covers the accumulation of many waste products — garbage, trash, junk, and air and water pollution. It includes increasing salinity in agricultural systems, release of biocides and other poisons into the environment, discharge of biological wastes, and biological pollution by the introduction of pests and diseases.

Positive material needs center around basic maintenance and support. We need food, water, and shelter; also, we need services. At one time in human history, our populations were small, and our material needs were met from renewable resources. Our ancestral nomadic hunter-gathering societies merely had to move on, and the resources which had been utilized locally to meet these needs would be regenerated. Now our populations are immense and we are no longer nomadic. We irreversibly degrade the areas of our settlements, and exponential increase in the use of the materials required to satisfy the needs of these urban concentrations is making serious inroads into nonrenewable as well as renewable resources. It is only a matter of time now that some items at least will become exhausted.

The next chapter pursues this issue of the *duration* of exponential growth phases, and the nature of the limits and constraints by which exponential growth is eventually always curtailed — usually before it reaches the realm of the ridiculous, and all too often, in commercial ventures, before we have even received back our original investment.

Bibliography and References

Boulding, K. E. "Gaps between Developed and Developing Nations." In *Toward Century 21: Technology, Society and Human Values,* edited by D. C. Wallia, pp. 125–34. New York: Basic Books, 1970.

Chapman, Duane; Tyrrel, Timothy; and Mount, Timothy. "Electricity Demand Growth and the Energy Crisis." *Science* **178**: 703–708 (1972).

Forrester, J. W. In paper presented to the Joint Computer Conference, Anaheim, California, February 1975.

Kuznets, Simon. *Economic Growth of Nations.* Cambridge, Mass.: Harvard University Press, 1971.

Lapp, R. E. *The Logarithmic Century: Charting Future Shock.* Englewood Cliffs, N.J.: Prentice-Hall, Inc., 1973.

MacArthur, R. H., and Connell, J. H. *The Biology of Populations.* New York: John Wiley & Sons, Inc., 1966.

Stearns, F. W., and Montag, Tom (Eds.). *The Urban Ecosystem: A Holistic Approach.* Stroudsburg, Pa.: Dowden, Hutchinson and Ross, Inc., 1974.

Wilson, E. O., and Bossert, W. H. *A Primer of Population Biology.* Stamford, Conn.: Sinauer Associates, 1971.

Chapter Three

Resource Limits

A little reflection will lead to the logical conclusion that exponential growth, as it has been discussed so far in this text, obviously must be largely a theoretical concept. The duration of a period of exponential increase in any portion of a real-world system must clearly be very brief. No system, large or small, could contain within its own boundaries the final explosive phase of exponential growth in any of its component elements. Many projections designed to illustrate the quantitative absurdity of the dimensional magnitude of this final phase of exponential growth have been published; some were provided in Chapter 2. Mostly, as noted there, these examples take the form of theoretical increases in the size of populations of living organisms, such as bacteria, elephants, or people, assuming a positive natural increase and therefore an exponential one. Growth in such theoretical populations eventually reaches a point where the mass of the population is greater than that of this earth, and it is continuing to increase at a rate greater than that of the calculated rate of expansion of the universe.

On a lesser scale, but at a more pragmatic level, many people as students in high school or college will have been exposed to a laboratory experiment in which a small amount of yeast is inserted into an appropriate nutrient liquid culture, including among its ingredients some simple sugar. The yeast converts the sugar to alcohol, and the number of yeast cells and the amount of alcohol in the culture solution increase for several days. Eventually, however, the concentration of alcohol inhibits further growth of the yeast, and its population size is stabilized. Accumulation of one of its own waste products has halted further population growth.

Logistic Growth

Ecologists have expressed such a decline in — and finally the halting of — exponential growth by the stylized diagram illustrated in Figure 3−1. As shown in this figure, the exponential growth initially exhibited by a population of organisms sooner or later becomes modified by one or more factors that have been described in their totality as "environmental resistance." Eventually, this environmental resistance factor brings all growth increase to a halt. This type of growth that begins slowly, accelerates, and finally comes to a halt at an asymptote is known as *logistic growth*. The form of curve which results is described as S-shaped because — as may be observed in Figure 3−1 — it is roughly in the form of the letter *S*. It is also known as a sigmoid curve. The asymptote at which logistic growth stabilizes is called by ecologists the *carrying capacity*. In any ecological or sigmoid form of growth, sooner or later there is a leveling-off at some carrying capacity asymptote as determined by one or more limiting factors.

When we examine the exponential growth in certain major elements of our global system as it was described in the first two chapters, we can observe trends that indicate that this exponential growth pattern already is in many instances beginning to be replaced by a logistic one.

> Peace, population, pollution and resources are the central interlocking variables whose unsatisfactory management threatens our options. Views about this threat tend to be pessimistic or optimistic, depending on the extent to which they focus on the magnitude and ecological complexity of the problems or on the technological capabilities with which we confront these same problems.
>
> *Preston Cloud, 1969*

For example, as regards size increases in national populations, with the exception of a few countries such as Morocco, Rhodesia, Brazil, and Venezuela, where recent improvements in medical care may presently be markedly affecting the rate of population growth, all national populations are now showing a decrease in their crude rate of natural increase. Figure 3−2 charts this decrease during the present decade for selected examples of industrial, agrarian, and intermediate countries. World population growth as a whole began to slow in the seventies, falling from an annual average rate of natural increase of 2 percent in 1970 to an estimated 1.7 percent in 1975. Nevertheless, unless this world figure can be reduced to 1.0 percent in the next ten years, it will be virtually impossible to provide sufficient food for all on most estimates, as will be discussed later.

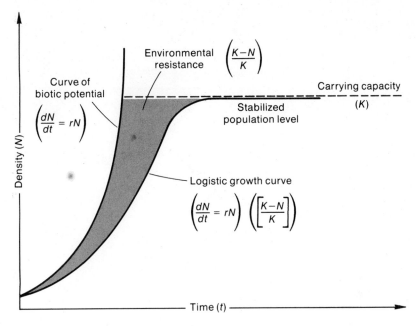

Figure 3–1 Relationship between logistic and exponential growth. The initial exponential growth as exhibited by a population is very rarely maintained. More usually, environmental feedbacks, customarily known under the collective term *environmental resistance,* slow this growth and finally bring it to an equilibrium position at a level known as the *carrying capacity.* From *Ecology of Populations,* 2nd ed. Copyright © 1973 by Arthur S. Boughey. The Macmillan Company, New York.

Limits to Economic Growth

On the economic side, K. E. Boulding several years ago pointed out that the rate of increase in the gross national product (GNP) was beginning to decline in those industrialized nations with the highest values for this index. When these increases are plotted on a graph, as in Figure 3–3, they are seen to be distributed along a curved line in which the rate of increase is negatively correlated with the value of the GNP. Thus the United States, with until 1974 the highest GNP on a per capita basis, has the lowest rate of increase. Indeed, in the first three quarters of 1974, no increase at all was recorded, although a slight total increase is forecast for 1975. Japan, the last of the major industrialized nations of the world to accomplish the industrial revolution, and with presently the lowest GNP per capita of this group, is still increasing its GNP at a rate higher than in any other industrialized nation. It would thus appear that both in the case of exponential growth in national population size and in the case of exponential growth of GNP, some factors not immediately obvious are reducing

40

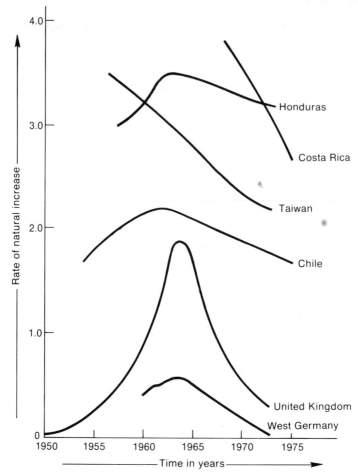

Figure 3–2 The current decline in the rate of natural increase. The graphs shown here for a selected number of countries illustrate the steady decline in the rate of natural increase throughout the world. This decline is almost universal, although the level of the rate of natural increases varies appreciably. Thus industrial nations (United Kingdom, West Germany) have low rates, agrarian nations (Honduras, Costa Rica) high ones, and countries in an initial stage of industrialization (Taiwan, Chile) intermediate ones. Several countries, for example Mexico and Morocco, are exceptional in that they currently still show increasing rates of natural increase, almost certainly the result of the recent provision of improved health care services.

the previously exponential rate of increase and converting this to a logistic mode. Boulding coined the term *cowboy economics* for the exponentially expanding type of economy, and *spaceship economics* for the dynamic equilibrium type which has leveled off in a logistic mode.

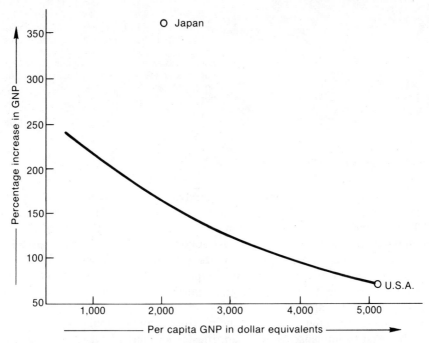

Figure 3–3 Declining rates of increase in the gross national product. In-creases in the GNP on a per capita basis are plotted against actual values of the GNP; the data for various industrialized nations fall along a curved and declining line, in which Japan is at one end and the United States at the other. This suggests that the older industrialized nations are reaching some kind of limit to further in-crease in per capita GNP (see also Table 2–1).

When we examine human social systems, there are two types of en-vironmental restrictions that can be identified as likely to cause such a change from an exponential to a logistic mode of growth, from cowboy to spaceship economics. The first of these types is physical — that is, material needs; the sec-ond type is psychological — that is, the factors resulting from human crowding and density. Both were discussed briefly in Chapter 2. In the preparation of their global system dynamics model, the Meadows team examined the physical or material type of restrictions in relation to five basic quantities — population, capital, food, nonrenewable resources, and pollution. These can be further defined, as has been seen; moreover, others can be added — for example, energy and space resources. Psychological aspects of crowding have been examined ex-perimentally in some animals; but as noted already, the data on human social systems is still scattered and scanty, and much more difficult to insert into models based on causal relationships as they influence logistic growth rates.

> Although it is true that man has repeatedly
> succeeded in increasing both the space he oc-
> cupies and its carrying capacity, and that he will
> continue to do so, it is also clear that both the oc-
> cupiable space and its carrying capacity have
> finite limits which he can approach only at great
> peril.
>
> Resources and Man, *1969*

Food Production

Of these various factors, the most extensively investigated and the one that has been studied for the longest time is that of food. Thomas Malthus in 1790 presented his classic dissertation on food as a resource that limits increase in human populations. Malthus noted that population increased by a geometric (exponential) rate, whereas food supplies grew at an arithmetic (linear) rate. His prediction that the size of national populations would thus continue to rise until food resources became limiting and famine incipient has now been incorporated into the language as *Malthusian disaster.* Many predictions that continuing exponential growth on the part of national populations would inevitably lead to immense Malthusian disaster, primarily as a result of famine situations, have continued to be made right through to the present time. A consensus of current estimates holds that despite an anticipated virtual doubling of the global population size before the end of this millennium, improvements in food production techniques will ensure that the total world production of food will be adequate to prevent famine, *assuming that food distribution procedures are adequate.*

However, it is patently obvious that even now food distribution procedures are *not* equal to the task of preventing *local* famines, and these have been occurring throughout the decade of the sixties and the early years of the 1970 decade in ever-increasing and alarming intensity. In 1974, although actual figures are inadequate and unreliable, it would appear that tens of thousands died of famine or other causes immediately resulting from starvation in the Sahel region of West Africa, and possibly by the hundreds of thousands in parts of Ethiopia and the Indian subcontinent. Therefore, despite the overall reassurance for the general food production outlook through to the end of this millennium, food has clearly become — at least on a local scale — a limiting resource. It can thus be expected to inhibit the continuation of exponential increase in the human populations of at least the famine areas concerned.

Limiting Factors in Food Production

Despite the apparent recent occurrence of periodic local famines, the current attitude toward the possibility of the world continuing successfully to feed an expanding global human population is, as noted, generally optimistic.

The Harvard Population Center, in a recent report by Roger Revelle, argues that the world could feed a global population of 38−48 billion at an adequate nutritional level. A survey by a group principally composed of agricultural economists at the University of California suggests that there need be little anxiety as to *total* world food production during the rest of this century. The agrarian nations themselves, the ones most likely to suffer first from general famines, appear on the whole to be under no urgent internal pressure to reduce their population growth to obtain a more realistic conformity with their more slowly increasing rate of food production. A recent report on the world food situation by the Economic Research Service of the U.S. Department of Agriculture draws the same optimistic conclusion that despite a growing population the world is not yet in danger of universal famine. It bases this conclusion on the fact that in the twenty-year period from 1954 to 1973, world per capita food production increased 17 percent. In industrialized nations over the same period the per capita increase was 33 percent, as against the 8 percent increase achieved by underdeveloped countries. Notably, in Africa, even this small gain was not universally recorded, and some countries suffered an actual decline in per capita food production.

> Foreseeable increases in food supplies over the long term . . . are not likely to exceed about nine times the amount now available. That approaches a limit that seems to place the earth's ultimate carrying capacity at about 30 billion people, *at a level of chronic near-starvation for the great majority* (and with massive immigration to the now less densely populated lands) . . . there could be 30 billion people by about 2075 in the absence of controls beyond those now in effect.
>
> Resources and Man, *1969*

Thus, while there is a consensus of optimistic opinion as to immediate global food prospects, there is also a general agreement that through the remainder of this millennium there will be great differences between national performances both as to current per capita food production and as to future prospects. The latest estimate by the U.S. Department of Agriculture considers that as little as 26 percent of the 45 percent of the global land surface of potential agricultural use is presently cultivated. There exists in some areas either a potential for increased acreages or the possibility of increased yields, more particularly through fertilizer application. What is needed to even out regional food production disparities is quite commonly believed to be, as a first step, a concerted effort to increase food production in areas where the potential is high, in order to redistribute food supplies to areas of lower potential. Later in this text, this issue will be discussed again, as well as the matter of increasing agricultural acreages; some early attempts to implement a policy of increasing agricultural acreages, such as the ill-fated British "Groundnut Scheme" in Tanzania, ended in complete failure.

This generally optimistic attitude toward food supplies may originate from the continuing promise of what is now usually called the *Green Revolution.* Very briefly, the Green Revolution is the production and introduction of higher yielding varieties of local food crops in areas where the cash or other incentive to do so was previously lacking. The introduction of the new strains of wheat and rice that were recently produced to permit this major agricultural innovation, together with the use of hybrid corns, enabled India, for example, according to Revelle, to obtain a 265 percent increase in corn, a 140 percent increase in wheat, and a 105 percent increase in rice production in the last two decades. This spectacular and, for that country, unique rate of increase led to forecasts that India would in a few years' time become a *food exporter.* Similar dramatic increases in food production were obtained earlier in Mexico. However, in this case, it was acknowledged that one contributory factor to the increased agricultural output was an increase in the area of land cultivated. It has recently become known that in the People's Republic of China, a country where little potentially arable land remains undeveloped, comparable increases in food production have been obtained by breeding improved wheat and rice varieties.

Few nations still have a readily exploitable reserve of potential arable land remaining. President Lyndon B. Johnson's Science Advisory Committee, in a 1967 report on "The World Food Problem," estimated that less than one half (43 percent) of potentially arable land was currently cropped. Unfortunately, there is some obvious and immediate difficulty over extension of food growing into these unutilized areas. The thin acid sandy soils of the vast Amazon Basin now opened up by the trans-Amazon highway produce disastrous crops when cultivated by peasant small-holding techniques. So do the soils of the "Cuvette Centrale" of Zaire and the great stretches underlying "miombo" woodland in Central Africa, presently on a "chitamene" regime. Other similarly still undeveloped areas may be too subject to rainfall perturbation, to salt accumulation, to tsetse fly infestation, or to locust attack. Vast regions are not available for agrarian development because they do not have a climate providing the minimum of ninety frost-free days per year required for raising an agricultural crop through to harvest. The Canadian Shield and the Siberian plains of Russia provide two good examples of this.

The 1967 Science Advisory Committee report considered that development of the remaining potential arable land would proceed only slowly because of the great cost of overcoming these several difficulties. However, while there is unanimity as to the certainty of such costs, there is a wide divergence of views as to the *actual* cost involved. The Meadows group estimated a relationship such as is shown in Figure 3−4A. The cost of developing virgin acreage rises exponentially as the remaining fraction is steadily reduced. The Sussex group maintains that while this relationship is exponential, it may well be of the form shown in Figure 3−4B. In the same way, the Meadows group considers that

A   B

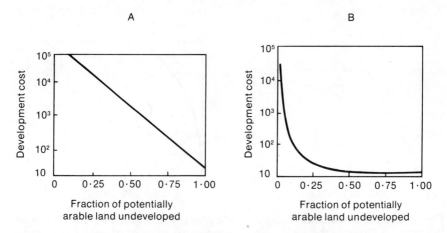

Figure 3–4   Diminishing returns from breaking further arable land.   Of the potentially arable land surface of the earth, less than one-half is presently cultivated. Various difficulties have prevented utilization of the remainder. One view presents the cost of developing this remainder as conforming to the graph shown in example A (Meadows group). Another suggests that ever-improving cultural technologies will provide a relationship more like that shown in example B. Both relationships are of exponential form for the values on the vertical axes of these graphs are plotted in logarithmic form. The issue is clearly critical in any consideration of potential world food supplies.

after an initially reasonable yield from new arable areas, there are ever-diminishing returns from the capital expended on breaking additional arable acreage (Fig. 3–5A). The Sussex group, by contrast, considers that continuous improvements in cultural technology will permit the initial yields to be maintained for a much longer period (Fig. 3–5B).

Perhaps the last word on the future of food supplies belongs to Lester Brown, an acknowledged leader in the assembling of accurate food production data. In a very recent position paper on food he states ". . . it is clear that we are in a position of having to come to terms with negative trends — falling fish catch, falling grain yields, falling food reserves, the loss of cropland, increasingly expensive fuel and fertilizer — at the very same time that the causes of those negative trends remain unchecked. Unless population growth, overconsumption, overfishing and ecological deterioration are arrested, it will not be possible to maintain even the present quality of life."

Mineral Resources

During virtually the whole of this century, much attention has also been paid to the remaining reserves of the 92 naturally occurring elements on this

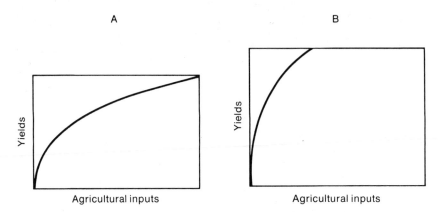

Figure 3−5   Relationship between agricultural input and output. There are two ways of charting the relationship between the amount of capital invested in agricultural operations and the agricultural yields. Example A shows the graph as illustrated by the Meadows group, which almost immediately begins to have serious feedback from the law of diminishing returns. Example B shows an interpretation that the Sussex group offers, in which there continues for a much more substantial period of time to be a large benefit from additional inputs into agricultural operations in terms of agricultural yields.

earth, all of which are now used in one form or another for industrial production. More especially, attention has been directed toward some 36 elements that are currently considered indispensable for industrial development. Linked with this issue is the question of the amount of those nonrenewable natural mineral resources that are utilized not for the elements they contain, but because of their chemical structures which, when rearranged by combustion, provide a source of energy. This last category includes coal, natural gas, oil, radioactive isotopes, and numerous less important compounds. Several authoritative statements of the remaining reserves of all these essential substances, both energy and nonenergy producers, have been prepared. One of these appeared a few years ago in book form under the general editorship of Preston Cloud, as has already been noted; it was compiled by the Committee of the U.S. National Academy of Sciences on Resources and Man. The specific material needs of the United States were reviewed by a national commission in 1973.

Even if comprehensive information were available on the geochemistry and configuration of the earth's crustal materials, we could still not assess the likely eventual reserves of ore for specific mineral commodities at the level of confidence we might like.

T. S. Lovering, 1969

Nonrenewable Energy Resources

When we turn to nonrenewable energy resources, we find that the situation already has become critical. The use of coal, natural gas, and oil as major energy resources by Western-world nations as they industrialized was not initially significant in relation to the total global reserves of these fuels. As reflected in Figure 3−6, this bountiful supply of energy sources permitted the major industrialized nations to establish an industrial base which, as measured by their GNP on a per capita basis, was directly related to their energy use. Meanwhile, the major part of the human population remained stranded at the stage of an agrarian society. Figure 3−7 illustrates the system bioenergetics underlying this situation. In agrarian societies the sole source of energy is that derived from sunlight in the biological process of *photosynthesis*. With very minor exceptions, no mineral sources of energy ever are utilized. Such agrarian societies are caught in a vicious circle in which the population has to do work to capture photosynthetic energy and raise food in the form of crop plants, which are used for feeding the population, enabling them to do agricultural work to raise more food, which will nourish more people so that they can raise more food. There are two limits to the growth of such a bioenergetic system, both energy limits. The one is dependent on the fact that the total cropping area that

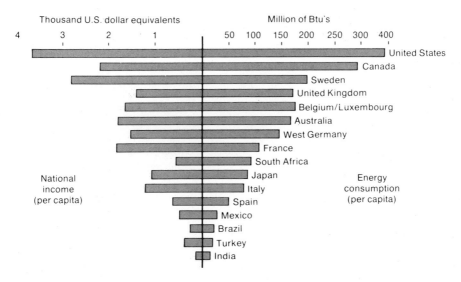

Figure 3−6   National per capita income and energy consumption.   The heavy use by extensively industrialized nations of auxiliary energy is paralleled by a high per capita income. As energy use diminishes, so does per capita income. United States Energy: A Summary Review, U.S. Department of the Interior, 1972.

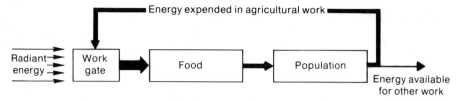

Figure 3-7   The bioenergetic block of agrarian economies.   An agrarian society utilizes only the radiant energy which falls as sunlight on its territory and is in part acquired in the photosynthetic processes of its crop plants. As this formalized diagram shows, this bioenergetic regime is a vicious circle in which a limited number of people can be supported by the radiant energy acquired in this way; they must devote virtually the whole of the energy they obtain to raising more crops to acquire more energy for more people.

can be occupied by a society is finite; the limit to the area determines the total amount of sunlight that can be utilized. The second limit is the amount of energy that can be input by the activities of the people themselves, after consuming the food which they raise. There is an optimum body size for individuals in any given agricultural system; large individuals consume too much energy in mere body maintenance for the amount of agricultural work they perform. Small individuals are not powerful enough to achieve the necessary agricultural work quota. The generally low stature of cultivators indigenous to the area of the Old World tropics lying within the ten-inch rainfall zone bears witness to the operation of natural selection on human stature in this way.

**Bioenergetic Limits on
Human Societies**

> Predictions about how much petroleum, natural gas, coal and uranium, the principal energy fuels, remain to be recovered in the United States vary widely, depending upon one's assumptions. But there is a consensus that unless growth slows, we are approaching a point at which most of the economically recoverable reserves of natural gas and petroleum in the United States will be exhausted within a very few decades.
>
> *D. B. Large, 1974*

This limiting energetic cycle restricting the growth of agrarian societies can be broken only by the insertion of some new form of energy other than direct photosynthetic energy. Initially, this auxiliary energy was acquired on a small scale by wind- or waterpower through windmills or waterwheels. Then, first coal — and finally oil — was utilized as an auxiliary energy source and was introduced into the energy cycle. It is true that both these fossil fuels are a stored form of photosynthetic energy, but they represent for all practical purposes a nonrenewable, instead of a renewable source. It appears that once this energetic cycle change has been introduced, not only can this auxiliary energy be inserted into the agricultural production energy cycle, substituting for human energy and releasing it for other activities, but the auxiliary energy can also be combined with human energy in an *industrial energy cycle* (Figure 3–8). In this new cycle the amount of industrial production is related primarily to the amount of auxiliary energy inserted into the system.

Thus, all the nations as yet underdeveloped — that is, those in the lower GNP per capita values of Figure 3–6 — are now striving to obtain auxiliary energy sources in order to break out of the agrarian energy cycle. The industrialized nations seek for ever-increasing supplies of auxiliary energy from an ever-diminishing global base of energy resources in order still further to augment industrial output. The world has thus suddenly come starkly face to face with a limit to economic growth in the form of finite supplies of mineral energy resources. The projected energy requirements for the maintenance of continuing exponential growth in the American economy are illustrated in Figure 3–9. These requirements are broken down in Figure 3–10 into projections of sources from which this energy may be obtained. It will be very apparent that all of these sources are now imposing a limit on industrial growth of varying intensity.

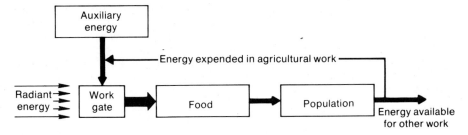

Figure 3–8   The bioenergetic regime of an industrialized society. By contrast with the system shown in Figure 3–7, an industrialized society has succeeded in incorporating into its bioenergetic cycle an auxiliary supply of energy. This releases much of the energy of the people, which was previously utilized in working the land, for other purposes. Combined with supplements from the auxiliary energy supply, this energy surplus can then be devoted to the production of industrial products. A second cycle develops in these industrialized nations in which most of the people are involved in the utilization of auxiliary energy supplies for the production of industrial goods, as shown in Figure 6–11.

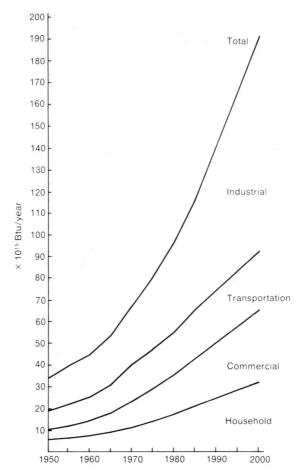

Figure 3–9   The use of energy by various sectors of the American econo-my.   In these projections, prepared by the Department of the Interior in 1972, the use of energy is broken down into its industrial, transportational, commercial, and domestic components. In this governmental forecast, the exponential increases shown by all these sectors of the economy since 1950 were projected through to the end of this millennium. U.S. Energy through the Year 2000, U.S. Department of the Interior, 1972.

> An energy crisis has already begun. It is
> real, not contrived. . . . It is going to get worse
> before it gets better, and even if it does, it will not
> get better much before the end of this century.
>
> *R. W. Comstock, 1974*

Unfortunately, the securing and insertion of an auxiliary supply of energy into the bioenergetic system of an underdeveloped nation is likely to be not the

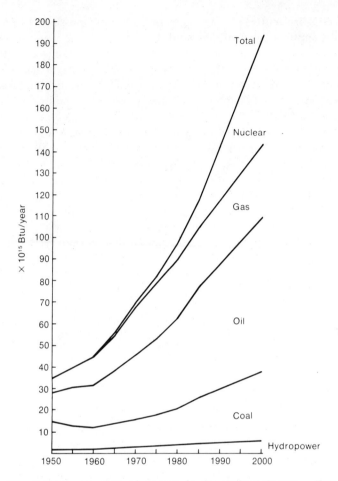

Figure 3-10 Primary sources of energy in the United States. This government projection, provided by the Department of the Interior in 1972, continues the historic exponential growth in supplies from the several energy sources, except hydroelectric power. While natural gas is not shown to expand very considerably, oil use is more than doubled; so is the use of coal, and nuclear power sources show an enormous increase. U.S. Energy through the Year 2000, U.S. Department of the Interior, 1972.

end but only the beginning of its industrialization problems. Industries require not only energy supplies, but also continuous inputs of mineral elements of one kind or another. Few countries are so well endowed naturally as to be provided with all the 36 vital industrial elements, let alone the totality of the 92 naturally occurring elements on this earth, all of which, as has already been observed, are now in one form or another exploited by modern industrial processes. For those elements that it does not possess as reserves within its own frontiers, a nation has to trade in the international market. Quite recently, with the example of the oil consortium (OPEC) as their model, nations possessing minerals that are in short supply have begun to hold the industrializing world to ransom by artificially raising the price of these scarce mineral resources without any reference to their intrinsic market values. That this particular commercial operation of upward price manipulation is capable of almost infinite extension may be seen by analyzing a table of remaining reserves of nonrenewable natural resources presented in Table 3–1. For example, Jamaica, Guinea, Guyana, and Surinam provide 95 percent of the world bauxite market; Malaysia and Bolivia 70 percent of the tin; and Zambia, Zaire, Chile, and Peru 80 percent of the copper. Such natural resource tables are compiled from figures of *proven* reserves. These are the quantities of each particular element that have been presently located, the deposits of which in these discovered locations have been estimated. It is usual to calculate what is commonly referred to as a *static reserve life index*, presenting the number of years that these proven reserves might last if they continue to be utilized at current rates.

> . . . although there may be temporary improvements, it seems certain that energy shortages will be with us for the rest of the century, and that before 1985 mankind will enter a genuine age of scarcity in which many things besides energy will be in short supply.
>
> *P. R. Ehrlich and A. H. Ehrlich, 1974*

Reference to any such compilation of remaining reserves indicates that for many of the more extensively used elements, it is impossible to foresee any substantial unexpended reserves remaining within a century from now. Indeed, there seem very real prospects that exponential industrial growth must grind to a halt before the end of the present millennium because of critical shortages in such elements as chromium, nickel, cadmium, and so forth.

Until this time, industrial societies have not had to consider long-term nonrenewable resource availability. Essentially, the assumption was always made that the amount of such resources on the earth was virtually infinite. During the Industrial Revolution in Western Europe, this quite unwarranted assumption did not have any untoward results. The annual usage rate of nonrenewable resources was such a small fraction of the total world reserves that this assumption was never in practice shown to be incorrect. The situation has radically changed, however, during the past few years. First, in the utilization of many nonrenewable resources, we are now beginning to exhaust the richer and more easily available deposits. Second, developing nations are commencing to implement plans for their own industrialization, and will also need to tap into remaining reserves of nonrenewable resources. Third, developed nations such as the United States have production industries of so great a size that they are

Table 3–1 Estimated life of some critical nonrenewable resources. Excluding fossil fuels, some thirty-six mineral elements are considered essential for industrial production. This table lists the expected life of proven global reserves of a selection of about one third of the commonest of these critical nonrenewable resources, calculated on present usage rates.

Resource Element	Static Reserve Index (Years)	Resource Element	Static Reserve Index (Years)
Aluminum	100	Mercury	13
Chromium	420	Molybdenum	79
Cobalt	110	Nickel	150
Copper	36	Silver	16
Iron	240	Tin	17
Lead	26	Tungsten	40
Manganese	97	Zinc	23

beginning to exhaust national supplies of certain minerals like chromite, columbium, mica, and tantalum, and metals such as cobalt, manganese, aluminum, platinum, cadmium, asbestos, zinc, and nickel (Fig. 3–11).

Reserve Indices

The controversial issue of resource availability is one of the most disputed elements of the Meadows global model World 3. Some of the criticisms are considered further in Chapter 6. While these several criticisms were being developed, the Meadows group was clarifying its treatment of nonrenewable natural resources. An account of the basic work, actually completed before the construction of World 3, has appeared in a paper by W. W. Behrens III. The *static reserve life index* concept developed by the Meadows resource economists group indicates the number of years current known reserves of a given nonrenewable nature would support consumption if present demand remains unchanged. Such a concept assumes that demand will not change, and that ore grades remain constant, no new deposits are located, extraction technologies are not improved, and no alternative materials are substituted for the particular resource.

In the real world, with its burgeoning populations, each with its own set of ever-increasing resource needs, none of these premises can remain true. Exponential growth in resource needs is now occurring, thereby invalidating the static reserve life index. The rate of this exponential growth in resource demands is difficult to estimate precisely; but as Figure 3–12 indicates, its exact

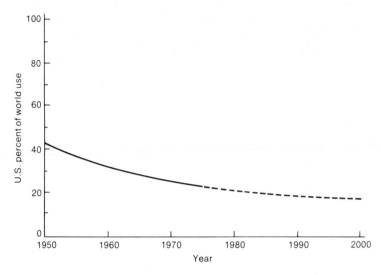

Figure 3–11 Actual and projected U.S. consumption of nonrenewable resources on a proportional world basis. As shown in this illustration, the U.S. consumption of mineral resources, although still rising exponentially, is now a diminishing proportion of the total world use, because this also is rising exponentially. The U.S. requirements are proportionally much less than the potential world demands. U.S. supplies of such resources as mica, tantalum, and tin are already exhausted; and more than 90 percent of others, such as aluminum, antimony, cobalt, and manganese, have to be imported, as do more than half of certain others, such as asbestos, cadmium, nickel, and zinc. The United States also now imports more than a third of its requirements of iron ore, lead, and mercury. Commercial and political leverage for negotiating further imports of these essential mineral resources into the United States and other industrialized countries is continuously diminishing.

estimate determination is unnecessary, for variations have but a relatively small effect on total resource life. The Meadows group took a different rate value for the mean annual increase in individual resource utilization. The consequences of this increase on the total time a reserve will last are calculated from the formula:

$$e = \frac{\ln(r \times s + 1)}{r}$$

where:

e = Exponential reserve life index
s = Static reserve life index
r = Annual growth rate of demand

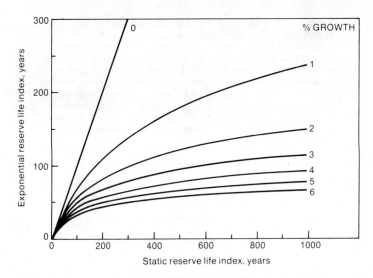

Figure 3-12   The effects of reserve underestimation.   When remaining reserves of a nonrenewable resource are expressed in terms of an exponential
reserve life index, instead of the static reserve life index, additional demands arising from underestimations of the rate of industrial growth have a comparatively
slight effect on the actual time left before remaining supplies of the nonrenewable
resource are exhausted. (Reprinted from) William W. Behrens III, "The Dynamics
of Natural Resource Utilization" in *Toward Global Equilibrium: Collected Papers,*
ed. D. H. and D. L. Meadows, Copyright © Wright-Allen Press, Inc., Cambridge,
MA 02142 USA.

Table 3-2 shows a selected list of nonrenewable resources contrasting the
static reserve life index and the exponential reserve life index calculated in this
manner. It should be noted that location of further reserves of a given resource
do not greatly increase the exponential reserve life index. Behrens cites a
theoretical resource with a static reserve life index of 40 years. If new discoveries were to raise this static index ten times — that is, to 400 years — the exponential reserve life index would rise only from 26 to 86 years.

Dynamic Resource Models

In a real-world situation a resource will not be run down to either its static
or its exponential index limit. Usually, long before either point is reached, extraction costs become uneconomic because remaining ore bodies are too remote
or too dilute. The actual cost increase is shown as a logistic curve in Figure
3-13. On this same illustration are also shown the logistic decline in remaining
resource reserves as indicated by the exponential index, and a curve of the usage
rate.

Table 3−2   Static and exponential reserve life indices compared. This table lists a selection of fourteen commonly used nonrenewable resources, contrasting the expected life of proven reserves at present rates of utilization (static reserve life index) with the calculated life based on an exponential increase in the rate of usage, as calculated by the Meadows group in *The Limits to Growth*. At this adjusted rate of utilization, as expressed by the *exponential reserve life index*, no element vital for industry will still be available in its unmined mineral resource reserve within a hundred years from now.

Resource Element	Static Reserve Life Index (Years)	Exponential Reserve Life Index (Years)
Aluminum	100	31
Chromium	420	95
Cobalt	110	60
Copper	36	21
Iron	240	93
Lead	26	21
Manganese	97	46
Mercury	13	13
Molybdenum	79	34
Nickel	150	53
Silver	16	13
Tin	17	15
Tungsten	40	28
Zinc	23	18

This curve of usage rate, shown in Figure 3−14, is, however, a theoretical rather than a real chart of resource utilization. As costs rise, there will be an incentive to industry to undertake research and development activities designed at least to stabilize costs and prevent further rise. But there is a time lag in this process, with a delay that can be set at about twenty years before research findings can be applied to extraction technologies. A closer approximation to what actually occurs in the history of the utilization of a given nonrenewable resource is shown in Figure 3−15.

As research and development activity responds in this way to extraction cost increase, so other research and development work is simultaneously developing a substitution technology, locating different sources for the element involved, or other elements to substitute for this particular one. The gradual increase in the fraction of the resource for which a substitute is located is shown in Figure 3−16.

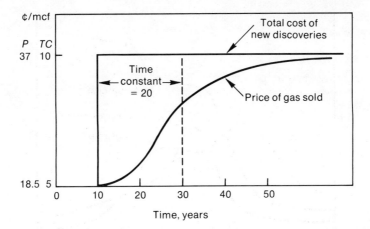

Figure 3-13   The increased costs of extracting diminishing supplies of a non-renewable resource.   The response of price to total cost has a time-lag situation built in. As long as we continue to locate plentiful fresh supplies of the resource, there is no problem. When the availability of additional supplies is appreciably diminished, the time lag begins to overtake the rise in cost. Price increases then tend to become prohibitive. (Reprinted from) Roger F. Naill, "The Discovery Life Cycle of a Finite Resource: A Case Study of U.S. Natural Gas" in *Toward Global Equilibrium: Collected Papers,* ed. D. H. and D. L. Meadows, Copyright © Wright-Allen Press, Inc., Cambridge, MA 02142 USA.

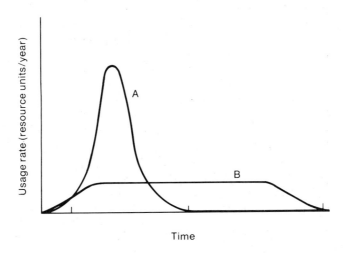

Figure 3-14   Theoretical curves of resource utilization.   A nonrenewable resource can be used at various rates. Maximum utilization regardless of cost will produce a usage curve of form A; controlled utilization will result in a utilization rate leveling off at some cost threshold as in form B. Most usage rates probably lie somewhere between these two extremes. Reprinted, with permission, from Meadows, Dennis L., William W. Behrens III, Donella H. Meadows, Roger F. Naill, Jørgen Randers, and Erich K. O. Zahn, *Dynamics of Growth in a Finite World,* Copyright © 1974, Wright-Allen Press, Inc., Cambridge, MA 02142 USA.

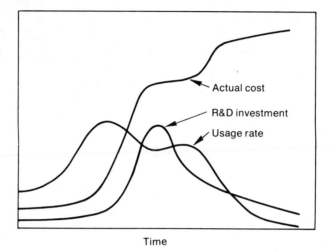

Time

Figure 3–15   Actual curves of resource utilization.   Increasing costs of extraction promote industrial research and development which eventually reduce the rate of further increase in extraction costs. Usage rate reflects the eventual fluctuations in extraction costs. (Reprinted from) William W. Behrens III, "The Dynamics of Natural Resource Utilization" in *Toward Global Equilibrium: Collected Papers,* ed. D. H. and D. L. Meadows, Copyright © Wright-Allen Press, Inc., Cambridge, MA 02142 USA.

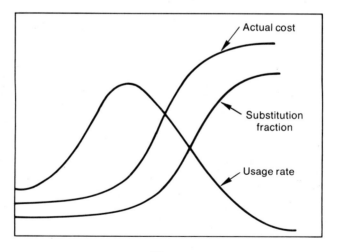

Time

Figure 3–16   The introduction of a substitute for a nonrenewable resource. The usage rate of a nonrenewable resource falls away as the actual cost of extraction increases. After a lag time which is necessary to develop the needed technology, a substitute for the original nonrenewable resource is introduced. (Reprinted from) William W. Behrens III, "The Dynamics of Natural Resource Utilization" in *Toward Global Equilibrium: Collected Papers,* ed. D. H. and D. L. Meadows, Copyright © Wright-Allen Press, Inc., Cambridge, MA 02142 USA.

Case History of a Mineral Resource

The Meadows group illustrated the exhaustion of these essential mineral elements by taking the case history of chromium. The world's proven reserves of chromium are about 775 million metric tons. Present industrial use of chromium requires the mining of about 1.85 million metric tons annually. At this rate of use the reserves would last about 420 years. Unfortunately, the world consumption of chromium is increasing at the annual rate of 2.6 percent. As shown in Figure 3−17, this exponential rate of use of chromium would exhaust world supplies in 95 years. This is very different from the linear rate of depletion that would take 420 years totally to deplete proven reserves. The Meadows group points out that even if further exploration increased the amount of proven chromium reserves by a factor of 5, at an exponential rate of exploitation, this would extend the availability of chromium only from 95 to

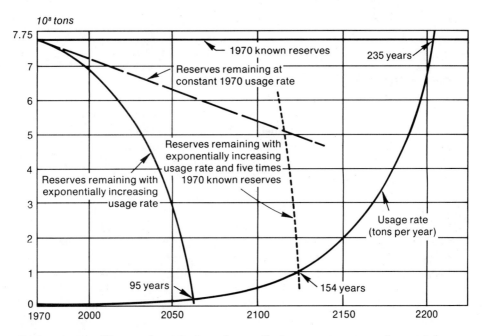

Figure 3−17   The usage of chromium. If the usage rates of remaining chromium reserves continue to be constant, it will be available for a little over 400 years. If usage increases exponentially at its present growth rate of 2.6 percent per annum, reserves will be exhausted in 95 years. Even if actual remaining reserves of chromium are five times as great as the present estimates of proven reserves, this period can only be extended to approximately another 150 years. Even were all chromium used in industrial products to be completely recycled, this would extend the life of chromium less than another 100 years to approximately 235 years from 1970.

154 years. Moreover, they note that even had it been possible from 1970 onward to recycle 100 percent of the chromium used in industry, demand would exceed supply in 235 years.

In producing its world models, the Meadows team included the assumption that proven reserves of all essential mineral resources would be expanded fivefold by new discoveries. Such calculations provide, for example, for the exhaustion of aluminum in 55 years, copper in 48, and chromium — as has been noted — in 154 years.

> For the first time in history, the nation's energy supply is failing to keep ahead of the ever-growing demand. America's factories and consumers are increasing use of electricity, natural gas, coal and other fuels faster than the suppliers of energy can boost their output. Some analysts see the problem as temporary, but others view it as a historical turning point in which the energy resources that always have been taken for granted become a limiting factor in national growth.
>
> *Anon.,* Wall Street Journal, *1970*

Costs of Mineral Extraction

Before the new era in which prices of mineral ores are artificially maintained, and during the period when markets were allowed to respond to supply-and-demand balancing, prices of mineral ores tended to remain low and constant because extraction methods became increasingly more efficient. Sooner or later, however, rising costs of labor, technical difficulties of ore extraction, and mounting costs in exploration cause price increases. Once the price begins to rise, it does so exponentially, because each price rise in one item of the extraction process interacts with the cost of every other one. Under the traditional marketing system, this was still of no major concern, for usually some much cheaper alternative element was available. This substitution process is well illustrated, for example, by the history of our coinage, where the original gold was replaced by silver, silver by nickel, nickel by copper, and copper by even cheaper alloys. After running through a series of such element changes, we can, however, eventually come to the end of the possibility of change. Thus, even in instances such as that of chromium, where the exponential reserve life index may exceed one hundred years, and some substitution is possible, it is unlikely that this element will be available to industry for that long, because the price of its extraction and distribution would have become excessively high, even without the price-fixing maneuvers lately introduced into the marketplace. During the last decade the prices of mercury, which has gone up 500 percent, and of lead, which has increased 300 percent, provide familiar illustrations of this price rise phenomenon.

The Effects of Pollution

For an industrializing nation the difficulties unfortunately do not end with the need to secure sources of energy and of essential mineral elements. The process of industrialization itself may create such an increase in the amount of polluting wastes as to operate a negative feedback inhibiting the whole industrial process. Because pollution constraints on industrial societies are comparatively recent, having scarcely been registered until after the Second World War, the extent of negative feedback from pollution is quite inadequately known. It is assumed that pollution will increase exponentially, but we have no knowledge of the upper limits of this exponential growth. We know that natural systems can tolerate considerable overloads of pollution, until they reach what is called a nonlinear dosage threshold and quite suddenly collapse. Moreover, many pollutants do not produce their feedback effects on the geographical areas in which they are generated, but can disturb other regions or, even worse, feed into the whole global system. It is only in this last instance that feedback loops cannot be displaced; use of the global system as a universal sink inescapably involves both innocent and guilty parties alike.

One of the commonest pollutants arising from industrial processes is carbon dioxide. The amount of carbon dioxide in the atmosphere has been monitored since 1958 by a station on the until recently quiescent volcano Mauna Loa on the island of Hawaii. The increase in the amount of carbon dioxide that has been recorded at this station suggests that since the Industrial Revolution began, there has been an exponential increase in the amount of carbon dioxide in the atmosphere, and that before the end of this millennium the amount will reach 160 parts per million, an increase of nearly 30 percent. Very similar figures have been produced, for example, for waste heat generation in the Los Angeles Basin, and nuclear wastes and lead contamination in the Greenland ice cap. Comparable exponential increases have also been demonstrated for pollutants that are deliberately rather than inadvertently released, such as pesticides and other forms of biocides. The one pollutant that has been the subject of extensive investigation and much controversy is the persistent chlorinated hydrocarbon DDT, still the most extensively used insecticide in the world. It is estimated that 150,000 metric tons of DDT a year are released into our global system.

DDT Distribution in the Global Environment

DDT is not readily biodegradable; it may persist for several decades in soil. It is stored in fatty animal tissues, and has been found in the tissues of Arctic Eskimos and Antarctic penguins far from its release points in agricultural and residential areas. The Meadows group attempted to model the flow of DDT in the environment. When it is applied to a target, much of the DDT released remains in the atmosphere. Some subsequently finds its way there by

evaporation from soil or some other target surface. In the air, it may be
transported over long distances before once more being carried to the earth's
surface by rain or snow, or merely settling out of suspension. Moreover, it
enters ecosystem food webs, usually becoming more and more concentrated as
it passes from one member of a food web to another.

The effect of continually increasing the universal use of DDT as a general
insecticide is shown in Figure 3−18A, in terms of the residues that will accumulate in the soil, and in fish as representing a midway section of a food web.
Figure 3−18B shows the amounts of residues accumulating if no increase were
permitted in the global amount of DDT released from 1971, and Figure 3−18C
shows the effect of phasing out the use of DDT from this date. Even if its use
could begin to be phased out in 1971, which is what indeed did happen at about
this time in many industrialized countries, the DDT level in fish would not peak

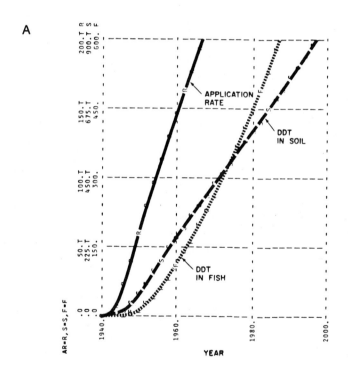

Figure 3−18   DDT use and its persistence in the ecosphere.   Example A shows
that increasing exponential use of DDT will result in similar increases in DDT per-
sisting in the soil and occurring in fish. Even were the use of DDT to be leveled off
at existing values in 1971, levels in fish and in the soil would continue to rise for a
time until they also stabilized (example B). If, starting in 1971, the use of DDT is
gradually reduced (example C), reaching zero in the year 2000, there still will be
further rises in the amounts of DDT in fish and in the soil for a very considerable
time. (Reprinted from) Jørgen Randers, "DDT Movement in the Global Environment" in *Toward Global Equilibrium: Collected Papers,* ed. D. H. and D. L.
Meadows, Copyright © Wright-Allen Press, Inc., Cambridge, MA 02142 USA.

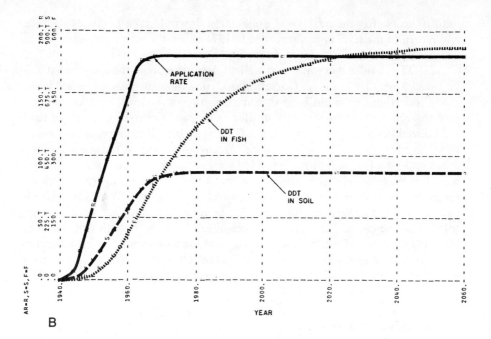

B

C

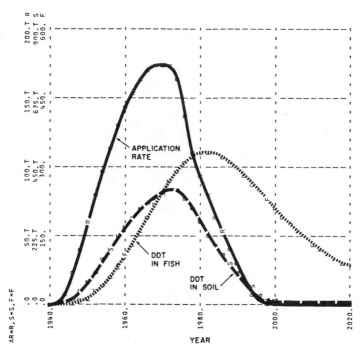

until 10 years after the peak DDT application. It would take 25 years to reduce and return to the level in fish recorded in 1971, when the action to phase out its use was instituted.

DDT provides a familiar and well-studied example of the use of what can be called a *negative resource.* Garrett Hardin describes such resources as "common," referring to the old English common grazing grounds. Such communal facilities represent resources only insofar as they are not overexploited. If they are utilized beyond their tolerance limits for system maintenance, they cease to be of any further use for any purpose for anybody. One of the more famous comments on a frequent attitude toward such negative resources was made by a high Los Angeles official in describing that city's garbage and trash disposal methods. He told how that city had devised a system of filling canyons with such wastes and remarked with pride that as yet only about one thirtieth of the total available canyon capacity had been filled. It seems that this official was blissfully unaware of the "commons" value of the wild canyons with which his city has been generously endowed by nature. Unfortunately, he is far from unique in his attitude toward commons, or negative resources, of various kinds.

Bibliography and References

Anderson, A. A., and Anderson, J. M.   "System Simulation to Identify Environmental Research Needs: Mercury Contamination." In *Toward Global Equilibrium: Collected Papers,* edited by D. L. Meadows and D. H. Meadows, pp. 85–115. Cambridge: Wright-Allen Press, 1973.

Anderson, J. M.   "The Eutrophication of Lakes." In *Toward Global Equilibrium: Collected Papers,* edited by D. L. Meadows and D. H. Meadows, pp. 117–40. Cambridge: Wright-Allen Press, 1973.

Anon.   *Wall Street Journal,* June 2, 1970, p. 25.

Barkley, P. W., and Seckler, D. W.   *Economic Growth and Environmental Decay.* New York: Harcourt Brace Jovanovich, 1972.

Behrens, W. W., III.   "Determinants of Long-Term Resource Availability." In *Toward Global Equilibrium: Collected Papers,* edited by D. L. Meadows and D. H. Meadows, pp. 291–306. Cambridge: Wright-Allen Press, 1973.

Borgstrom, Georg.   *World Food Resources.* New York: Intext, 1973.

Brown, L. R.   "The World Food Prospect." Paper presented to the Limits to Growth '75 conference, Woodlands, Texas, October 21, 1975 (since published in *Science* **190**:1053–59 (1975)).

Cloud, Preston.   "Realities of Mineral Distribution." In *Texas Quarterly* **11**:103–26 (1968). Reprinted in *Readings in Man, the Environment, and Human Ecology,* edited by A. S. Boughey, pp. 509–24. New York: Macmillan Co., 1973.

Cloud, Preston (ed.).   *Resources and Man.* San Francisco: W. H. Freeman and Co., 1969.

Comstock, R. W.   "Energy Crisis: Fact or Fiction." In *Energy Crisis,* edited by V. J. Yannacone, pp. 343–359. New York: West Publishing Co., 1974.

Council on Environmental Quality.   *Energy and the Environment.* Washington, D.C.: U.S. Government Printing Office, 1973.

Economic Research Service, U.S. Department of Agriculture. *The World Food Situation and Prospects to 1985.* Foreign Agricultural Report No. 98. Washington, D.C., December, 1974.

Emmett, J. L.; Nuckolls, J.; and Wood, L. "Fusion Power by Laser Implosion," *Scientific American* **230**(6):24—37 (1974).

Flohn, H. "Der Wasserhauchalt der Erde," *Naturwissenschaften* **60**:310—48 (1973).

Gough, W. C., and Eastlund, B. J. "The Prospects of Fusion Power," *Scientific American* **224**(2):50—64 (1971).

Hayami, Yujiro, and Ruttan, V. W. *Agricultural Development: An International Perspective.* Baltimore: Johns Hopkins Press, 1971.

Inglis, D. R. *Nuclear Energy: Its Physics and Its Social Challenge.* Reading, Mass.: Addison-Wesley Publishing Co., Inc., 1973.

Lappé, F. M. *Diet for a Small Planet.* (Rev. ed.) New York, Harcourt Brace Jovanovich, 1972.

Large, D. B. "Conserving Energy: Opportunity and Obstacles." In *Energy Crisis,* edited by V. J. Yannacone, p. 317. New York: West Publishing Co., 1974.

Lerza, Catherine, and Jacobsen, M. *Food for People, Not for Profit.* New York: Ballantine Books, 1975.

Lovering, T. S. "Mineral Resources from the Land," in *Resources and Man,* edited by Preston Cloud, pp. 109—34. San Francisco: W. H. Freeman and Co., 1969.

Maddox, J. *The Doomsday Syndrome.* New York: McGraw-Hill, 1972.

Naill, R. F. "The Discovery Life Cycle of a Finite Resource: A Case Study of U.S. Natural Gas," in *Toward Global Equilibrium: Collected Papers,* edited by D. L. Meadows and D. H. Meadows, pp. 213—56. Cambridge: Wright-Allen Press, 1973.

National Commission on Material Policy. *Material Needs and the Environment Today and Tomorrow.* Final Report. Washington, D.C.: U.S. Government Pring Office, 1973.

Perry, H. "The Gasification of Coal," *Scientific American* **230**(3):19—25 (1974).

Quigg, P. W. "Alternative Energy Sources," *Saturday Review World,* February 23, 1974, pp. 29—32.

Quigg, P. W. "New Energy Sources," *Saturday Review World,* February 8, 1974, pp. 47—50.

Randers, Jørgen. "DDT Movements in the Global Environment." In *Toward Global Equilibrium: Collected Papers,* edited by D. L. Meadows and D. H. Meadows, pp. 49—83. Cambridge: Wright-Allen Press, 1973.

Revelle, Roger "Food and Population," *Scientific American* **231**(3):160—70 (1974).

Science, Vol. 184, no. 4134, April 16, 1974, collected papers on "Energy."

Woodwell, G. M., and Pecan, E. V. (eds.). *Carbon and the Biosphere.* Springfield, Va.: U.S. Atomic Energy Commission, 1973.

Yannacone, V. J. *Energy Crisis.* New York: West Publishing Co., 1974.

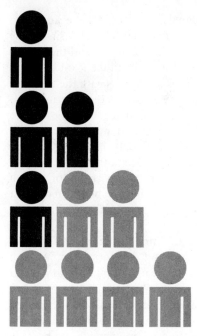

Chapter Four

Model Characteristics

Most people believe that modeling is something new, that it is a novel and modern process that sprang into being with the development of computers some thirty years ago. In fact, it is not a new process, nor need it involve the use of computers. Everything that enters our own cognitive perception has to be intuitively modeled, for without such symbolic processing we would be unable to translate sensory perception into cognitive perception. As we mature, we build up an ever-increasing store of such mental models. In colloquial language, we say the more we learn, the smarter we get. In psychological terms, we are creating in our minds an intricate web or *schema* of coupled intuitive models.

As our experience widens, the interconnecting web of mental models becomes ever more complicated. If further kinds of environmental signals come in too fast for us to form new models coupling to the old ones, our cognitive system breaks down. When this happens, we are said to suffer from *cultural shock,* or *nervous breakdown,* whichever terminology we are employing. The number of unfamiliar environmental signals coming in has to be temporarily reduced while we catch up with our intuitive model building. Individuals who have constructed a coupled mental model system that enables them to cope immediately with all environmental signals they receive are said to have balanced personalities.

Written Models

With the invention of writing, we were relieved of some of the need to build, each for ourselves, an intricate individual web of coupled mental models. Some models could be set down as *written models* to which we could refer when necessary in order to interpret particular signals. We could have access to libraries of written models prepared by other individuals. When using these libraries, we need to know only the input environmental signal and the output result; the written model itself does not matter, for we can take it on trust, on the *authority* of the person who prepared it. This is analogous with the way that we can jump into a car and drive off without any knowledge of the internal-combustion engine. All of us have to take some things on trust, for if we were to challenge every written model to which we are now exposed, one lifetime would be a totally inadequate time for the task. Some individuals, however, seem to prefer the negative task of challenging established models; others, the positive task of constructing new ones. This is just as well, for the superiority of written models resides in their examinable nature. They do *not* have to be taken on trust as is the case with verbal models; their *logic* can be reexamined and either confirmed or refuted.

Thus, once we begin to set down our mental models in written form, we expose them to a greater degree of organization and categorization. We can start constructing a peripheral storage device of great power, a library bank, immensely increasing our model-forming capacities. Written models, by virtue of being set out in some form of language, have thereby acquired a formalized structure that makes them more readily comprehensible than mental models, for they follow methods of symbolic representation with which we can become familiar if we are not already so aware.

Traditionally, written models are nestled into a hierarchical arrangement according to type, as set down in Figure 4–1. The hierarchy commences with the simplest form of written model, the *process model* (Fig. 4–2). Many examples of process models are provided in this text. These are *qualitative* models only — that is, they merely show us the *nature* of the interactions in the systems modeled, not the *quantities* and *rates* involved. To insert quantities and rates, we have to proceed further along the model hierarchy.

Multiple Regression Analyses

In order to develop the earliest forms of quantitative models, we had to identify cause and effect. When we could examine the cause-and-effect relationship under the controlled conditions of a laboratory, it was relatively easy to isolate the causal factor involved, vary it, and determine the extent of its effect. From the results, we could develop correlation coefficients, the quantitative expression of the cause-and-effect interaction.

Development of more sophisticated statistical techniques in the twentieth century permitted us to explore cause-and-effect correlations without this laboratory control. We could examine a multivariable system with several independent but interacting cause-and-effect relationships, and statistically "control" all but one cause, while we quantitatively determined the partial regressions describing its statistical effects. This powerful statistical technique of

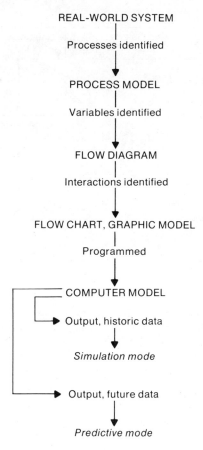

Figure 4–1 **Hierarchical categories of written system models.** The construction of a written system model proceeds in a logical series of stages, as shown here. When the interactions in the model represent information feedback loops, the model is of the form described as a *system dynamics computer model.* If the interactions are represented by constants and all the input variables are known, the model is called *deterministic;* if some input variables are unknown because their values are determined by chance or some unknown determiner, the model is defined as *stochastic.*

regression analysis spawned a multitude of empirical correlations, many of which have remained uninterpreted in terms of primary cause and effect. In other words, lacking the basic process models, the regression observations could not be incorporated into rational system models. Moreover, this technique of multivariate analysis could not be used to study the effect of closely related variables.

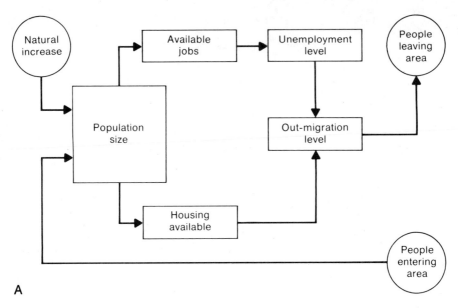

A

Figure 4−2 Process models. The process model of a simple socioeconomic system is shown in example A. It identifies natural increase and in-migration as adding to a population, and out-migration as reducing it. It further recognizes the available jobs and housing as related to out-migration. The process model B represents the global socioeconomic system as analyzed for the Meadows model World 3. Reprinted, with permission, from Meadows, Dennis L., William W. Behrens III, Donella H. Meadows, Roger F. Naill, Jørgen Randers, and Erich K. O. Zahn, *Dynamics of Growth in a Finite World,* Copyright © 1974, Wright-Allen Press, Inc., Cambridge, MA 02142 USA.

Simulation Models

Some partial regressions, however, did respond to cause-and-effect analysis; they thus became accepted regressional models of the third hierarchical order of what can legitimately be termed *system models* (see Fig. 4−2). In some instances, it was considered that visual presentations of these third-order system models would provide for easier comprehension, and *graphic models* of regressional interactions were constructed (see Fig. 5−3). Without the invention of the computer some thirty years ago, system models would have remained at this regressional or third-order stage. The limitations of linear regression equations were recently described by R. W. Poole. Our system-modeling capability would have been determined by a computational limit on human capacity, for a regressional model allows for only one iterative run of the system model before a new set of calculations must be made. Directional

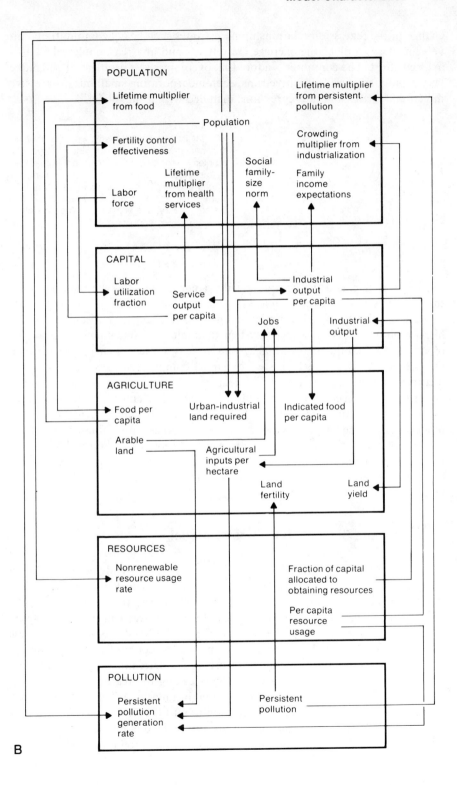

B

change of the regression relationship necessitates such heavy computational involvement as to place the exercise entirely beyond any reasonable calculator-assisted effort. The computer is a tool that overcomes this problem. It will make very rapidly a series of iterative runs, each incorporating small but progressive directional changes in the regressions included within the model.

> Investigators with many kinds of training and background are approaching . . . systems problems, some concentrating on human relations systems alone, some concentrating on simple ecological models . . . which do not include man, some trying to develop general systems theory, and some working on the electrical computer models.
>
> *H. T. Odum, 1971*

Forrester called the computerized system models that he developed for the simulation of socioeconomic systems, *system dynamics computer models* because of this capacity for directional interactive change, or *dynamism,* which his computer models provided. System dynamics computer models have not obviated the need for regressional system models; these still have a useful place in system analysis. However, system dynamics computer models provide for the incorporation of varying interactive relationships into a system model that is closer to reality because of this built-in capacity for change. Predictive system models of the future will have to be of a system dynamics form when they model total socioeconomic systems, for the variables within these systems are always potentially modifiable by changes in the feedback pressures that govern them. Thus, socioeconomic systems cannot be adequately represented within the rigid framework of traditional regressional models.

A Simple Simulation Computer Model

The system dynamics computer models that have already been mentioned and are to be considered later in more detail in this text are very complex. Although they all possess a common basic structure, their very complexity tends to obscure their essential features. These features can more readily be perceived in a greatly simplified model. Figure 4—2A shows a basic process model of a socioeconomic system that simulates a region of any given dimensions. This region has a population whose size is determined by three factors: the natural increase, the number of people leaving the region (out-migrants), and the number of people entering the region (in-migrants). The model does not concern itself with the cause of in-migration, but takes it as a fact. Nor does it attempt an explanation of out-migration, although this might be ascribed to one of two factors: either failure to find a job, or failure to find a dwelling place.

The Process Model

A process model such as this differs from a mental model only in that it is written down. Some process models are so simple that they do not need to be diagrammatized. For example, the positive feedback model illustrated in Figure 2−4 can be readily pictured and remembered as a mental model. As process models become progressively more complicated, they become increasingly difficult to visualize without graphic illustration. A system model is nevertheless a system model whether it remains a mental model or is set down as a written model. Some system models are first prepared graphically and then memorized as mental models — as, for example, a football play, or a procedure for winning at blackjack.

The variables in a system model are of two kinds. When they refer to a quantity, they are known as *state* variables; these contrast with *rate* variables that indicate the rate at which an interaction occurs. When a process model consists entirely of rate variables, it can be converted into a system model by direct substitution of rate values for each interaction recognized. This is the procedure in all empirical multiple regression analyses of social relationships. Most systems, however, have system state variables as well as input rate variables. Process models of systems are thus much more than assemblages of partial regression relationships. The effects of input and system rate variables on system state variables must be individually determined and then totaled.

> Formal models can be expressed in words, pictures, or other symbols, but they are probably best stated in mathematical equations, for two reasons: mathematics is a precise and a neutral language, . . . and assumptions expressed in mathematical notation can be processed by a computer. . . .
>
> *D. L. Meadows et al., 1974*

The Flow Diagram

The next stage of model preparation is to draw up a flow diagram based on the process model. Before proceeding to do this for the simplified urban system used as an example here, an even more basic system — the law of supply and demand — can be used to establish the basic flow diagram features. In a simple flow diagram the flow of material or of people is shown by continuous lines, the flow of information by dotted lines. *Quantities* or *levels* — that is, numbers of such items as people, jobs, and houses — are inserted into rectangular boxes, *rates* into a formalized symbol that looks like a bottle on its side. When a line runs to a triangle, it means there is a flow into or from another system that is not considered a part of the one being modeled. There is a convention to indicate whether this external system is a receiving or contributing one, and the arrows showing direction of flow make it clear which is which. An external information source can be indicated.

Figure 4—3 illustrates how a flow diagram can represent the operation of the law of supply and demand. A metal, X, is stockpiled after being mined. It is mined at a variable rate from a system that is not considered here. It is used to manufacture goods (Y). The goods are sold at a variable rate to a system also not considered here. A solid line will link the flow of the metal X into the system by mining at an unspecified rate, to a stockpile of an unspecified quantity, to manufacture into goods at an unspecified rate, accumulating in unstated quantities for sale at unspecified rates to outside the system that is being modeled.

This is already a written system model for metal X, but it provides little information. It can be converted to a dynamic model by inserting two information feedback loops, as shown in Figure 4—3. One relates the rate of mining more metal X to the quantity already stockpiled. The other feedback loop relates the rate of manufacture of goods to the accumulation of Y — that is, goods already manufactured. The system can be made responsive to demand by inserting a third information feedback loop from a market situation outside the system being modeled (Fig. 4—3).

This model is now a perfectly sound system dynamics model. We can research the system to obtain the regression equation for the effect of the level of the metal X stockpile on the mining rate, the effect of the inventory of goods Y on the manufacturing rate, or both.

A metal substitution loop can be added to this working model very simply, as is shown (Fig. 4—3). When there is a run on the stockpile of metal X, substitute metal B is used to manufacture the same goods. Information feedback loops will swing in this substitute when supply and demand require it.

> Making a formal systems model is a non-linear process that involves many experiments, regressions, and reiterations. Nevertheless, the process must cycle through a number of logical steps in sequence; each step is dependent on the successful completion of the one before.
>
> *D. L. Meadows et al., 1974*

The running of a simple dynamic system model such as the one just described is subject to the prior determination of the operating level of the information feedback loops in the system, in this instance four. There is no need for a computer model to be developed; the four separate calculations from the corresponding regression equations, plus the fifth feeding in from the outside market, could be done by hand with but five calculations per iteration. However, a twenty-year run with yearly iterations would involve a hundred separate calculations. Even the simplified urban model developed in this chapter would involve far more than that number.

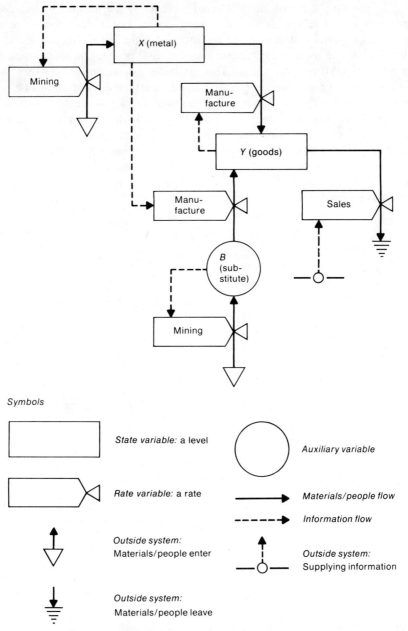

Symbols

State variable: a level

Auxiliary variable

Rate variable: a rate

Materials/people flow

Information flow

Outside system:
Materials/people enter

Outside system:
Supplying information

Outside system:
Materials/people leave

Figure 4–3   Flow diagram of a simple system.   The law of supply and demand can be represented in operation in the simplified economic system modeled in this flow diagram. The symbols employed in this diagram are commonly encountered, some being used, for example, in the DYNAMO language of the Forrester-Meadows school. One symbol only — that representing a materials flow from the outside, often called an *exogenous* source — is not so commonly indicated in this manner.

In the flow diagram modeled in Figure 4—4, the nature of the several categories of variables in the simplified urban system can be perceived. Statistics on births and deaths can be obtained from census figures. These are *rates* that can be used to estimate changes in total population size, which also can be obtained from census data. The number of houses and jobs, if these were to be inserted in an expanded model, can be ascertained from similar or other sources; there are ways of determining the number of in-migrants (such as the number of changed car registrations). All these variables are what are known as *input variables*. The number of out-migrants is what is known as a *system variable,* for it can be estimated from the input variable values and their interactions as shown in the flow diagram. Having selected the variables to be included, and their interactions, the next stage in the construction of a system dynamics computer model is to prepare a *flow chart.*

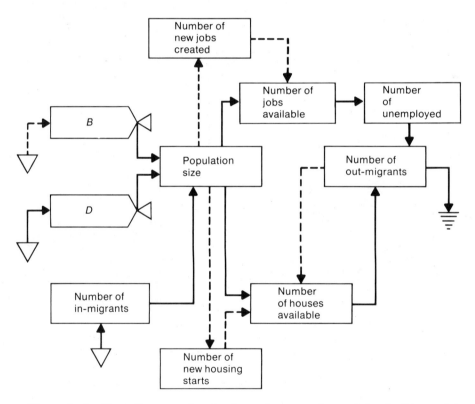

Figure 4—4   Flow diagram of a simple socioeconomic model. In this model, developed from the process model shown in 4—2A, there are two rate variable inputs (birth and death rates), one state variable input (net migration), and three system state variables (population size, numbers of jobs, and numbers of dwellings). Run with historic values for all input system variables, the model can be validated. It becomes a predictive model when present values for two input rate variables (births and deaths) and one state variable (net migration) are projected into the future to calculate the one system state variable (population). All interactions in such a simple model are assumed to be linear.

The Flow Chart

The flow chart must analyze the interactions between variables as shown in the flow diagram until each one is broken down into a single interaction that can be repeated over and over again after the lapse of a given time, or *iterated.* The flow chart must show each of these iterated interactions arranged in a logical sequence of events. A flow chart that can be developed from the flow diagram in Figure 4—4 is shown in Figure 4—5. It should be noted that this is only one of several ways in which this system can be flow-charted; the same results can be obtained from other variants of this particular flow chart.

In Figure 4—6, what each iterative computational procedure shown in the flow chart represents is briefly explained. The READ and PRINT variables are the input data variable and the output system variable, respectively. The other system variables are for computational purposes only; there is no need to have their values recorded in the output information.

The Computer Program

Once the flow chart has been prepared, a computer program can be written. The computer language used for this purpose can be selected from many, or can be specially made up. Fortran IV was selected for use in this example because it is the most commonly used computer language in the United States, indeed in the world. There are languages especially designed for use with computer models — for example SIMSKRIT. Jack Pugh of Forrester's group designed its own modeling language, DYNAMO, now developed into the DYNAMO 3 version.

The Fortran IV program for the simple model developed here is shown in the appendix. When the model is to be run, the values for all the input variables listed in the READ statement must be entered. Those selected for this exercise are statistics from Orange County, California. As these values represent actual data, the model can be set to run in historic time. The output values will also then be in historic time, and can be checked against actual data. Validation by historic replication is an initial step in the verification of a simulation model. A validation run on this simple system model is shown in Table 4—1. As the model shows a fair approximation of output data to the actual data, it can be regarded as having been validated in this initial sense. It is a reasonable simulation model; indeed, it is so simple it could not be far wrong, but neither can it be very accurate. For comparison, a validation run on the Meadows World 3 population subsystem is given in Table 4—2.

The model having thus been validated, it can now be set to run in a *predictive* mode, using historic input data, but generated system variables that provide output values for future years.

The particular predictive mode output from this model set for twenty years is shown in Table 4—3.

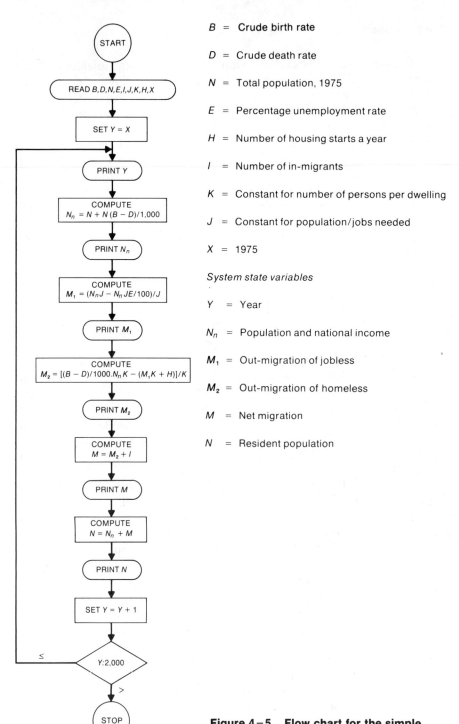

B = Crude birth rate

D = Crude death rate

N = Total population, 1975

E = Percentage unemployment rate

H = Number of housing starts a year

I = Number of in-migrants

K = Constant for number of persons per dwelling

J = Constant for population/jobs needed

X = 1975

System state variables

Y = Year

N_n = Population and national income

M_1 = Out-migration of jobless

M_2 = Out-migration of homeless

M = Net migration

N = Resident population

Flow chart elements:

START

READ $B, D, N, E, I, J, K, H, X$

SET $Y = X$

PRINT Y

COMPUTE
$N_n = N + N(B - D)/1{,}000$

PRINT N_n

COMPUTE
$M_1 = (N_n J - N_n JE/100)/J$

PRINT M_1

COMPUTE
$M_2 = [(B - D)/1000.N_n K - (M_1 K + H)]/K$

PRINT M_2

COMPUTE
$M = M_2 + I$

PRINT M

COMPUTE
$N = N_n + M$

PRINT N

SET $Y = Y + 1$

$Y : 2{,}000$ $\leq$ $>$

STOP

**Figure 4–5   Flow chart for the simple
socioeconomic urban model.**

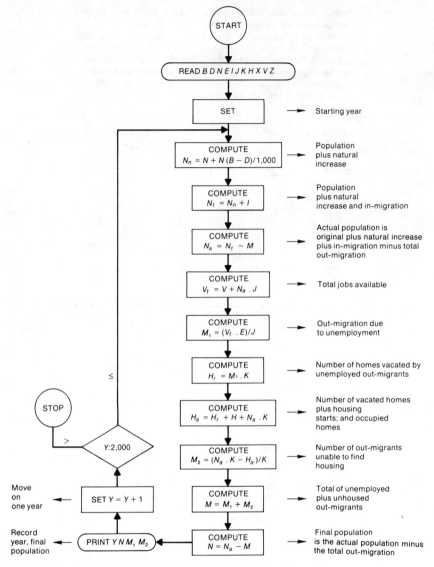

Figure 4−6   The flow chart of Figure 4−5 explained.

Table 4-1   Simulation mode output from the simple socioeconomic system model.   When comparing the estimated population of Orange County with the actual data from 1950 through 1970, the first part of the model run is usually less than 10 percent off. Greater discrepancies occur later because of the simplistic and deterministic, that is, nondynamic nature of this system model; but even then, it is never more than 25 percent out.

Population (in thousands)			Population (in thousands)		
Year	Model Estimate	Actual	Year	Model Estimate	Actual
1950	216	216			
1951	257	231	1961	680	763
1952	299	250	1962	723	840
1953	340	273	1963	767	939
1954	382	308	1964	810	1,093
1955	424	336	1965	854	1,124
1956	466	448	1966	899	1,190
1957	508	504	1967	943	1,250
1958	551	551	1968	988	1,306
1959	593	611	1969	1,032	1,363
1960	636	703	1970	1,078	1,421

Table 4-2   Population data from a historical run.   When the Meadows World 3 model is run in historic time, it can be validated against historical data. This table compared world population size, as calculated by the model, set against United Nations estimates. The model final figure differs from the estimate by 4 percent, a minor discrepancy in the context of the model.

Year	World Population (in millions of persons)	
	Meadows Model	United Nations Estimate
1900	1,610	1,610
1910	1,760	. . . . .
1920	1,910	1,860
1930	2,080	2,070
1940	2,380	2,300
1950	2,740	2,520
1960	3,210	3,000
1970	3,790	3,660

Table 4-3 Predictive output from the simple socioeco-nomic system model — nondynamic form. This *predic-tive* output is from the system model shown in Figure 4−5, and run in its *simulation* mode for the output shown in Table 4−1. This simple deterministic model puts the 1990 population of Orange County at 2,412,000, which lies within the spread of 2,196,000 to 2,445,000 that is provided by the estimates of various planning authorities.

Year	Estimated Population (in thousands)	Year	Estimated Population (in thousands)
1975	1,750	1985	2,189
1976	1,793	1986	2,233
1977	1,837	1987	2,278
1978	1,881	1988	2,322
1979	1,924	1989	2,367
1980	1,968	1990	2,412
1981	2,012	1991	2,456
1982	2,056	1992	2,501
1983	2,100	1993	2,546
1984	2,145	1994	2,591

The time horizon of a model is the period over which the modeler is interested in the system's behavior. That period usually cor-responds either to the time necessary for the system to manifest a behavior mode of interest or to the time required for the system to respond fully to some proposed new set of policies.

D. L. Meadows et al., 1974

Dynamic Variables

The simple model so far described is not truly a system dynamics com-puter model because it does not allow for any change over time in input values. With each successive iteration the model is thus likely to run further and further from reality; and as can be seen, in this form it rapidly gets us into one of the ridiculous exponential growth situations described in Chapter 2. In this form the model is described as a *deterministic* one, that is, it is capable of only one solution. System dynamics computer models are also deterministic within this usually accepted meaning of the term.

Dynamism can be inserted into the model very readily, as shown in Figure 4−7. First, the flow diagram is modified so as to allow for a progressive decline in fertility and migration. In this instance, assuming the model runs from 1975, the crude birthrate is set to decline by one person each year until 1985, when it will equal the unchanging crude death rate, and replacement fertility levels will

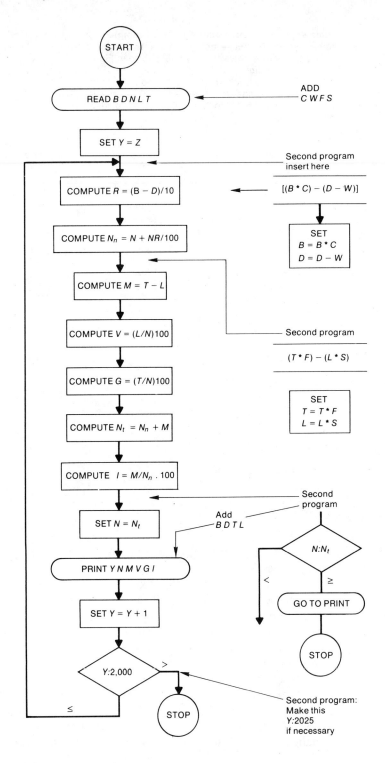

START

READ $B\ D\ N\ L\ T$ ← ADD $C\ W\ F\ S$

SET $Y = Z$

Second program insert here

COMPUTE $R = (B - D)/10$ ← $[(B * C) - (D - W)]$

SET $B = B * C$ $D = D - W$

COMPUTE $N_n = N + NR/100$

COMPUTE $M = T - L$

COMPUTE $V = (L/N)100$ — Second program

$(T * F) - (L * S)$

COMPUTE $G = (T/N)100$

SET $T = T * F$ $L = L * S$

COMPUTE $N_t = N_n + M$

COMPUTE $I = M/N_n\ .\ 100$

SET $N = N_t$

Second program

Add $B\ D\ T\ L$

PRINT $Y\ N\ M\ V\ G\ I$

$N{:}N_t$

$<$ $\geq$

GO TO PRINT

SET $Y = Y + 1$

STOP

$Y{:}2{,}000$ $>$

$\leq$

STOP

Second program: Make this $Y{:}2025$ if necessary

have been reached. Natural increase is then held from 1985 at this level. Similarly, in-migration levels are set to decline by 2,000 persons annually continuously throughout the run of twenty-five years.

Table 4−4 shows the effects on the output of running this simple model in this new form. Even now, it is not truly a system dynamics computer model in the full sense; it is still an oversimplified deterministic model and not yet a system dynamics model in the Forrester-Meadows meaning. There is no feedback loop in the model to drive the changing rate values. Also, for example, people without dwellings are unlikely all to out-migrate immediately; they will stay with relatives or friends, live in a motel, rent a mobile home, and so forth. People without jobs are equally unlikely immediately to depart. For a while, they will go on unemployment insurance or welfare, draw down savings, obtain loans, and somehow or other hang on for a while. Appropriate modifications of the several interactions would have to be made to allow for time lags of this nature. However, what will make this model finally a system dynamics model in the Forrester-Meadows sense is to provide two information feedback loops. One such can go from the number of people unemployed to the number of new jobs created, the other from the number of people unhoused to the number of new housing starts.

Table 4−4 Predictive output from the simple socioeco-nomic system model — dynamic form.   This is the predictive output from the system model shown in Figure 4−7, which provides for dynamic interaction between variables. Because of this dynamism, and contrary to any other presently existing projections, the projected population of Orange County levels off in 1987 and after several years starts to decline. It never reaches the 1990 figure of any of the planners' projections, or of the nondynamic model output of Table 4−3. Deliberate changes in the socioeconomic system could, however, prevent this predicted population decline.

Year	Projected Population (in thousands)	Year	Projected Population (in thousands)
1975	1,750	1985	1,930
1976	1,793	1986	1,933
1977	1,828	1987	1,934
1978	1,855	1988	1,934
1979	1,876	1989	1,934
1980	1,892	1990	1,934
1981	1,904	1991	1,933
1982	1,914	1992	1,932
1983	1,921	1993	1,930
1984	1,926	1994	1,928

◄ **Figure 4−7   The flow chart of Figure 4−6 with further variation introduced.**

Model Sensitivity

Now that the simple model constructed here has a dynamic form, it is possible to test its sensitivity, that is, to determine how responsive it is to changes in the nature of the interactions represented by particular mathematical expressions. One further advantage of a system dynamics computer model over a multiple regression model is that great precision in input data is not required. Considerable approximation in the input data may be tolerated without great detriment to the output data of the model.

In the population model run illustrated in Figure 4−7, whose output is provided in Table 4−4, the rate of out-migration is estimated as declining by 5 percent. This figure could be twice too much, or it could be one half of what it should be. When the results of adjusting this expression to 2 ½ percent are run there appears to be not too much difference in the elapsed time before the population stabilizes. Alternatively, the out-migration rate may be increased by 5 percent instead. Again, the results of making this adjustment do not change the elapsed time to equilibrium very greatly. It would appear that insofar as this particular interaction is concerned, the model is not highly sensitive; minor errors in assumptions in this portion are thus of little significance.

> One way to predict the consequences of change in a system is to draw a systems diagram as a model, including values for flows and storages. Then the relative magnitude of the change can be compared with the normal.
>
> *H. T. Odum, 1971*

Structure of System Dynamics Computer Models

Any system dynamics computer model, however complex, has to conform to the same basic structure as the example just illustrated. It must include *variables* and *interactions* between them. The variables may be *states* (*quantities*) or *rates*. The interactions may be predictable (*deterministic*) or *unpredictable* (*stochastic*) in form; but without a minimum of two variables and one interaction, we do not have a system model. No matter how complicated the system model, it must be constructed from the same basic units, *variables* and their *interactions*. When values for variables are entered into the system model as data, such variables are known as *input variables*. When the values are calculated from the interaction within the model, they are called *system variables*.

> The system dynamics computer modeling methodology is based on a theory of system structure which permits the symbolic and math-

ematical representation of the variables and their
interactions which govern the behavior of social
and physical systems.

A. S. Boughey

When the value of the system variables that are output are known
historically, and the model is run in historic time, the use of historic data for the
input values will permit the model to be checked, that is, *validated.* Assuming a
continuation of existing levels for the input variables, and the same interactions
and feedback loops, the model can then be used in a *predictive* mode by projecting it forward into the future. If a continuation of existing levels for input
variables cannot be assumed, various adjustments, as described later, must be
made.

Mathematical Expression of Interactions

Each of the interactions in the simple model under consideration in the
last few pages is *deterministic.* It can be represented by a mathematical expression. *Stochastic* models can also be represented by mathematical expressions. A
stochastic model, previously known as a Monte Carlo model, by contrast with a
deterministic model has more than a single solution. Currently the study of
topology — the mathematics of surfaces — is greatly contributing to the
development of sophisticated stochastic models. It has led to the formulation of
what is presently called "Catastrophe Theory." Some deterministic relationships we already have considered in Chapter 2 — for example, the one between
births and deaths and population, where:

$$\frac{\Delta N}{\Delta t} = B - D$$

To substitute a mathematical calculation for the population growth interaction on an annual basis in Figure 4–4 using input rates for B and D, we
merely have to convert this mathematical expression to:

$$N_1 \text{ (New population)} = N + 1 \left([B - D]/1000 \times N\right)$$

The other interactions in the simple model are not ready-made, but
likewise can be represented by mathematical expressions. Taking the present
population, the number of jobs (J_O), the number of employed (U), and the
population size (N_O), we might find that the population of, say, 2 million has
500,000 jobs and 10 percent unemployed. Then:

$$J_1 = \left(N_1 \times \left(\frac{1 \times 10^6}{2 \times 10^6}\right)\right) + \left(J_0 + \left(J_0 \times \frac{10}{100}\right)\right)$$

In this simple deterministic model the several interactions are all of a
linear type. Few biological or social systems can be adequately simulated by a
simple model of this type; usually, the interactions are of a nonlinear form.

> If our information and assumptions are right, a computer can enable us to work through the consequences or the preconditions for a range of events, some of which might not be detected or predicted by the naked, uncomputerized eye. But if our assumptions are wrong, then we shall be just as wrong with a computer model as without one.
>
> *H. G. Simmons, 1973*

Nonlinear Interactions

a. Simple Curves.   The simplest type of nonlinear interaction can be illustrated from the Meadows model by the interaction that relates nutritional level to life expectancy (Fig. 4—8). The greatest effect of nutritional level increase is at the lowest end of the scale. Thereafter the effect diminishes continuously until, beyond a certain nutritional level, further increments are without effect on life expectancy. The segment of the Meadows model that covers this phenomenon distinguishes between mortality occurring at the prereproductive, reproductive, and postreproductive stages. Increases in nutritional levels that extend longevity into and through the reproductive years are more significant in considerations of population growth than those occurring in either of the dependent classes.

Relationships like this are shown by consumption of industrial metals such as copper and steel, and the market prices of raw materials. The inverse or declining form of this relationship is shown by mineral extraction costs and some expressions of pollution like oxygen depletion.

b. Logarithmic Relationships.   Causal relationships of an exponential form have already been extensively discussed in Chapter 2. The mathematical expression of this relationship is:

$$\frac{dN}{dt} = rN$$

This expression states that the *rate* of change (*r*) in the amount of *N* is determined by the amount of change (*dN*). A typical curve of such an exponential relationship is shown in Figure 4—9.

Apart from the familiar logarithmic growth rate of human populations and of compound interest money deposits, and similar instances cited in Chapter 2, there are many other examples of this form of interaction, including rate of urbanization, increase in industrial production, use of agricultural fertilizer (Fig. 4—9), consumption of some industrial requirements such as mercury, and air pollution (Fig. 4—10).

Inverse interactions — that is, logarithmic reductions — are illustrated by declines in the population of hunted endangered species like whales, and by remaining reserves of nonrenewable resources.

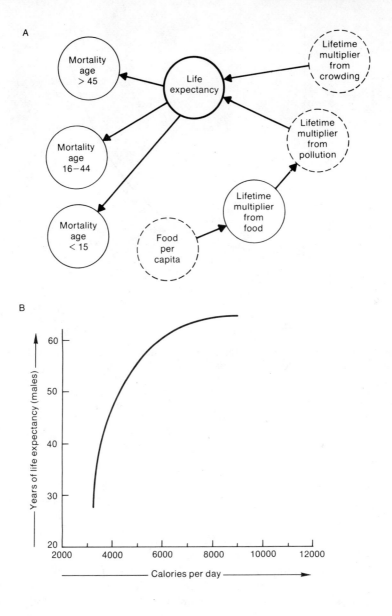

Figure 4–8   A simple nonlinear interaction.   When the mean national nutritional level is plotted against the average national expectation of life for a number of countries, a simple nonlinear relationship is exhibited showing a continuous decline in extension of life expectancy for specific increments of nutritional levels. Eventually, there is no effect from further increments (example B). This interaction is entered in the Meadows model as shown in example A, which depicts the relevant portion of the model flow diagram; mortality is separated into three age groups: the prereproductive, reproductive, and postreproductive segments of the population. Diagrams incorporate material from several sources.

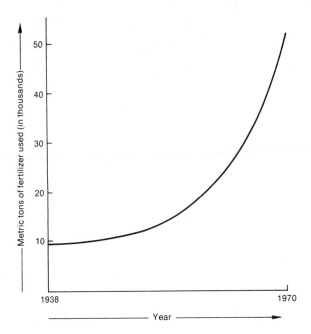

Figure 4–9 Logarithmic relationships: Fertilizer demands.   World fertilizer consumption is of this logarithmic or exponential form. Unfortunately, some predictions as to improvement in future agricultural yields as a result of the Green Revolution have failed to recognize the possibility of this logarithmic increase in world fertilizer demands. Figure prepared from several sources.

c. Logistic Interactions.   The logistic or sigmoid type of growth represents exponential growth proceeding until it encounters limiting factors. It has already been considered in Chapter 3. Mathematically, the type of interaction is represented by the expression:

$$\frac{dN}{dt} = \left(\frac{K - N}{K}\right) N$$

where K is the maximum value of N that the limiting factors will permit.

Besides the familiar example of this provided from human population growth, logistic forms of interaction are shown between availability of resources and resource usage (Fig. 4–11), steel consumption in various nations, recycling costs, and returns on investments. Inverse logistic relationships are shown, for example, by numbers of whales killed, the effect of industrialization on birth rates, and price gains when demand exceeds supply.

Most importantly, logistic interactions are the only ones considered here that are significantly disturbed by *time lags.* The logistic relationship is not always immediately responsive to the limiting factors involved, and overshoot may result. The effects of time lags and consequent overshoots are considered more fully in later chapters.

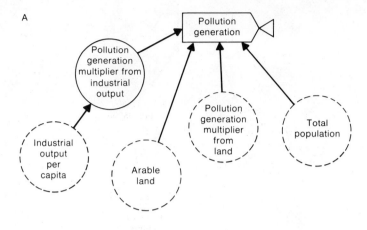

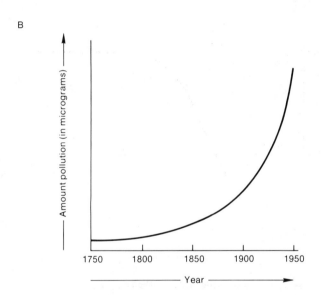

Figure 4–10 Logarithmic relationships: Pollution generation. Pollution generation as influenced by the variables shown in this portion of the Meadows World 3 flow diagram (example A) increases logarithmically (example B). Diagrams prepared from several sources.

d. Compound Interactions. It is not always possible or practicable to break down a particular interaction into its most basic relationships in terms of the several linear or nonlinear forms already described. The result of this partial separation is a compound interaction whose mathematical expression is too complicated for most practical usages. A good example of such a compound interrelationship is provided by Meadows et al. (Fig. 4–12).

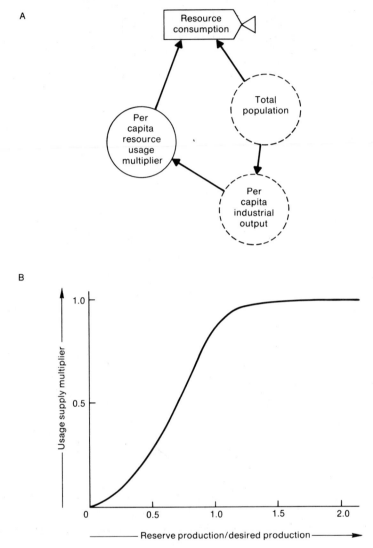

Figure 4-11   Logistic relationships: Resource usage.   The rate of consumption of a nonrenewable resource as entered in the flow diagram of the Meadows World 3 model is shown in example A. Eventually, this usage rate will level off at an asymptote (example B), thus exhibiting a logistic form of increase. Diagrams prepared from several sources.

e. Unknown Relationships.   While it is possible to analyze some resultant interactions as just described, others may — at least momentarily — defy definition; their causal interrelationships cannot be perceived. Such resultants can be treated in one of two ways: The first is to "black-box" them; the second, to follow the "Kane" procedure.

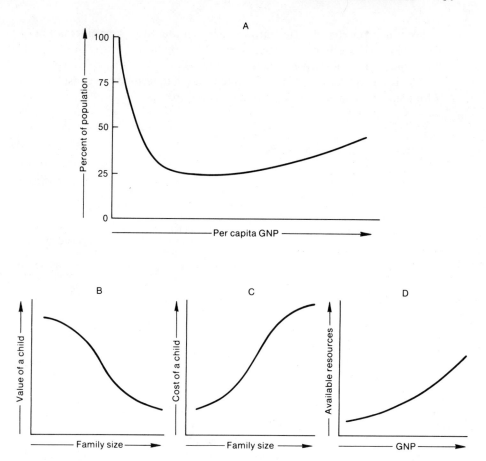

Figure 4-12 A compound interrelationship. The effect of increasing per capita prosperity on the average percentage of the population desiring families of four or more children is initially expressed by a decline. One data point suggests, however, that there may with further prosperity be an upturn. Assuming the validity of this interaction as expressed in the resultant curve A, this can be broken down into component curves B, C, and D. Curve B is of inverse logistic form and expresses the value of each child. Curve C is of logistic form, reflecting the cost of each child. Curve D is of exponential form, indicating the increase in available resources as prosperity increases. Diagrams prepared from several sources.

Engineers have long used the black box technique. It is a very convenient expedient when proceeding with system analysis of the type that they commonly perform. In the black box procedure, it is not necessary to understand the causal relationships of an interaction; it is sufficient to obtain empirical data as to output values at different levels of input variables. Indeed, such empirical correlations provide the initial entry also into many social interrelationships. In the classical days of human ecology, many empirical correlations were explored, such as the effect of population density on crime, juvenile delinquency, divorce, longevity, fertility, and income. More recently, with an increasing study of ecological and social systems, raw field data on particular relationships have been incorporated directly into models, without any prior elucidation of underlying causal mechanisms. There is no objection to this procedure, provided that some stated objective is thereby achieved.

The Kane procedure is a sophisticated tool that need not be considered in this fundamental exposition of modeling procedures.

Potential Uses of Models

> There are many approaches to computer models. Some are naïve. Some are conceptually and structurally inconsistent with the nature of actual systems. Some are based on methodologies for obtaining input data that commit the models to omitting major concepts and relationships in the psychological and human reaction area that we all know to be crucial. The key to success . . . is not to computerize a model but to have a model structure and relationships that properly represent the system that is being considered.
>
> *J. W. Forrester, 1973*

For some purposes, it is sufficient in itself to construct a simulation model. It is very satisfying to be able to reproduce by a man-made device the complex of interactions that occur within, for example, a social system. However, with all simulation models, the real potential is not achieved until some degree of prediction has been obtained from the model.

In the case of the Meadows global model World 3, the desired prediction was an estimate of the ongoing levels of the five input state variables when the model was run forward as far as the year 2100. This would provide as output graphs for population, industrial production per capita, food production per capita, pollution as a multiple of the 1970 level, and the remaining nonrenewable resources as a fraction of the 1900 reserves. Additionally, the model would output three system rate variables: the crude birth rate, the crude death rate, and the services per capita as the dollar equivalent per person per year.

Figure 5−5 on page 108 illustrates the first run, the *Standard Run,* from a run of the Meadows model projected to 1970 as a simulation model and continued from there to 2100 as a predictive one. It will be observed from this printout that global nonrenewable resources begin to show about halfway through the run a dramatic decrease. This creates a severe shortage of raw material for the expanded industrial world system, and per capita industrial production begins to fall away. Almost simultaneously, so too does the level of food per capita because this is influenced by the industrial output of machinery, pesticides, fertilizers, and so forth. Once these declines are initiated, they continue very rapidly. So also do services, which had increased during the earlier expansive phase of the model run. A combination of food and medical service scarcities promotes a rapid rise in the death rate, and an abrupt curtailment of the exponential rate of population growth. Indeed, the population shortly proceeds into a crash phase. In this particular run, this crash phase has still not ended when the run ceases. According to the model, the world system is by 2100 at the point where the population is roughly half of what it was within less than a century previously.

The authors of the Meadows model emphasize that it is not intended to express specific times or precise values. It would be quite illegitimate, therefore, to say that a population crash will occur at some specific year, or that when this crash occurs the population will be one half or one quarter or some specified fraction of the maximum number of individuals that was attained before the crash. The Mesarovic-Pestel regional models, to be considered later, try to avoid the same possibility of misrepresentation by offering conclusions in the form of *scenarios*. By this procedure, they can avoid making a statement such as "By the year 2100 the nation of Japan will have only a 2 ½ years' supply of coal reserves remaining within its home islands." Instead, Mesarovic and Pestel can build a scenario in which regions relying on domestic reserves of fossil fuels will have begun to experience very serious depletion of remaining reserves of fossil fuels, with consequent serious energy problems in supplying industrial power. The SPECULATER model of California, prepared by K. E. F. Watt, is by contrast much more specific in its output (Fig. 4–13).

In its predictive operation the Meadows World 3 model shows primarily the mode of increase or decrease that will be followed in the future by the five input state variables. It can be seen from Figure 5–5, which is usually referred to as the world model *standard run,* that the world system will collapse before reaching 2100. Whether it will do so 15 years or 100 years before the end of this period is really immaterial, at least for the model purpose. Nor is it any more relevant that the population will fall from a figure of x to that of y. The point is that if the world system continues to operate in the future as it does today in the first half of the 1970 decade, industrial growth and food production will go on increasing as they have been doing recently until a serious shortage of resources causes the curtailment of further increase. Because of a time lag, pollution will continue to rise even after this event. Then, primarily because of food shortages, the population growth will not only actually be contained, but it will fall so dramatically that its decline comes into the category of what can be called a population crash.

> If technology is defined not just as machines, but as a rationalistic attempt at problem solving using machines, then the new intellectual technology — system analysis, simulation, decision theory, linear programming, stochastic models — based on the computer will become increasingly important in the analysis of problems and the laying down of alternative solutions.
>
> *Daniel Bell, 1969*

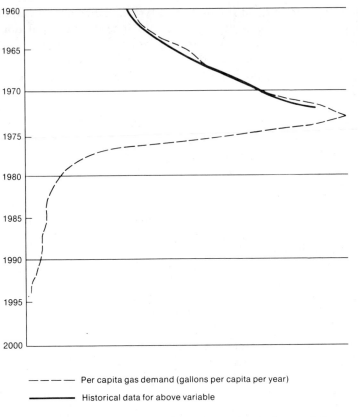

— — — — Per capita gas demand (gallons per capita per year)

———————— Historical data for above variable

Figure 4—13   A systems model run in both its simulation and its predictive modes.   The SPECULATER model of California, constructed by K. E. F. Watt and his associates, is shown in this redrawn and simplified output in both its simulation (solid line) and predictive (broken line) mode. The simulation mode, where historic data (solid) and predicted variables (broken) overlap, is seen to produce a reasonable agreement. This lends verisimilitude to the predictions of the output after 1970 as to per capita gasoline demand.

The conclusion that we have to draw from the predictive capability of the Meadows model is thus that the world system cannot continue unchanged with its present growth ethic. How it must be modified to avoid the crash situation it will otherwise encounter within this time span is a matter for further exploration utilizing this and other models. Not everyone is prepared to admit the possibility that the growth ethic is wrong, and continued exponential growth in industrial output and population is indeed impossible. However, among those who do concede that there is some limit to both types of growth, there is a great diversity of opinion as to how the system may be adjusted in order to avoid this catastrophic situation, in other terms, as to the nature of intervention. Almost all of these suggestions are based on intuitive models that have been learned or devised, and that operated very well in the less complicated past. There is, for example, an economic rule that assumes that there is no economic collapse that cannot be avoided by administering a good stiff dose of unemployment. It was in the hope of securing advice as to which of such dicta were most applicable to our present situation that President Gerald Ford, soon after assuming office in 1974, called a conference of economic consultants to the White House. It was clear then that the majority of those consultants invited did indeed possess intuitive models; each provided his own conventional mental model solution to the trade recession into which in 1974 the country and the world were rapidly sliding.

The potential use of system dynamics computer models has been illustrated here principally from a simple basic model, but also from a much more complicated one — the Meadows global model. It must be emphasized that numerous other such models of varying complexity have been prepared and described. Some have already been mentioned, others will be discussed later. This text is concerned more especially with dynamic models of social systems. The final objective of all such kinds of system dynamics computer models, of which the Forrester-Meadows series of models provided the first published examples, has to be the prediction of what will happen in these social systems in the future unless specific changes are made, and the determination of the likely effects on these systems of any particular specified changes.

Bibliography and References

Bell, Daniel. "The Balance of Knowledge and Power," *Technology Review* **71**(8): 38–47 (1969).

Bell, Daniel. *The Post-Industrial Society: A Venture in Social Forecasting*. New York: Basic Books, 1973.

Forrester, J. W. *Principles of Systems*. Cambridge: Wright-Allen Press, 1968.

Goodman, M. R. *Study Notes in System Dynamics*. Cambridge: Wright-Allen Press, 1974.

Kane, Julius. "A primer for new cross-impact language — KSIM," *Technological Forecasting and Social Change* **4**:129–42 (1972).

Kirk, Dudley. "Computerized Prophecy: The Limits to Growth." *Contemporary Psychology* **18**(1):1–3 (1973).

Mass, N. J. (ed.). *Readings in Urban Dynamics,* Vol. I. Cambridge: Wright-Allen Press, 1974.

Poole, R. W. "The Use of Simultaneous Linear Regression Equations as Empirical Models of Community Structure," *Mathematical Biosciences* **20**:105–16 (1974).

Pugh, A. L., III. *Dynamo II User's Manual*. Rev. ed. Cambridge: M.I.T. Press, 1973.

Schroeder, A., and Schroeder, S. (eds.). *Readings in Urban Dynamics,* Vol. II. Cambridge: Wright-Allen Press, 1975.

Watt, K. E. F., and Brewer, J. W. *Land Use, Energy Flow and Decision Making in Human Society*. Progress Report, Interdisciplinary Systems Group, University of California at Davis, 1974.

Watt, K. E. F., et al. "A Simulation of the Use of Energy and Land at the National Level," *Simulation,* May, 1975, pp. 129–53.

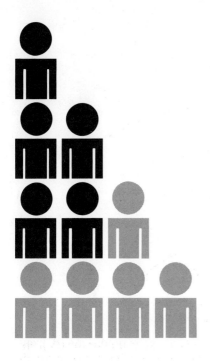

Chapter Five

Modeling the World System

Attempts to model the global socioeconomic system in one form or another are by no means new. A century ago the economist John Stuart Mill presented the law of diminishing returns, fashioned from classical economic theories such as were espoused by Thomas Malthus and others. In terms of agricultural production, the law of diminishing returns proposes that incremental increases in work applied to the same area of land eventually reach a point where each further increment generates a successively smaller amount of crop yield. Assuming the validity of this classical word model, J. Overbeek and other economists considered that the economies of at least some industrialized nations, between the time of World Wars I and II, had evolved beyond their optimum productivity. Evidence for this was considered to be provided by the general rise in commodity prices.

Graphic Models of Productivity

A number of graphic models were constructed to represent the operation of the law of diminishing returns on socioeconomic systems. Several of these were reproduced in a recent paper on population theory by Nathan Keyfitz. The graphic relation between industrial or agricultural productivity and population size on the basis of the law of diminishing returns is shown in Figure 5−1. It can be seen from this graphic model that after an initial exponential increase in the amount of production, as population growth proceeds, further

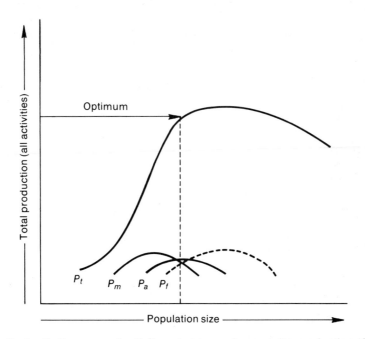

Figure 5–1   Optimum productivity. In terms of per capita production (P_t), optimum production will occur at the inflection point where further increase in population size in the agrarian or industrial system modeled here would begin to operate the law of diminishing returns. This point, moreover, coincides with the peak production point for any average activity (P_a) within a diversified economy. Any marginal activity that has peaked before this (P_m) will be eliminated if its production at this point is not at least that of the average activity. On the other hand, any new activity with a later peak that has already reached at or above this level (P_f) will be favorably selected, for it will raise the optimum level of total production and permit further increase in population size.

population increase results in successively smaller increments of production. In terms of efficiency, there is an optimum population at the inflection point where the amount of incremental increase begins to decline.

If this model represents a complex society with diversified activities, the average industry will have its productive peak at this inflection point. Any activity that peaks before this, and achieves a production less than that of the average activity at the inflection point, will be eliminated. Likewise, if a new activity develops that at the inflection point has a production at least equal to the average, and it has not yet peaked, it will be favorably selected. This graphic model illustrated in Figure 5–1, in fact, is one way of demonstrating the favorable selection of new technologies providing for higher productivity. The process model in Figure 5–2 illustrates this same process of selection in a different way.

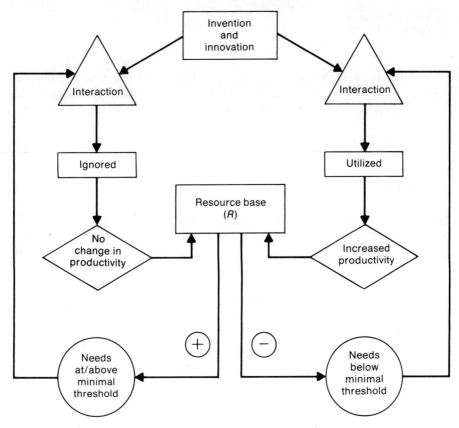

Figure 5–2   **Production and needs.**   When per capita production falls because of the operation of the law of diminishing returns once the optimum productivity point has been reached (Figure 5–1), unsatisfied needs force the introduction of improved technology. This permits a further increase in population size, as shown in the model in Figure 5–1. Alternatively, if there is no further population increase, the per capita resource base for the population would increase. (Reprinted from) Boughey, 1974, with the permission of Gordon and Breach, Science Publishers Ltd.

Some people recoil at the thought of designing social systems. They feel that designing a society is immoral. But we have no choice about living in a system that has been designed. The laws, tax policies, and traditions of a society constitute the design of a social system. If we lament the functioning of our cities, or the persistence of inflation, or the changes in our environment, we mean that we prefer a social system of a different design.

J. W. Forrester, 1970

Graphic Models of
Carrying Capacity

The two graphic models in Figures 5−1 and 5−2 illustrate how the continuous introduction of new technologies into socioeconomic systems provides for greater productivity and permits a steady upward escalation in population size. Even without any such improved technology, however, the carrying capacity of a given area for a human population can vary. It is a question of the amount of surplus production desired, and the duration of the time period involved. The effect of these two considerations is illustrated in Figure 5−3. The model shown in this figure is very important because it provides a determinable point for estimating when a given population will reach its optimum size and its maximum size. Many authorities dispute the real existence of such determinable values. If a maximum surplus of production is desired, it is possible to assess the size of the *optimum population* that will provide it. This level will be determined by the point at which the law of diminishing returns begins to lower the total productivity. It is possible to envisage two circumstances in which a human society requires an optimum population. The first is where a dictatorial dynasty or elected bureaucracy is exacting the maximum toll for its own support. The second is where a society of its own volition elects to support an economically nonproductive class engaged in humanistic activities. Anthropologists consider that a civilization cannot evolve further culturally without such an available reserve production — or *surplus,* as they call it — to devote to the one purpose or to the other.

The second population point in the graphic model illustrated in Figure 5−3 is the *maximum sustainable population.* This is the point at which all the production of the population is used up in its support. There is no surplus. Another way of expressing this second equilibrium level is shown by the graphic model already illustrated in Figure 3−7. This model describes a population whose sole energy source is solar radiation captured in its food-crop plants. Nearly all the photosynthetic energy captured in this way is utilized as human food for the support of the population, which has virtually no surplus energy available for activities other than those of food-crop raising. As will be discussed later, this model presents the Third World dilemma: Without an auxiliary source of energy to supplement the photosynthetic supply, no further societal evolution is possible.

The third condition for a population in the graphic model shown in Figure 5−3 is not an equilibrium level; in fact, it is both a transitory and a terminal one. By utilizing productivity below the maintenance threshold limit, the population has condemned itself to extinction. Such a situation can readily be comprehended by referring to a one-crop subsistence economy. At the end of each harvest, sufficient food will be put into storage to sustain the population until the next harvest, and a supply of seed for this next crop will be set aside. Any surplus beyond these two needs will be donated as tribute to dependent

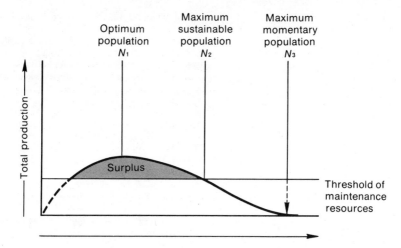

Figure 5−3 Human carrying capacities. There are three definable carrying capacity limits, identified in this diagram as N_1, N_2, and N_3; the first two are at equilibrium points, and N_3 is a momentary position. N_1 is the optimum population at the peak of production before the law of diminishing returns has begun to operate; surplus productivity is at a maximum. N_2 is the population when total production balances the minimum maintenance production necessary to sustain the system. The population maximum can rise beyond this to N_3, but only at the expense of the production necessary to maintain the system.

members of the society, or perhaps fermented and drunk. If the population between harvests rises beyond expectations, and excess individuals are also to be fed, not only will the reserve food supply be consumed, but also the seed supply for the next crop. What more often happens in practice is that the planting rains are delayed and so therefore is the harvesting of the first yields from the new crop. This has the same effect; the system cannot maintain the population at this maximum size. A maximum population of this type is thus achieved at the expense of the society's continuity. This situation is not infrequent in Third World areas. Another example is provided by the former Eskimo socio-economic system, which incorporated female infanticide. In a year of bad hunting a family may not have accumulated sufficient food supplies to carry it over the winter. The drain on these food supplies is lessened by placing female infants out on the ice to perish. Alternatively, the sled dogs could have been slaughtered, providing both fresh meat and a savings of the rations allocated to them. However, without the sled dogs, it would have been impossible to range out to hunt, so the whole family would in the end have perished. Thus, population size must be reduced by any means whatever to avoid fatal inroads on the maintenance part of the Eskimo system.

Many world models have been developed in the past. Every person carries in his head a mental model, an abstraction of all his perceptions and experiences in the world, which he uses to guide his decisions about future actions. Two mental models in particular have been shared by so many individuals that they have been the basis for social policy at various times throughout history. . . . The ecological world view depicts mankind as an integral part of larger, natural systems, limited by physical laws and a finite earth. . . . The technological model pictures the earth's natural systems as created expressly for the use of man, who is a creature apart, endowed with an intelligence that lifts him above the constraints of nature.

D. L. Meadows et al., 1974

Business Cycles

It has been known for many years that Western industrialized societies exhibit cyclic phenomena of varying amplitudes (see Fig. 5—4). Attention has once more been focused on empirical models of these business cycles by J. W. Forrester, who described them in two presentations in February and in November of 1975.

First there is a short business cycle of four or five years' duration, due to interaction between sales and inventories. Then there is the Kuznets cycle, seemingly an expression of a relationship between business activity and capital investment. It has a span of fifteen to twenty years. Finally, there is a much longer cycle, the Kondratieff cycle, with an amplitude of about fifty years. This cycle was detected by the Russian Kondratieff in the early part of the 1920 decade. Obviously he had only two previous cycles to go on, before he reached backwards to a time preceding the Industrial Revolution. The recession that began about 1970 may be the return of the recessional cycle that began in the 1920 decade.

These three business cycles are shown graphically in Figure 5—4A. Forrester superimposed these on one another and produced the charts shown in Figures 5—4B and 5—4C. He suggests that we may presently be on the declining side of this composite cycle, continuing a downward slide punctuated by short periods of apparent but only temporary recovery. The study of such cyclic business phenomena in industrialized societies seems momentarily at least to have attracted Forrester's whole attention. Several major steps separate these cycles from system dynamics computer models that simulate the socioeconomic system displaying such cyclic behavior.

Global System Models

Apart from the business cycles just described, the several written, graphic, and process models described so far in this chapter simulate agricultural and industrial systems. They all illustrate the point that we must construct such simulation models in order to understand where we now stand in relation to human population size and carrying capacity. It was thus inevitable that, sooner or later, system dynamics computer models of our global socioeconomic system would be constructed, even though the deductions as to the finiteness of growth already perceivable in these earlier types of models and in intuitive environmental models had essentially been ignored for many years. What regenerated interest in possible limits to global growth was, in the first place, the impact of the several publications referred to in Chapter 1, which induced a "doomsday syndrome" of dimensions too large to be ignored. The well-entrenched growth ethic that had arisen with the Industrial Revolution, and had remained relatively unchallenged for several centuries, suddenly became widely questioned. Doubt arose as to the validity of the technological intuitive model. There was also, in the second place, the disquieting circumstance that the operation and control of the immense and complex cybernetic system created to accommodate our ever-accelerating industrialization and urbanization processes began to suffer sporadic failure. Generally, these failures were patently triggered by unusual coincidences of natural occurrences; this was the case, for example, with the electricity blackout of New York City and much of the Northeast of the United States on November 9, 1965. The blackout left 30 million people without electricity for up to 14 hours and marooned 800,000 persons in the New York subways. A partial telephonic communications failure followed the California earthquake of 1970; in the same year, weather precipitated a temporary breakdown of the Penn Central Railway system. Sometimes, these systems failures arose from human action, deliberate or accidental. Moreover, it seems likely that no industrial nation could now maintain its essential production level in the face of a general strike; the strike of coal miners in Britain in 1973 virtually collapsed the economic and social life of that nation. Industrialized nations, in fact, are presently continually confronted with the possibility of at least local system failures. Any of these breakdowns — potentially, at any rate — could develop into a total system failure — the "knockout," as Europeans describe it — especially if there were to be an unhappy coincidence of natural disasters and human errors. Doomsday scenarios predicting the nature of these general system collapses have come from both sides of the Atlantic. Roberto Vacca sees such a collapse as inevitable; perhaps he has been unduly influenced by the extremely precarious situation of the Italian monetary system. Alvin Toffler projects an essentially similar collapse, and likewise is perhaps strongly influenced by the gradually deteriorating monetary situation of the United States, whose dollar continues slowly to weaken in the world monetary market, even against the currencies of nations

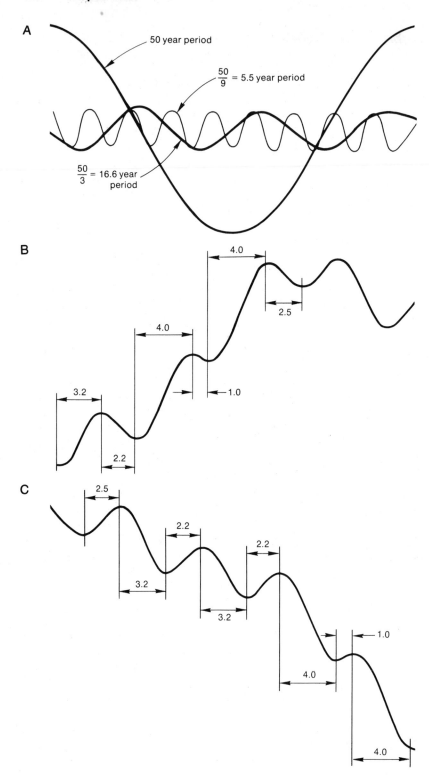

A

50 year period

$\frac{50}{9}$ = 5.5 year period

$\frac{50}{3}$ = 16.6 year period

B

4.0

2.5

4.0

1.0

3.2

2.2

C

2.5

2.2

2.2

3.2

3.2

1.0

4.0

4.0

whose economic health appears less sound. The same is true of the Ehrlichs, who presented one of the latest disaster scenarios.

The Forrester Models

Although the procedures of system analysis have been known and adopted for some time, the idea of applying this approach to social systems did not develop until the middle of the last decade, as described in Chapter 1. As stated there, credit for initiating this approach in its most recent form is usually given to J. W. Forrester, working in the Sloan School of Management at the Massachusetts Institute of Technology.

> Unfortunately, neither the ecological nor the technological model provides an adequate basis for increasing human understanding of the world. Both theories are based on simple mental models, intuitive generalizations from observations of real-world events. Those observations are partially correct. . . . However, since mental models can incorporate and process only a few observations at a time, they are necessarily incomplete. . . . To manage complex social systems effectively, policy makers must bring together a variety of mental models, both ecological and technological; translate them into a common language; and determine simultaneously all their important implications.
>
> *D. L. Meadows et al., 1974*

Forrester considers that socioeconomic systems are in a category he calls *multiple loop nonlinear feedback systems.* He believes that until computers for iterative operations were available, the behavior of this category of systems could not be estimated except by contemplation, discussion, argument, and guesswork. Nor, it may be added, was there until recently any real need for us to understand this behavior, anyway, for selection of the most appropriate system could occur by trial and error. Now, however, the effect of any erroneous interpretation of the behavior of our socioeconomic system is potentially so monstrous, as the various doomsday scenarios have dramatically portrayed, that we have to understand clearly what we are doing before we attempt to manipulate the system.

◀Figure 5–4   **The business, Kuznets, and Kondratieff economic cycles.**   These diagrams, modified from J. W. Forrester, 1975, show the three principal cycles in economic activity currently recognized as occurring in industrialized societies (A). Forrester made a composite chart of these, producing an upgrade shown in B and a downgrade shown in C. He suggests that we may have begun on the downhill slide about 1970.

The early system dynamics work that Forrester developed, like other system-modeling exercises, was applied to simulation models of corporate policy. Forrester first began to apply his approach to socioeconomic systems in 1968, developing a model that related industry, housing, and people within an urban system. In 1970, he prepared a dynamic model showing the interaction between the global population, industrialization, depletion of natural resources, agriculture, and pollution. An account of this world model in book form appeared the next year; this model is often referred to as World 2. The Meadows global model developed from this Forrester world model; it is commonly referred to as World 3.

The Meadows Model

> The model . . . called World 3, is an example of a formal mathematical model of a complex social system. It combines elements of both the ecological and the technological world views, as well as theories derived from many traditional disciplines. Like all models, it simplifies the great complexity of the total socioeconomic system. . . . However, it is considerably more complex than any mental model. . . .
>
> *D. L. Meadows et al., 1974*

The Meadows model briefly discussed in earlier chapters — like its progenitor, the Forrester world model — was limited to the examination of five basic entities: population, industrial capital, food, nonrenewable resources, and pollution. The function of these entities as limits to growth in the world system was among those constraints described in Chapter 4. These five entities were selected as the system variables in the Meadows system dynamics computer model because they were considered the most critical. As with any model, these input variables, all in the form of state variables, interacted with one another in varying degrees through a series of rate variables. When the model with all of its entries of historic input values of state variables and historic rate variables was run in past time, it functioned as a simulation model, monitoring the operation of the world socioeconomic system. As long as all the state and rate variables were based on historic data, and the model operated in past time, it remained a simulation model whose validity could be checked against already known statistics. The Meadows group started its model with data from the year 1900 and ran it through to 1970; it thus had the form of a simulation model when run over this time period. However, the main purpose of the Meadows model was to project the operation of the world system into the future and examine the possibility of growth continuing in its present form. For this, it was decided to run the model through in its projection mode to 2100, a further 130 years beyond the historic data ending in 1970. The two centuries spanned by the model have witnessed the beginning of the demographic transition, passage from labor-intensive to capital-intensive industry, insertion of biocides into ecosystems, resource substitution, widespread soil erosion, and enormous progress in health care — a palette of changes which have to date been unrivaled over any similar period.

It was possible in the model, for example, to project birth rates and death rates and so arrive at a system variable of population size over future time based on historical data. Running the model forward from 1970 then provides for calculated interactions with other state variables similarly based on historic input rates. The programed interactions within the model produce a series of system variables quantifying continuing progress in the level of the five state variables as the model continues to run to 2100.

> The patterns of dynamic value change included in the [World 3] model . . . were limited to the patterns of change historically observed over the last hundred years or so. During that time, the major global force behind value change has been the process of industrialization . . . the values that both shape and respond to the development of the model system follow the historical patterns observed during industrialization. As industrialization increases in the model — measured by the level of industrial output per capita — the aggregate social demand shifts in emphasis from food to material goods and finally to services.
>
> *D. L. Meadows et al., 1974*

These calculated progressive projected values for the five state variables in such a run are shown in Figure 5−5, known as the *standard run.* This is the most critical single output of the Meadows model, for it illustrates that without some future change in the historic levels of the several input states, the world socioeconomic system cannot continue to the year 2100 without collapse to a world system very different from the present one. It is easier to understand how such a global system collapse could eventuate if the state variable relationships which are input to the model are examined in more detail.

**The Relationship between
Population and Carrying
Capacity**

As was seen earlier, a human population cannot in actuality long sustain exponential growth without encountering some carrying capacity limit. As was also noted, there are two equilibrium positions for this limit, at the *optimum* and at the *maximum* population. The effects of the carrying capacity limit may not always be sensed in time to halt population growth at either of these population levels. There is a built-in time lag in human population growth. In the

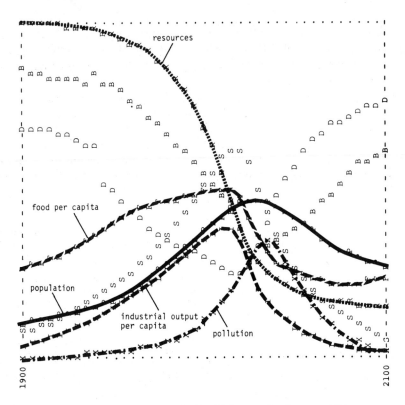

resources

food per capita

population

industrial output
per capita

pollution

1900

2100

Figure 5-5 The Meadows model World 3 standard run. This assumes no major change in the physical, economic, or social interactions which have determined the operation of the world system from 1900 to 1970. Food, industrial output, and population continue to grow exponentially until a rapidly diminishing resource base slows industrial growth. Per capita food production is then drastically reduced; the death rate rises because of starvation and inadequate medical services, and the population crashes.

first place, there is an interval of nine months between conception and parturition. In the second place, infants and juveniles do not usually consume adult quantities of a resource until they attain the age of approximately 15. A carrying capacity responding to a resource limit such as food, for example, would fail to halt in time the later addition to the population of new individuals still in various stages of gestation. Nor will it prevent those individuals already present as infants or juveniles from eventually requiring more of the food resource as they mature to the adult stage.

A human population, and indeed any population, increasing exponentially thus tends, because of time lags from these and other causes, to overshoot its food carrying capacity, as shown in Figure 5–6. Because when it does so there is not sufficient food to sustain all the individuals in the population, some will die of starvation. There will also be a time lag in that the population size will have to fall below the limit imposed by the food-carrying capacity. The deceased individuals do not have any further food requirements; some food is thereby released for consumption, and the population may after a time take a further upturn in growth and again overshoot its carrying capacity. The result may be a series of diminishing oscillations about the carrying capacity, as shown in Figure 5−7, until eventually the population levels off at the asymptote defining the food-carrying capacity. Such an oscillating pattern is characteristic of logistic growth in which time lags operate. The particular delays in response time in human population are considered further in Chapter 7.

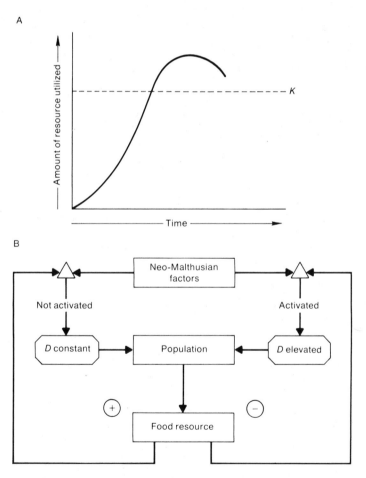

Figure 5−6   Carrying capacity overshoot.   In this overshoot mode, shown in curve A, a delayed response in the operating feedback mechanisms has prevented curtailment of population growth before the carrying capacity has been exceeded. This situation is modeled in the system model shown in curve B.

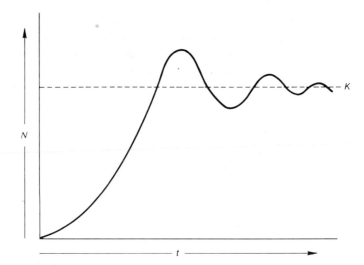

Figure 5−7 Oscillation about a carrying capacity limit. This mode is initially similar to the situation shown in Figure 5−6; the carrying capacity has been exceeded by an overshoot of population growth because of delayed response, but there is also a delayed response to cessation of a consequent decline in population (*N*), so that this falls below the carrying capacity (*K*) and then recovers again. The subsequent alternation of overshoots and undershoots of the carrying capacity produces a series of diminishing population oscillations about this value.

The Meadows model could be described, in a technocratic sense that was surely not intended, as an exercise reflecting on the problem of the introduction on a world basis of cultural controls on population and industrial growth in such a way as to ensure a leveling-off of growth before the values of either cause the world population to exceed the carrying capacity of the global environment. In order to do so, the system dynamics computer model the group constructs has to set forth all the interlocking feedback interactions that represent the relationship with the five state variables selected to represent determiners or indicators of the state of the world's system. Estimation of the value for the input variables that these states represent has made a number of quantitative assumptions.

Interactions between Growth and Limiting Factors

It is likely that in the initial overexploitation of the food-carrying capacity, a given population may have damaged its own food production capabilities. There may have been resultant soil erosion, as in the Dust Bowl days of Oklahoma, when much of the topsoil of that state literally blew away. Laterization may have occurred, forming an impenetrable hardpan on or near the soil surface; this is likely to happen more especially in tropical areas with distinct rainy and dry seasons. The soil water table may have been lowered beyond the limit of economic pumping operations, or made too saline to be of further use for agricultural purposes; fossil water supplies may have been entirely exhausted.

> Until the Industrial Revolution, society was a low-energy operation, depending on human muscle and beasts of burden for most of its energy. Not too far in the future, a few hundred years at most, we will have exhausted our limited supplies of fossil fuels . . . and we will face the choice of developing alternative forms of energy or of returning to a low-energy mode of existence which will last until the end of time.
>
> *J. W. Andrews, 1974*

Whatever the nature of the environmental degradation, the original carrying capacity will have been reduced to much lower values, and the number of deaths from starvation and resultant diseases must be correspondingly greater until the population has been brought once more into balance within the lowered carrying capacity. This situation is illustrated in Figure 5−8, and it is a familiar situation in nonhuman ecology. The classical case that will be found in many general ecology texts is that of the Kaibab deer (Fig. 5−9). It may well also be the situation with the Sahel savanna regions of West Africa, which recently suffered severe drought for a period lasting five or six years. With the decreased annual rainfall, the productivity of this sub-Saharan zone was insufficient to support its human populations and their domestic stock. The consequent degradation of the Sahelian ecosystem through overgrazing and overfarming is probably for all practical purposes irreversible. The ground cover has gone, the topsoil has blown away; breeding herds and planting seed stocks have been lost. This kind of process was described several decades ago by Anton Aubréville in a classic work entitled *Climats, forêts, et désertification de l'Afrique tropicale*. The word *desertification* is now beginning to be used more extensively with its adoption unchanged in form or meaning into the English language. It describes the process of degrading a marginally dry human ecosystem by overpopulation until its carrying capacity is reduced to that of an actual desert area.

Challenges to the Meadows Model

> The major weakness of the world dynamics models is that they illustrate the pessimistic consequences of exponential growth in a finite world without taking account of politics, social struc-

> ture, and human needs and wants. The introduc-
> tion of an extra variable — man . . . may entirely
> change the structure of the debate which these
> models have so far limited to physical properties.
>
> *Marie Jahoda, 1973*

The so-called *standard run* of the Meadows model forecasts a systems crash at some time before the end of the run in 2100, primarily because of the rapid depletion of nonrenewable resources, including energy supplies. With increasing shortages of raw materials, the global industrial machine slows down and then goes into a steep decline. The decline in industrial production reduces the per capita food production level and the extent of available services, especially medical services. The death rate begins to climb as food and services become scarcer, and the population numbers start to crash.

The key to the systems collapse is the scarcity of nonrenewable resources, and this is precisely the state variable of the World 3 model that the Sussex group of H. S. D. Cole and his coworkers most vigorously challenge. They claim that the Meadows group grossly underestimates the reserves of nonrenewable resources. In fact, the Meadows group in sensitivity tests had run its model with twice the quantity of reserves in 1900 that was originally estimated. Because in this case, as also when resources are recycled and reused, as seen in the illustration of the output in Figure 5−10, industry is able to increase to a point well beyond its level in the standard run, pollution gets out of hand. The system crashes because pollution reaches levels where it both lowers per capita food production and directly causes great increases in the death rate.

> There are no substantial limits in sight either
> in raw materials or in energy that alterations in
> the price structure, product substitution, antici-
> pated gains in technology and pollution control
> cannot be expected to solve.
>
> *F. W. Notestein, 1970*

The Sussex group maintains that the present world system will *not* collapse within the time span of the Meadows model. The Sussex version of the *standard run* is shown in Figure 5−11. The group claims it is *not* legitimate to model a world system that does not allow for continuing technological response to resource shortages and pollution increases. By predicating a mere 2 percent rate of new resource discovery and a 2 percent increase in technological ability to control pollution, the Sussex group can run a modified Meadows model through 2200 without its experiencing system collapse.

The work of an independent Dutch group, reported by T. W. Oerlemans and coauthors, made rather similar observations on the Meadows standard run

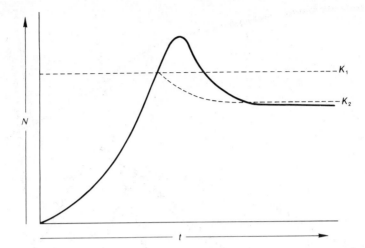

Figure 5–8 Degradation of carrying capacity. A population overshoot of carrying capacity such as is illustrated in the last two figures may result in permanent degradation of the environment. When this occurs, the carrying capacity (K_1) is permanently lowered so that population decline must continue until the new and lower population carrying capacity (K_2) is reached.

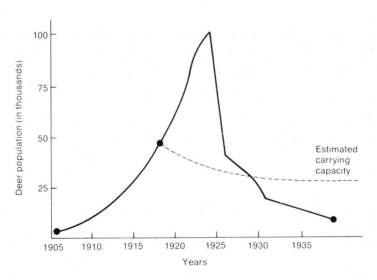

Figure 5–9 Population fluctuation in the Kaibab deer. Eradication of the main predators — coyotes, cougars, and wolves — permitted an exponential growth of this isolated population of deer. Consequent damage to grazing, linked with an apparent increased stocking level of domestic herds, so degraded the environment that the carrying capacity for grazing animals was drastically lowered. Ultimately, the size of the Kaibab deer herd was considerably lower than before the removal of the main predators.

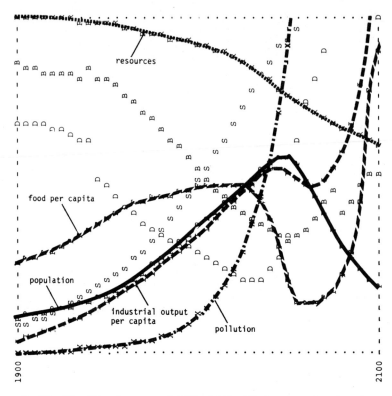

Figure 5–10   The Meadows model World 3 with increased natural resource reserves.   In this model run the remaining resource reserves in 1900 were doubled, and three quarters of the minerals used were recycled, keeping all other input variables at the same level as in the standard run. This permits industrialization to reach a higher level; consequently, pollution increases exponentially. This drastically increases the death rate, which is still further augmented because of a decline in food production due to pollution effects. At the end of the run, population has crashed, and nonrenewable resources have been severaly depleted, despite the fact that initially the reserves were doubled.

by introducing feedback mechanisms that continually improved resource extraction capacity and pollution control. This whole question of avoidance of system collapse by technological innovations is pursued further in Chapter 6.

Bibliography and References

Andrews, J. W.   "Work, Energy, and Power." In *Energy Crisis,* edited by V. J. Yannacone, pp. 3–39. New York: West Publishing Co., 1974.

Aubréville, Anton.   *Climats, Forêts et Désertification de l'Afrique Tropicale.* Paris: Muséum d'Histoire Naturelle, 1949.

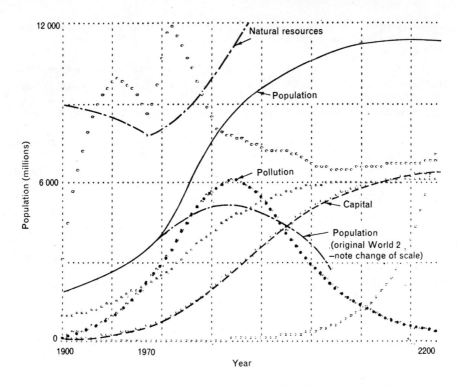

Figure 5–11   The Sussex group's adjustment to World 3.   By including a 2 percent rate of new resource discovery, a 2 percent increase in the technology of pollution control, and a 2 percent annual increase in food production, the Sussex group ran World 3 here without encountering system collapse. The possibility that agricultural technology was "overcounted" is conceded, however; that is, global food production might not increase by the 2 percent per annum needed to prevent system collapse. The matter of global food production was extensively explored in Chapter 3.

Bourgeois-Pichat, J., and Taleb, Si-Ahmed.   "Un Taux d'accroissement nul pour les pays en voie de developpement en l'an 2000: Rêve ou realité?" *Population* **25**:957–972 (1970).

Chenery, H. B., and Taylor, L.   "Development Patterns: Among Countries and over Time," *Review of Economics and Statistics* **50**(4) (1968).

Cole, H. S. D., et al.   *Thinking about the Future.* London: Chatto and Windus, 1973.*

Forrester, J. W.   "Systems Analysis as a Tool for Urban Planning," *IEEF Trans. Systems Sci. and Cybernetics* **55c–56**(4):258–65 (1970).

Forrester, J. W.   *World Dynamics.* Cambridge: Wright-Allen Press, 1971.

Jahoda, Marie.   "Postscripts on Social Change." In *Thinking about the Future,* edited by H. S. D. Cole et al., pp. 209–15. London: Chatto and Windus, 1973.

*Please note that the American version is *Models of Doom* published by Universe Books, New York.

Keyfitz, Nathan. "Population Theory and Doctrine: A Historical Survey." In *Readings in Population,* edited by William Petersen, pp. 41–69. New York: Macmillan Co., 1972.

Kuznets, Simon. *Modern Economic Growth.* New Haven: Yale University Press, 1966.

Meadows, D. L., et al. *Dynamics of Growth in a Finite World.* Cambridge: Wright-Allen Press, 1974.

Mill, John Stuart. *Principles of Political Economy.* 5th ed. New York: Appleton-Century-Crofts, 1876.

Notestein, F. W. "Zero Population Growth: What Is It?" *Family Planning Perspectives* 2(3):20–24 (1970).

Oerlemans, T. W.; Tellings, M. M. J.; and de Vries, Hans. "World Dynamics: Social Feedback May Give Hope for the Future," *Nature* 238:251–255 (1972).

Overbeek, Johannes. *History of Population Theories.* Rotterdam: Rotterdam University Press, 1974.

Randers, Jørgen, and Meadows, D. H. "The Carrying Capacity of Our Global Environment: A Look at the Ethical Alternatives." In *Western Man and Environmental Ethics,* edited by I. G. Barbour, pp. 253–276. Reading, Mass.: Addison-Wesley Publishing Co., Inc., 1972.

Schneider, S. H., and Meisrow, L. E. *The Genesis Strategy: Climate and Global Survival.* New York: Plenum, 1976.

Toffler, Alvin. "Beyond Depression," *Esquire* 83(2), no. 495:53–57, 130–40 (February, 1975).

Vacca, Roberto. *Il medioevo prossimo venturo.* Rome: Arnoldo Mondadori, 1971. Translation: *The Coming Dark Age.* New York: Doubleday & Co., Inc., 1973.

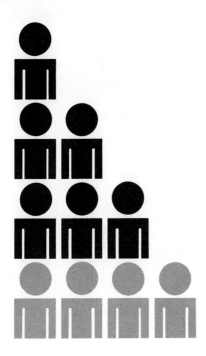

Chapter Six

Technological Innovations

The history of our global civilization has been charted by a progressive series of technological advances. The pace at which such advances have appeared has not been constant; there appears historically to have been an exponential decrease in the time interval between each step. It took us half a million years to progress from our first tool culture to our second. By contrast, within the 10-year span President John F. Kennedy alloted in 1962 for the achievement of the first American landing on the moon, a whole new space technology was developed and implemented. In the 1960 decade over 250,000 inventions were granted patent rights, taking the total numbers recorded by all nations.

There is, indeed, no shortage of inventions anywhere in the modern world. However, whether or not particular inventions are utilized depends not so much upon their intrinsic merit, but rather on the particular need of the society at any one moment of time. This relationship between invention and utilization is shown graphically in the illustration in Figure 6–1. A society that has developed an educated middle class is believed to generate a steady flow of inventive concepts and ideas. These gradually accumulate in the information store of the society — that is, in the libraries, the patent offices, and the computer banks — until the need arises that initiates their retrieval and application. As already discussed, the technological intuitive model assumes the existence of such information ready and waiting for utilization in achieving yet one more triumph over the environment.

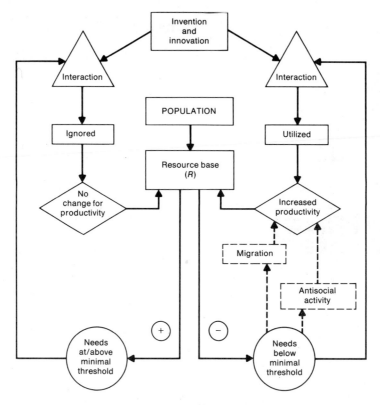

Figure 6–1   Relationship between inventions and their utilization.   As long as the resource base for a population remains adequate and the population has no unsatisfied needs, it will ignore all inventions, and there will be no change of productivity. When the resource base is inadequate because the population size has passed the threshold of maximum supportable population, the needs of the population can be fully met only by the utilization of inventions and innovations. These will permit the increase of productivity until the resource base is raised to the point where it satisfies the needs.

There are two methods of avoiding the negative feedback mechanism: migration and antisocial activity. The population, by migration, can move to an area where the resource base will be adequate; or it can take the resources it is lacking from other populations. (Reprinted from) Boughey, 1974, with the permission of Gordon and Breach, Science Publishers Ltd.

Deeply imbedded in all of us is the notion there are no limits to man's activities which somehow, someway cannot be overcome. Western cultures have particularly idolized the goddess of technology. Indeed the great American dream and the good life were equated with limitless opportunity based on limitless growth. It is upon this often unspoken concept we have founded not only corporate and governmental policy but the very fabric of an economic system.

R. W. Comstock, 1974

The knowledge that such a store of inventions and innovations exists is probably the reason for the customary belief in industrialized societies that technology will always find a solution, which is merely a different way of defining the intuitive technological model. Modern industrial society is viewed by economists as a cybernetic system rapidly responding to supply and demand. When the pressure of a need exceeds a required threshold, the cybernetic feedback triggers the necessary response, and a new technology is developed to provide for the meeting of that need. The negative feedback loop in Figure 6–1 symbolizes this pressure. Because of the operation of this feedback loop, estimates of resource reserves have sometimes been viewed with a certain extent of skepticism, bordering on cynicism. The history of most major nonrenewable resources reveals that as the point of exhaustion of supplies is approached, some new process or discovery causes this point again to recede into the future.

The Natural Resource Base

Nevertheless, as the vast industrial production of the Western world places ever-increasing strains upon nonrenewable resources, a growing general apprehension is expressed as to the remaining reserves of these natural resources. The apprehension is commonly reinforced by current estimates of remaining *proven reserves*. These are reserves that have actually been located by geological exploration and that can be exploited by a known process. The nature and extent of such proven reserves was described in Chapter 3.

It is frequently stated that proven reserves of many nonrenewable resources provide grossly inaccurate figures of the actual remaining reserves of particular resources. Admitting this possibility, the Meadows group estimated the effect on the world system, as simulated by its model, of doubling all available proven resource reserves from 1900 onward. All other parameters were kept as in the standard world run (Fig. 5–5), so that this exercise tests the sensitivity of the World 3 model to errors of magnitude in resource estimation.

> The assumptions about the physical limits of the critical variables in the agricultural subsystem of World 3 are pessimistic. By making more optimistic but, on the basis of available information, equally plausible assumptions about them, any physical limits to agricultural production recede beyond the time horizon of the model. The major problems of feeding the less developed world are seen to lie in political rather than in physical limits.
>
> *P. K. Marstrand and K. L. R. Pavitt, 1973*

The effect on the Meadows model of a doubling of natural resource reserves is shown in Figure 6—2. It can be seen from this illustration that when the model is run with this new state variable input for available natural resources, industrialization can reach a higher level than in the standard run because resources are not so quickly depleted. The larger industrial base that results because of the delayed onset of serious resource depletion, unfortunately, eventually generates pollution at such an enormous level that it begins to rise exponentially at a very steep rate of increase. This steep rise in pollution causes an almost simultaneous and equally steep rise in the death rate, which soon exceeds the birth rate and causes a population crash. The decline in population resulting from increased pollution is reinforced by the effects of pollution on food crops, which cause a simultaneous decline in per capita food production.

Moreover, when the Meadows model is run with the input values just described, not only is there a catastrophic population decline, but at the end of the run resources are extremely severely depleted in spite of the fact that initially the amount of remaining reserves was doubled.

The next assumption explored in the Meadows model was the supposition that technology could provide an "unlimited" source of nuclear energy. Such an unlimited supply of energy would permit extensive reclamation and recycling of essential industrial elements, and thus reduce the need for the mining of virgin nonrenewable resources. This technological advance was assumed to provide for a reduction to one quarter of the virgin resources utilized by industries at the present time. With this new input value, and still leaving the static resource reserves at double their estimated 1900 figure, the model again runs to a system collapse because of an exponential pollution increase well before 2100. So with the parameters of the Meadows model, it appears that it will make comparatively little difference — perhaps a decade or so of postponement of the ultimate global collapse — if the available resources of nonrenewable elements, or the power of technology to gain additional resources, have been somewhat underestimated.

Additional Sources of Raw Materials

The behavior of the resources sub-system is critical to the overall behavior of World 3. One of its commonest modes of "collapse" results from resource depletion. The main reason for this is the assumption of fixed economically-available resources, and of diminishing returns in resource technology. Neither of these assumptions is historically valid. The relative cost of minerals has remained roughly constant, and has not increased over the past eighty years as a consequence of diminishing returns. And new economically exploitable reserves are being discovered all the time.

William Page, 1973

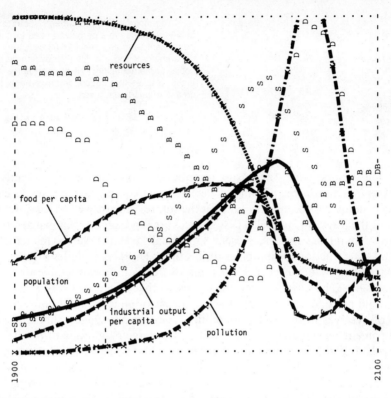

Figure 6−2 **The effect of doubling the natural resource base on World 3.** To test the effect of an underestimate of remaining natural resource reserves, the state variable input for natural resources available in 1900 was doubled. Industrialization reaches a higher level than in the standard run, but pollution is generated to such an enormous rate that it rises exponentially. The steep rise in pollution is reflected in a great increase in the death rate, which precipitates a population crash. This is reinforced by the effects of pollution on food crops, which cause a simultaneous decline in per capita food production.

As was briefly discussed in Chapter 5, the Science Policy Research Unit of the University of Sussex, England, in its recent publication, *Thinking about the Future,* has specifically challenged the Meadows assumptions as to mineral resource reserves. Under particular criticism is the figure of 250 years' supply for the average "current reserve life index" for every mineral in industrial use, and the assumption that the extraction costs of industrial materials from mineral ores will increase progressively in the future (see Fig. 5−7). The last is not a new criticism; it is one that was leveled earlier by some American economists such as Harold Barnett.

> Technological improvements seem to arise
> only in response to a perceived need for the im-
> provements and as a result of a costly and time-
> consuming period of scientific development and
> social implementation, not through some auto-
> matic process that causes improvements to in-
> crease regularly each year.
>
> *D. L. Meadows et al., 1974*

On the first issue, the Sussex group points to a number of presently un-
tapped *ultimate* sources of mineral elements that could provide reserves carrying expanding world industry far into the future, at least well beyond the time
span of the Meadows model. These sources are especially the known geological
deposits found beyond the present superficial layers of the earth's crust exploited by extraction technologies to this time. This also includes presently un-
detected shallow deposits that when discovered will be extractable by known
technologies. The Sussex group thus suggests that a factor of ×10 rather than
×2 would more likely represent the magnitude of underestimates of remaining
mineral reserves in the Meadows model. They further suggest that, combined
with some recycling and economy of use, this large magnitude of reserves can
be made available over the next hundred years by a mere 2 percent annual increase in resource discovery, presumably associated with development of the
appropriate extraction techniques. This statement could be viewed as comparable with the claim that an American could be put on the moon if sustained
annual progress over the distance toward that satellite could be maintained at 7
percent. Indeed, the fallacy in this type of argument arises from the all-or-
nothing nature of the progress required. Should there be a serious divergence
between the further supplies made available by recycling and economic and industrial needs before the new reserves can be tapped, then the system will
collapse before these new supplies ever become available. On a local scale, this
is comparable to the fate of project "Mohole" — the only attempt to date to
penetrate below the earth's crust. Support funds for this project were discontinued before the project had reached its primary objective, so that from this
point of view, it was a complete failure and a total waste of resources. Although
while it was a viable project, Mohole was making a steady annual percentage
progress toward its objective, all this progress was wiped out when the project
was discontinued before it had achieved its primary objective.

The arguments presented by Barnett and others as to the *price* of extraction are substantial and well documented. They appear valid for the examples
selected over the time span in question, which goes through to the mid sixties of
this century. Unfortunately, in the 1970s the circumstance that increasing demand for an item results in a *lowering* of its extraction costs no longer appears
the case. No material commonly used in industry presently is becoming cheaper, at least for industry to purchase. Perhaps an important determiner of this

circumstance is monopoly cartel manipulation; but whatever the reason, scarce raw materials are now becoming increasingly expensive for industry, as the Meadows model requires.

Specific Amendments to the Resource Variables of the Meadows Global Model

In view of the critical role that depletion of resources plays in the Meadows model, and the general criticisms of its approach already expressed, it is necessary to examine further and in more detail the specific challenges that have been leveled against its validity. The most extensively documented criticisms have been made by the Sussex group, some of whose general charges have already been presented.

As regards the nonrenewable resources subsystem, the Meadows model has two basic assumptions: first, that the world has 250 years' supply of minerals at current usage rates; second, that the costs of utilizing the remaining reserves will continually increase. The Sussex group proposes it is equally realistic to suppose that for the time period involved resources are for all practical purposes unlimited, and that the costs of extracting them can be set as a fraction of the total industrial capital involved. This fraction was fixed at 0.1 on a basis of the assumed 1970 level. The result of rerunning the Meadows model on this basis is shown in Figure 6–3. While a resource crisis is thereby avoided, there is soon a population crash following an unchecked rise in pollution levels, just as in the Meadows model.

The Sussex group then proceeded, as did the Meadows group, to control pollution in its model. Both industrial and agricultural pollution (which are combined in both the Meadows and the Sussex models) were set at 10 percent of the 1970 levels, on which the Meadows calculations were made. Run with this further modification, the Sussex model still provided a population crash (Fig. 6–4). This system failure developed because diminishing returns on further agricultural investment precipitated a food crisis.

The Sussex group then modified the lookup table in the Meadows model that related agricultural yields and agricultural land operation costs. The rationale for this change was the possibility that capital would be reallocated so as to provide the maximum return on agricultural land wherever it was, rather than be restricted to national territorial investments (see Fig. 3–5). With this further modification to the Meadows model, it now ran as shown in Figure 6–5. There is still a food crisis because of diminishing agricultural yields, and an industrial crisis is precipitated by a diversion of some capital investment to agriculture. Pollution rises but not, the Sussex group says, to dangerous levels, whatever they are. Population levels off; and with the model run through to 2200, the population size actually begins to decline.

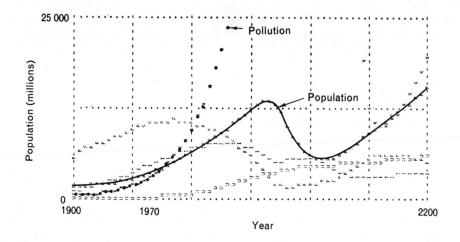

Figure 6–3 Sussex group modifications of World 3: Unlimited resources.
Assuming that resources are effectively unlimited, and costs of extraction will be
about the assumed 1970 level, the Sussex model still runs with the same crash
mode as World 3. Pollution rises unchecked and precipitates a population crash.

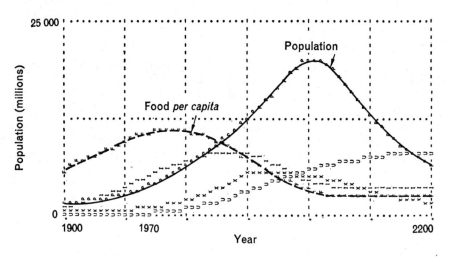

**Figure 6–4 Sussex modifications of World 3: Changed resource and pollution
assumptions.**   The Sussex modification shown in Figure 6–3 was further adjusted to set both industrial and agricultural pollution at 10 percent of the 1970
levels. With this additional modification, there still is a population crash because
of diminishing returns on further agricultural investment, catastrophically reducing the per capita food levels.

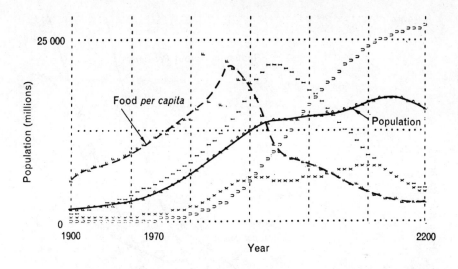

Figure 6−5 Sussex modifications of World 3: Maximized agricultural yields.
As the modifications shown in Figure 6−3 and Figure 6−4 still do not provide
equilibrium, the Sussex group then maximized the return on agricultural land to
provide the most efficient cost-effective returns upon agricultural capital inputs.
As this model run shows, this still did not prevent a food crisis from developing,
because of diminishing agricultural yields; and moreover, it provoked an industrial crisis, because of the diversion of some capital investment into agriculture. Population levels off, and by 2200 has actually begun to decline.

> Several fundamental assumptions deter-
> mine the behavior of the World 3 pollution sec-
> tor. One particularly important factor is the delay
> between the time a material is released into the
> environment and the time it is perceived or has
> its first impact on components of the global eco-
> system. The precise magnitude and source of
> the delay will vary from one material to another.
>
> *Jørgen Randers, 1973*

The last Sussex group adjustment to be considered here entails alterations
to a second lookup table, that concerning development costs per hectare of
agricultural land. Here again, it is argued, the Meadows assumptions may have
overestimated costs because the calculations are based on historical national experience rather than on a global approach to the problem (see Fig. 3−4). On
this run the model, presented in Figure 6−6, shows no crash in any state variable, but is described by the Sussex group as becoming unstable, with food, industrial production, and pollution levels increasing "unrealistically." The
Sussex group thus claims to demonstrate how all the constraints on growth can

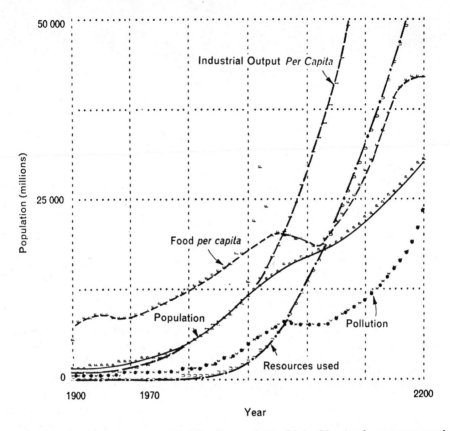

Figure 6-6 Sussex group modifications of World 3: Changed resource and pollution, agricultural, and capital distribution assumptions. The final adjustment in the Sussex group modifications shown in the last few figures was to lower the developmental costs per hectare of agricultural land. When this is done, there is no crash in any state variable of the model, but it has become highly unstable. Food, industrial production, and pollution levels are increasing "unrealistically."

be eliminated from the Meadows model, but concedes that the resultant modifications then provide an unstable and unrealistic model.

Further Technological Inputs into World 3

Unlimited Resource Availability

A primary cause of system failure in the Meadows global model, as it has so far been described here, is depletion of resources; and as has already been discussed, the rate of depletion of reserves remains controversial. When it was assumed that unlimited cheap power would be available, the model could be set with the assumption that three quarters of all nonrenewable resources could be reused and recycled from 1975. Serious depletion of resources was then halted, but pollution levels caused system failure.

Pollution Controls

> In the World 3 model, it is important to note that the effect of increased expenditure on anti-pollution equipment is to raise the capital use and so to increase pollution. Since the model is especially sensitive to marginal increases in capital investment this is particularly anomalous; and all the more so because it is clearly recognized among environmentalists themselves that "the technology required for pollution controls, unlike ordinary technology, does not add to the value of saleable goods. . . ."
>
> *P. K. Marstrand and T. C. Sinclair, 1973*

In the model runs of World 3 examined to this point, when unlimited resources permit the growth of a massive industrial complex, pollution intervenes to prevent its indefinite expansion. It was therefore assumed in this next model run that pollution generation by both industry and agriculture could be reduced by appropriate legislation to one fourth of its 1970 value. To assume a reduction beyond this would be unrealistic, for as Figure 6−7 shows, the costs of pollution control rise exponentially the more complete the level of control required. With these inputs in the Meadows model, the world system continued to operate successfully beyond the point previously reached, but eventually a limit of arable land imposed itself on the system. When this occurred, the per capita food production declined, the death rate started to climb until it exceeded the birth rate, and the population moved into a crash phase (Fig. 6−8). Previous to this population crash, industrial growth declined because capital input into new industrial enterprises slowed as capital was diverted toward agricultural production in an attempt to maintain the per capita output of food.

Increased Agricultural Production

In this last World 3 run the limit of arable land is reached, and food shortages become apparent because continuing population growth demands an ever-increasing total food production. The Meadows group therefore next determined the effect of increasing agricultural yields. This was done by doubling the average yield per acre from 1975, and the result is shown in Figure 6−9.

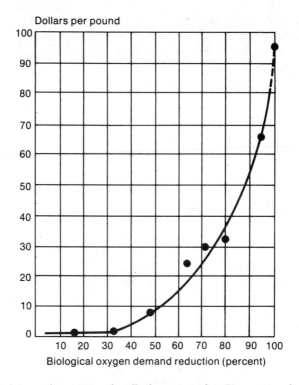

Dollars per pound

Biological oxygen demand reduction (percent)

Figure 6−7   Increasing costs of pollution control.   The costs of pollution control by the conventional methods rise exponentially with the level of control required.

It is not unreasonable to limit this increased agricultural production to a mere doubling, because as Table 6−1 shows, this ratio represents the present difference in agricultural crop yields in industrialized nations as compared with agrarian ones. Unfortunately, the animal protein production figures show greater disparities (Table 6−2). With this last adjustment, so many constraints to growth have been removed from the model that both population and industrial production reach very high levels. Indeed, average per capita industrial production approaches the 1970 U.S. level. Consequently, despite the introduction of pollution controls that hold relative levels to one quarter of their 1970 values, pollution values rise enormously, and the system collapses for the same reasons it did in the run shown in Figure 6−2.

> . . . even on the basis of the World 3 model and even with a very high population figure, continued growth, at least for the next two centuries, will not inevitably stop at an early date because of physical limits.
>
> *H. S. D. Cole and R. C. Curnow, 1973*

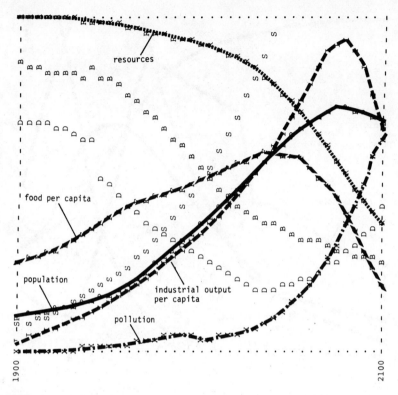

Figure 6−8   Modifications to World 3: Pollution control.   Assuming that pollution can be reduced to one-fourth of its 1970 value, the Meadows model runs successfully a few years longer, but eventually crashes because it reaches a limit of agricultural land. The per capita food production then declines, the death rate increases, and the population crashes.

Table 6−1   Grain yields in developed and underdeveloped countries.   The effect of the introduction of auxiliary energy supplies into agriculture is illustrated by the figures in this table for the average yield of cereal grains. In industrialized societies, yields are approximately twice those of essentially nonindustrialized ones. This is the basis for the modification shown in Figure 6−9, which determines the effect of doubling agricultural yields.

1972 Cereal Grain Yields	Average Kilograms per Hectare
North America	3,452
Western Europe	3,150
Latin America	1,439
South and Southeast Asia	1,337

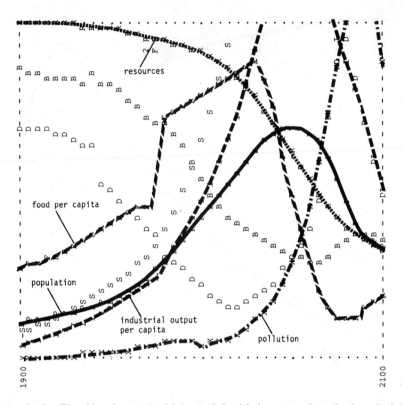

Figure 6−9   The Meadows World 3 model with increased agricultural yields.
Setting the average yield per acre at double from 1975 and attaining all the previous technological adjustments remove all population and industrial growth restraints. Pollution now rises enormously despite the partial control, and the system collapses as it did for this reason in the run shown in Figure 6−2.

Table 6−2   Per capita meat production in developed and underdeveloped countries.   Over the last decade, per capita meat production in developed countries has increased some 10 to 15 percent; the diet therefore contains yet more animal protein. In underdeveloped nations, by contrast, there has been no improvement in the amount of animal protein in the diet.

	1961−65	1970−71
North America	72	82
Western Europe	41	48
Near East	10	10
Far East	3	3
Africa	10	10

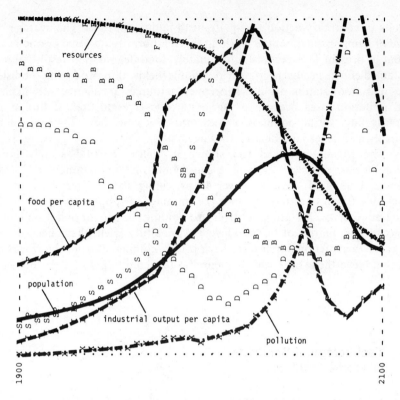

Figure 6–10   The final technological fix of Meadows World 3.   On the assumption that desired fertility is much lower than realized fertility, the effect of providing a perfect method of birth control was included in the model. As before, resources are fully exploited, and 75 percent are recycled. Pollution is set at one-fourth of its 1970 levels, and agricultural yields are doubled. In this run, population is for a time stabilized, but eventually it crashes because of cessation of industrial growth through resource depletion, and the death rate increases as pollution accumulates and food production declines.

Elimination of Unwanted Births

Finally, the Meadows group determined the effect of introducing completely effective birth control procedures, thus reducing the *realized fertility* to the *desired fertility* — that is, preventing the birth of unwanted children. The effect is to slow population growth; nevertheless the population does eventually crash as a result of food shortages (Fig. 6–10). This occurs about twenty years later than when the only adjustments to the model are to have resources made unlimited and pollution levels at a ratio of one quarter of 1970 levels. The population size becomes stationary for a short time because "perfect" birth control results in voluntary action to equate birth and death rates. The average standard of living throughout the world in this temporarily stationary population is about at present U.S. levels. Unfortunately, land degradation results from the sustained efforts necessary to provide double yields, thus producing food shortages and a population decline. Moreover, resources are significantly depleted, and pollution rises because of agricultural overproduction. Pollution temporarily falls as the population goes into a decline, but rises again uncontrollably as further land degradation occurs.

The Meadows model run shown in Figure 6–10 has fully utilized technology to remove four major constraints on population and industrial growth. Unlimited nuclear power is providing for the recycling of nonrenewable energy resources and the mining of previously unexploitable resource reserves. Pollution controls are holding the rate of pollution increase down to one quarter of its 1970 levels. Agricultural yields have been doubled overall. Unwanted children have been totally eliminated from the world population. Nevertheless the world system has turned into a decline before 2100.

Technological Solutions to World Problems

It was thus concluded from these several manipulations of the input variables in various runs of the Meadows model that the assumption that the world's problems are entirely technological, and that technological problems have technological solutions, is entirely fallacious. In fact, the model demonstrates that no presently known major technological process, operating either singly or in combination with others, can prevent the world's system from collapsing before the year 2100. The Meadows group therefore concludes, as we shall see in Chapter 8, that an equilibrium in the world system cannot be obtained unless some *social* controls are added to the various technological solutions. At the same time, there is considerable criticism of some of the input levels inserted in World 3; and there is an emphatic claim by the Sussex group that an equilibrium, admittedly a highly unstable one, could be achieved by technological adjustments alone.

In our human societies, we have in the last few centuries grown accustomed to expecting technological solutions to human systems problems. Our ingenuity in providing such solutions has indeed many times served us well. In the remote days of our early ancestors, cultural improvements in the way of more effective tool kits provided the technology that increased resource needs. In our urbanizing societies we increased specialization by further fragmentation of the division of labor. Associated with this specialization, improved tools and materials enable us to continue to introduce various technological fixes into our ever-expanding socioeconomic system. With the Industrial Revolution came the insertion into our bioenergetic system of auxiliary energy supplies. This represents the single greatest technological fix of all time (Fig. 6–11). With this assured external supply of energy, we were able to upgrade our tool kits into ever more sophisticated machines, often automated and minimizing the labor involved and maximizing industrial output — a capital-intensive instead of a labor-intensive system. Until the beginning of the last decade, most people believed that the industrial and population growth in our human system that these introductions permitted would continue indefinitely, as has been described by K. W. Back and Deborah Sullivan, among others. The growth ethic that grew out of this industrial development is not the central philosophical theme solely of industrial countries. The whole world has enthusiastically embraced this growth ethic, has measured social progress in terms of industrial growth and based national policies upon this concept. The standard run on the Meadows model may be interpreted as actually showing how unreal is this intuitive technological model, with its assumption of an infinite potential for perpetual growth, and how perilously close we are now fast approaching disaster through failure to appreciate the logical consequences of this form of growth. The various predictions forecast by runs on the Meadows model, after assuming certain technological advances, can achieve temporary increases in particular system variables, but the world system as a whole will not come into

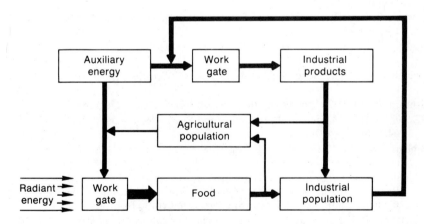

Figure 6–11   Bioenergetic cycle of an industrial society. Once auxiliary energy supplies are inserted into the bioenergetic cycle of a society, the main activity of the population can be directed into the utilization of this energy in industrial production. Some of this industrial production and a comparatively small proportion of the population can utilize a portion of the auxiliary energy to produce food both for themselves and for the ever-increasing industrial population.

equilibrium. Nor even if all the Sussex amendments are made, will it do so for long. All these model runs demonstrate that our global socioeconomic system has now progressed beyond the point where it can any longer be satisfactorily controlled by technology alone.

Bibliography and References

Ayres, R. U., and Kneese, A. V. "Economic and Ecological Effects of a Stationary Economy," *Annual Review of Ecology and Systematics* 2:1–22, (1971).

Back, K. W., and Sullivan, Deborah. "The Decline of the Ideology of Growth," *Population Reference Bureau Selection No. 41,* pp. 1–3 (1972).

Barnett, H. J., and Morse, C. *Scarcity and Growth: The Economics of Natural Resource Availability.* Baltimore: Johns Hopkins Press, 1963.

Behrens, W. W., III. "The Dynamics of Natural Resource Utilization." In *Toward Global Equilibrium: Collected Papers,* edited by D. L. Meadows and D. H. Meadows, pp. 141–61. Cambridge: Wright-Allen Press, 1973.

Borgstrom, Georg. "Food, Feed, and Energy," *Ambio* 2(6):214–19 (1973).

Bott, M. H. P. *The Interior of the Earth.* London: Edward Arnold (Publishers) Ltd., 1971.

Cole, H. S. D., and Curnow, R. C. "An Evaluation of the World Models." In *Thinking about the Future,* edited by H. S. D. Cole et al., p. 131. London: Chatto and Windus, 1973.

Colwell, R. N. "Remote Sensing of Natural Resources," *Scientific American* 218(1): 54–69 (1968).

Degens, E. T., and Ross, D. A. "The Red Sea Hot Brines," *Scientific American* 222(4):32–42 (1970).

Fine, M. M. "The Beneficiation of Iron Ores," *Scientific American* 218(1):28–35 (1968).

Groth, Edward, III. "Increasing the Harvest," *Environment* 17(1):28–39 (1975).

Heichel, G. H. "Agricultural Production and Energy Resources," *American Scientist* 64(1):64–72, 1976.

Hibbard, W. R. "Mineral Resources: Challenge or Threat?" *Science* 160:143–50 (1968).

La Que, E. L. "Deep Ocean Mining: Prospects and Anticipated Short-Term Benefits." In *Pacem in Maribus: Ocean Enterprise.* Occasional Paper 11(4). Santa Barbara, Calif.: Center for the Study of Democratic Institutions, 1970.

Marstrand, P. K., and Pavitt, K. L. R. "The Agricultural Subsystem." In *Thinking about the Future,* edited by H. S. D. Cole et al., p. 56. London: Chatto and Windus, 1973.

Marstrand, P. K., and Sinclair, T. C. "The Pollution Subsystem." In *Thinking about the Future,* edited by H. S. D. Cole et al., pp. 87, 88. London: Chatto and Windus, 1973.

Mero, J. L. "Oceanic Mineral Resources," *Futures* 1(2):125–41 (1968).

Page, William.   "The Non-Renewable Resources Subsystem." In *Thinking about the Future,* edited by H. S. D. Cole et al., p. 41. London: Chatto and Windus, 1973.

Pimentel, David.   "Extent of Pesticide Use, Food Supply, and Pollution," *Journal of the New York Entomological Society* **81**(1):13−33 (1973).

Singer, S. F. (ed.)   *The Changing Global Environment.* Boston: Reidel Publishing Co., 1975.

Tooms, J. S.   "Potentially Exploitable Marine Minerals," *Endeavour* **31**(114):113−17 (1970).

U.S. Bureau of Mines.   *Minerals Yearbook, 1970.* Washington, D.C.: U.S. Government Printing Office, 1970.

van den Bosch, Robert.   "The Cost of Poisons," *Environment* **14**(7):18−31 (1972).

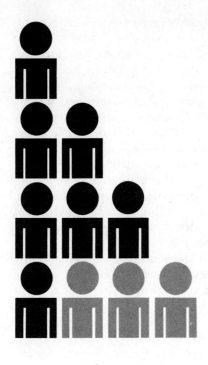

Chapter Seven

Population Control

The last chapter considered the proposition that appropriate technological changes could by themselves avert any possible collapse in the global socioeconomic system within the foreseeable future. It was observed that the Meadows World 3 model predicts that such a collapse cannot be avoided by application of any presently known technologies, while other models dispute this contention. As one of the two primary determiners of exponential economic growth is population increase (the other being a universal desire for a higher standard of living), this chapter addresses itself to the question of whether curtailment of population growth would by itself effectively prevent global system collapse.

> To think of population today is to think of growth. Although the science of demography deals with much more than population increase, it is the phenomenon of growth that commands the attention of experts and the public alike.
>
> *Nathan Keyfitz and Wilhelm Flieger, 1974*

It will be apparent that here and in Chapter 6 the same "bedroom versus boardroom" issue is being raised that was mentioned in Chapter 1. It is the same emotionally charged question that currently divides the world into two opposing camps, coinciding with the separation into developed and developing nations. Each camp seems determined not to recognize a circumstance that appears most obvious to the other. As the Meadows group remarks, America is a living monument to the immense powers of technology to override one societal constraint after another. When the cities of this nation were founded, land was cheap and plentiful; physical growth could be rapid and building unconstrained. When the city center was entirely covered with buildings, technology came to the rescue with skyscrapers. The city center was thereby enabled to continue its growth. Then traffic congestion snarled the ready passage of goods and people about the city. Again, technology came to the rescue by developing freeways and parkways. Technological solutions to fire and earthquake hazards were found, and skyscrapers could be built still higher, housing yet more people. Meanwhile, the crowded conditions of the burgeoning city centers developed social problems of crime, noise, drug addiction, poverty, and pollution. There were technological solutions to at least some of these social problems, too — better crime detection, improved security arrangements, closer personal surveillance systems.

Ultimately, however, people do not continue indefinitely to wait patiently for appropriate technological solutions; they respond in their own way, by moving when they can and burning when they cannot. The great cities of eastern and midwestern America have mostly had declining or stationary populations for a number of years (Table 7−1). Social behavior is taking charge of a situation that has temporarily, at least, defeated technology — the rehabilitation of aging urban centers. It is thus very pertinent to question whether our global system is likewise responding, or can respond, by social adjustment to the constraints that present technologies cannot circumvent without provoking system collapse. Any such investigation requires a forecasting of future population growth.

Table 7−1 Declining cities of northeastern America. Many of the larger cities in the northeastern states of the United States had at the 1970 census either negative migration rates or but slightly positive ones. Should the period total fertility rate in these cities fall much below replacement value during the 1970 decade, their populations will enter a decisive declining phase before the end of this century, assuming this migration pattern continues.

City (SMSA)*	Annual Net Migration	City (SMSA)*	Annual Net Migration
Pittsburgh	−167,000	Cincinnati	−36,000
New York	− 87,000	Newark	10,000
Buffalo	− 84,000	Chicago	10,000
Cleveland	− 45,000	St. Louis	17,000
Milwaukee	− 39,000	Kansas City	27,000

*SMSA = Standard Metropolitan Statistical Area (the area as defined by the Census Bureau for census purposes only).

The power of modern science and the force
of modern ideology are so great that we typically
pass over the fact that the species being shaped
by them is, like any other, fundamentally subject
to biological controls.

William Petersen, 1972

Population Forecasts

The most simple method of forecasting population growth or decline is by
taking the *current* crude birth and death rates and projecting any difference into
the future. Because the birth and death rates remain unchanged throughout the
projection, the inevitable result when births exceed deaths, as was noted in
Chapter 2, is exponential population growth. All the alarmist doomsday population projections from Thomas Malthus to P. R. Ehrlich are based on the
assumption that population growth will be of this kind. In actuality, changes
occur in either or both the birth and death rates as population growth raises
population size ever closer to perceived resource limits, as was described in
Chapter 3.

An empirical example of such a logistic curtailment of population increase incorporated into a population growth forecast is demonstrated by any
cohort type of population projection (Fig. 7–1). In this type of population
forecasting, each age cohort is moved on by the time interval it represents,
usually five years. The new size of the cohort, now five years older, is determined by the age-specific mortality known to prevail in the cohort at its original
age. The size of the youngest cohort is determined by summing the age-specific
fertility to be expected from the seven fecund female age cohorts containing
females 10–44 years old. As was the case with exponential growth, population
projections made following this cohort statistics procedure are liable to misrepresentation because of the fixed age-specific birth and death rates entered
into the model. If the age-specific birth rates were increasing over time, as was
the case during the decade of the fifties in the United States, the cohort projection would show an exponential population growth (Table 7–2). If the age-
specific birth rates were beginning to decrease over time, by contrast, as they
were during the 1960s in the United States (Table 7–2) after an initial population rise, the population size would begin to diminish, and would continue to
do so at an exponential rate (Fig. 7–1).

System dynamics models such as those of the Forrester-Meadows type
endeavor to avoid these intrinsic errors in exponential and cohort type population projections by providing for vital rate changes as the system operates over
time. A simplified version of the population section of the Meadows model is
shown in Figure 7–2. It will be observed from this diagram that fertility is
modified by the life expectancy and industrial output, both of which can vary
over time. Life expectancy, in its turn, is influenced by available food and services, and pollution and crowding levels. These effects are expressed as multipliers, whose values can change over time (Fig. 7–2). In this respect, even

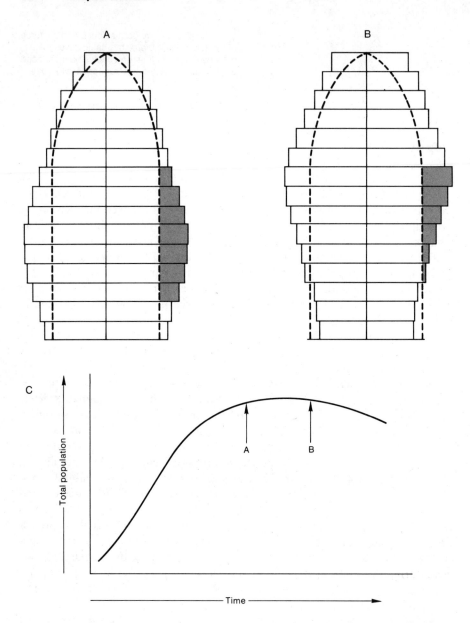

Figure 7–1   Cohort population projections.   When forecasts are made of population size on a basis of cohort natality and mortality, the future population size predicted will depend on whether the fecund female cohorts were progressively expanding or contracting at the starting time. During the early years of the decade of the 1970s, each new fecund cohort (shaded area) was diminishing (example A). As its size approached that required for zero population growth (broken lines), at the prevailing fertility rate population growth diminished. When cohort size falls below this threshold value (example B), total population size has to begin to decline (example C).

Table 7-2   Fluctuations in period fertility.   During the twentieth century the United States population shown here, like that of all other industrial nations, showed a marked decline in period fertility during the early 1930s, and a "baby boom" through the later 1940s and the decade of the fifties. During the early 1930s, the years of the Great Depression, the net reproduction rate (females born to surviving females) fell below 1.00, the replacement level value, and the population was at risk of declining.

Census Year	1919-21	1924-26	1930	1934-36	1940	1944-46
Period fertility rate	2.89	2.66	2.18	2.04	2.13	2.55
Net reproduction rate	1.14	1.10	0.96	0.88	0.95	1.16

Census Year	1950	1954-56	1960	1967	1970	1974
Period fertility rate	3.08	3.55	3.65	2.57	2.49	2.29
Net reproduction rate	1.43	1.66	1.71	1.21	1.17	1.14

without for the moment including discussion of the time lags in this simplified version, the Meadows model is more realistic in its population projections than forecasts using either exponential growth or cohort age-specific projections.

> The question is not if and when, but *by what means* will we elect to stabilize our individual national communities, including the population of the United States, and prevent any further increase in the size of the human global population.
>
> *A. S. Boughey, 1971*

An examination of population trends reveals that, in fact, changes in the rate of population growth are observable even before modifications occur, such as those that are compensated for by appropriate adjustment of multipliers in the Meadows model. Indeed, it is such fertility modifications that bring about changes in cohort vital statistics. The fertility levels are responding to one or more *social indicators* that represent needs but not necessities. Food is a necessity; a color television set, for example, is a need. The level of fertility in a population at any one time is a resultant of the combined effects of its total individual needs and necessities.

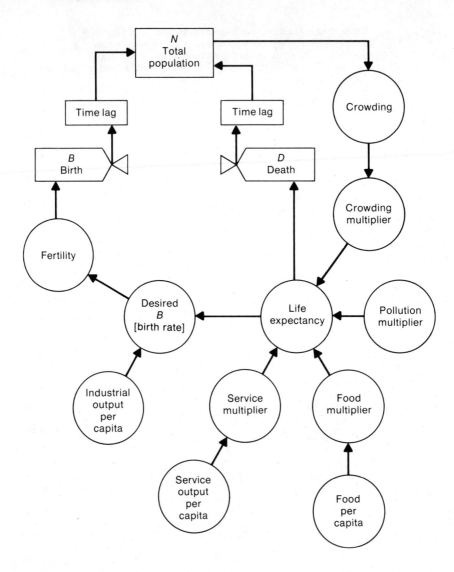

Figure 7 – 2   The flow diagram for population in World 3.   The population sub-section of the World 3 flow diagram illustrates the various factors which operate on population increase. Fertility is modified by economic factors relating to industrial output and controlled by desired fertility. Mortality is primarily related to life expectancy, which is modified by a series of factors basically arising from housing, pollution, and the amount of food and health services available.

Social Indicators

This particular interpretation of the term *social indicators,* and their effect on population growth, is illustrated in a recently published process model (Fig. 7—3). From this model, it can be seen how population size may be kept within essential resource limits without risking the possibility of these limits being periodically exceeded because of the occurrence of any time lags — or delayed responses, as they are now commonly called — in system response. This mechanism operates by monitoring the levels of resources that operate on the *reproductive activity* of individuals, but not on their actual survival from a life-and-death point of view. At the same time, these social indicators are coupled with essential resources that do constitute life-and-death requirements, so that they provide feedback information warning of imminent essential resource exhaustion.

Social Indicators in
Agrarian Societies

In some agrarian and other early forms of society, there is a custom known in English as bride price or dowry. The family of a bride-to-be must receive a payment in one form or another from the intended groom before a marriage can be formalized. Sometimes the currency in which this payment is made is domestic animals. If the society is approaching a stocking limit in terms of the numbers of domestic animals its land will carry, it will be difficult for the groom to raise the required number of animals. The marriage may be postponed because of this difficulty, and no additional human births will accrue to the population on account of it. Bride price requirements are then acting as social indicators of potential overpopulation, and triggering a mechanism to prevent it.

A typical example of the operation of social indicators on population control in such an early form of society was recently described by Laura Thompson. She studied fertility control among the southern Lau people who occupy a group of small islands in the South Pacific a little distance north and east of New Zealand. Briefly, an intending groom had to demonstrate that he had killed somebody before he could press his attentions upon the intended bride. Missionaries considered this practice unchristian and tried to discourage it. The government finally declared it illegal. Subsequently, there has been a population explosion on these islands.

A somewhat similar population control tradition in Ethiopia received momentary news coverage in 1974. A remote Ethiopian group until recently practiced infanticide by killing at birth all first-born children that were female. In families producing female first-born, further offspring were treated the same way if they were female, until a male child was born, when infanticide was discontinued. This effective but rigorous method of population control had recently increasingly been discouraged by missionaries, and a population explosion

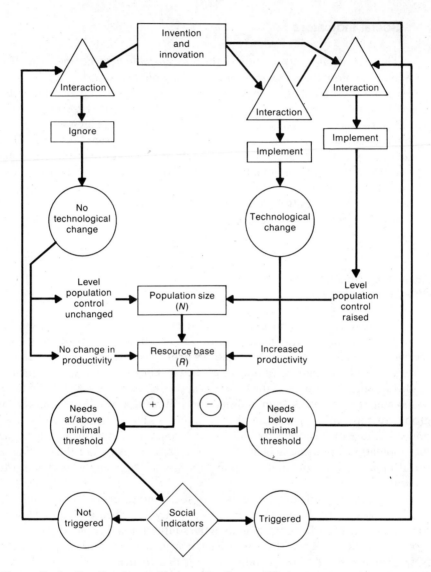

Figure 7-3 Feedback mechanisms in the equilibrium state. A society balanced by the feedback mechanisms shown in this scheme has a stationary population size, maintained by the interaction between social indicators and the birth rate. It also has a steady-state economics in which technological innovation operates to adjust material needs to the resource availability. (Reprinted from) Boughey, 1974, with the permission of Gordon and Breach, Science Publishers Ltd.

has now become evident because population size has finally exceeded the carrying capacity of the tribal land.

One of the best-documented and most-studied population control feedback mechanisms of this type was investigated and reported by R. A. Rappaport in a fascinating work entitled *Pigs for the Ancestors.* This traditional practice was worked up as a system dynamics computer model by S. B. Shantzis and W. W. Behrens III. The people modeled are a group of swidden agriculturalists (early agriculturalists in the terminology used in this text) belonging to the Tsembaga tribal group of eastern New Guinea. They are located in tropical rain forest in stationary populations at a carrying capacity level that has left portions of their area with virgin forest stands. In traditional practice the human population and domestic pig population are allowed to increase initially without check. Eventually, pressures on available cultivated land provoke so many confrontations between neighbors that factional warfare breaks out. Ritualized warfare continues until some casualties have been sustained, whereupon a truce is declared. As sexual intercourse and cultivation are both prohibited during warfare periods, these wars have limited duration. Truces are celebrated by a communal feast period during which every domestic pig that can be seized is eaten. The consequent drastic reduction in size of the pig population, coupled with a small reduction in the human population, takes pressure off the agricultural land, which is then for a time not so heavily used to produce either human food or supplementary food for a large pig population.

A flow diagram of this Tsembaga system is shown in Figure 7−4. Shantzis and Behrens quantified this into a system dynamics computer model by estimating the density-dependent threshold values that triggered the outbreak of warfare and declaration of a truce.

Social Indicators in Industrialized Societies

In our own industrialized societies, there are many economic social indicators that similarly trigger a lowering of the fertility rate. A. S. Boughey in 1971 called this the "Madison Avenue effect," because modern advertising techniques endeavor for commercial reasons to divert our resources into the purchase of nonnecessities, meanwhile inadvertently causing fertility postponement. In the current Western world, these economic social indicators appear to have brought about fertility postponement on an extensive scale, resulting at least once in a lowering of fertility rates to below replacement value. This phenomenon occurred in the Great Depression in the early 1930s (see Table 7−2). The eventual release of this postponed fertility was in part responsible for the baby boom of the 1950 decade, as Table 7−2 records. Whether the declining fertility rate that we are now experiencing in the Western world represents postponed fertility, which will eventually with changing feedback pressures become

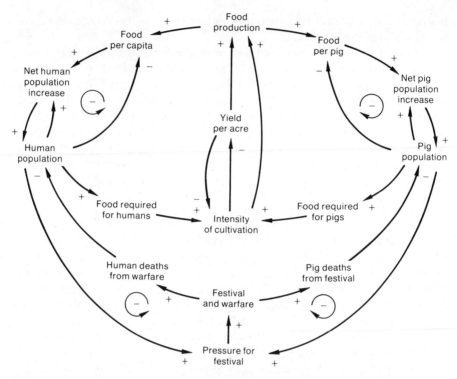

Figure 7−4　Process diagram of the Tsembaga system. This tribal group in New Guinea has a population control system which depends on feedback from the levels of the human and of the domestic pig population. This flow diagram indicates the operation of these feedback mechanisms. Reprinted, with permission, from Shantzis, Steven B., and William W. Behrens III, "Population Control Mechanisms in a Primitive Agricultural Society," in *Toward Global Equilibrium: Collected Papers* by D. H. and D. L. Meadows, Copyright © 1973, Wright-Allen Press, Inc., Cambridge, MA 02142 USA.

released fertility, Kingsley Davis and others have recently discussed. Examination of age-specific birth rate statistics for the United States, which are summarized in Table 7−3, suggest that this time, fertility rate decline is real. In technical terms, the *cohort fertility* as well as the period fertility is falling so low it may soon be below replacement value. The now widespread practice of vasectomy may effectively prevent postponed fertility from later becoming realized fertility.

> Raising the quality of life means releasing stress and pressures, reducing crowding, reducing pollution, alleviating hunger, and treating ill health. But these pressures are exactly the sources of concern and action that will lead to

Table 7–3   Fluctuations in cohort fertility. The period fertility shown in Table 7–2 does not reveal what is happening to the fertility of individual women taken as a mean. The cohort fertility for the United States shown here contrasted with the period fertility varies less. Moreover, for the cohort of females born in 1930–35, the cohort fertility was actually higher than at other times in this century. (Figures in parantheses are estimates; the actual figures cannot be known for some time yet.)

Age-Specific Birth Rates	Class of 1905	Class of 1930	Class of 1955	Period of 1930	Period of 1955	Period of 1970
10–14	.00031	.00067	.00099	.00048	.00093	.00099
15–19	.04696	.08145	(.06500)	.04788	.08821	.06653
20–24	.10463	.23966	(.15500)	.10463	.25676	.16414
25–29	.10590	.19811	(.13500)	.11639	.19811	.14000
30–34	.07721	.07934	(.06500)	.08646	.11333	.07638
35–39	.05471	.03842	(.03500)	.05585	.05618	.03842
40–44	.01471	(.01024)	(.01000)	.02164	.01543	.01041
45–49	.00111	.00056	(.00050)	.00243	.00094	.00064
Sum of age-specific birth rates	.40554	.64845	(.46649)	.43576	.74532	.49751
Total mean fertility rate	(2.02)	(3.24)	(2.33)	(2.18)	(3.73)	(2.48)

controlling total population to keep it within the bounds of the fixed world within which we live. . . . To try to raise the quality of life without intentionally creating compensating pressures to prevent a rise in population density will be self-defeating.

J. W. Forrester, 1973

Delayed Responses

The existence of such social indicator feedback mechanisms largely offsets the inevitable time lags to signal response inherent in human population growth processes. Some of the time lags have already been briefly discussed in Chapter 5. There are at least three such time lags to be considered when projecting human population growth and modeling a system that includes it, as already discussed. The first and most obvious time lag is due to the circumstance that conception and birth are not coincidental; the one normally precedes the other by nine months. An environmental signal operating to trigger a reduction in population growth because some limit has been reached will thus be nine months too late to prevent some measure of population overshoot.

A still more serious delayed response occurs because maximum resource utilization by individuals is not reached until adulthood. There is a period of juvenile dependency, conveniently reckoned at 15 years, during which an ever-increasing fraction of adult necessities are required. In the case of the most rapidly growing national populations, more than half the population is in this category of juvenile dependency (Table 7—3). Even if immediate replacement fertility can be established in such a population, it will still continue for 15 years to require additional essential resources as these juvenile dependents come to maturity.

> Although the existence of a relatively long delay in the reproductive response to changing environmental conditions does not imply that social norms regarding reproduction are totally rigid, it does suggest that they change only slowly, probably over several generations. This slow response is usually a source of system stability, ensuring a fairly steady renewal of the population regardless of sudden, random environmental fluctuations.
>
> *D. L. Meadows et al., 1974*

A third time lag also arises from this circumstance of juvenile dependency. Females do not usually all become fertile until attaining on average the age of 15 years or older. By the same circumstance as with resource needs, there is thus a delayed population increase built into the population structure of any still expanding population. The United States, for example, in 1975 had been below replacement value fertility levels for four years. Nevertheless, because of the large number of females entering the most fertile age cohorts 20—24 and 25—29, the U.S. population continues to increase in size. For this reason it is expected to rise to approximately 270 million before it reaches a stationary level in the next millennium. It is currently estimated at 215 million.

Postponed Fertility

As indicated a little earlier, there is a further form of delayed response that may develop in population growth — *postponed fertility*. This is presently a demographic phenomenon which is for all practical purposes exhibited only by industrialized societies, that is, those that have passed through the demographic transition and have lowered their birth rate to match the now lowered death rate. Why this is so becomes more obvious when reference is made to the diagram in Figure 7—5. Population control in underdeveloped countries, where it obtains, now generally takes the form of a curtailment of family size once a certain number of children have been produced. In industrialized societies, fertility control practices are operated as soon as sexual activity commences. Desired family size is attained by suspending these control practices at the

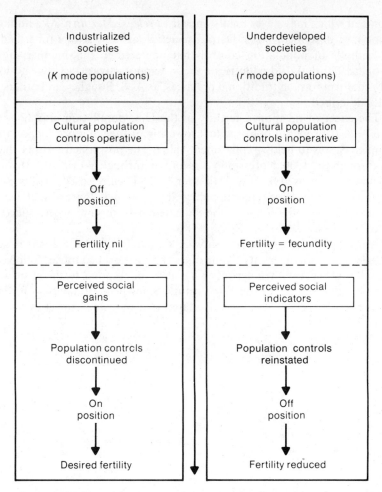

Figure 7–5   Fertility control in industrialized as opposed to agrarian societies.   In industrial societies, realized fertility is obtained at any point within the fecund period. In agrarian societies, restrictions on fertility are not usually applied until the later portion of the fecund period, when the cost of further children may be perceived. Postponed fertility will therefore not occur in agrarian societies, but the possibility of postponed fertility is always present in the earlier portion of the fecund segment of the life of a female in an industrialized society. (*K* mode populations are stationary, *r* mode populations remain in a phase of exponential growth.) (Reprinted from) Boughey, 1974, with the permission of Gordon and Breach, Science Publishers Ltd.

selected time, usually in passage through either the 20–24 or the 25–29 age cohort. An industrialized society thus normally contains a backlog of postponed fertility. When social indicators in such a society are operating particularly strongly, a very considerable amount of postponed fertility may build up, some of which may never finally appear as *released fertility*. As a number of authors have described, nonindustrial societies, at least at one time, had cultural methods of population control that operated in this manner; but the burgeoning Third World countries now — temporarily, at least — no longer closely conform to such traditional practices, as A. S. Boughey and others have recently described.

The effect of postponed fertility in the U.S. population may be seen in Figure 7–6. It brought about the first lowering of the net reproduction rate in the United States to below replacement value. The postponed fertility that accrued through the 1930 depression years and on through World War II was not translated into released fertility until after 1945. Then released fertility pushed the U.S. net reproductive rate into values approximately twice as high as in the previous decade, and produced the so-called baby boom of the succeeding decade (Fig. 7–6).

All industrialized countries showed similar fertility rate changes at this time due to postponed fertility. None of the Third World countries followed the same pattern, because their fertility rates did not respond to the same set, or perhaps even to any set, of social indicators. Some demographers — for example, Kingsley Davis — have recently stated that industrial societies may now

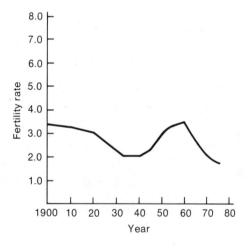

Figure 7–6   Total fertility in the United States during the twentieth century. The total fertility in the United States steadily declined through the twentieth century; superimposed on this decline is a very considerable additional drop in the Great Depression, partly the result of postponed fertility. When this postponed fertility was translated into realized fertility after World War II, combined with a brief return of higher fertility rates due to very prosperous economic conditions, there was a resultant baby boom which produced period fertility rates peaking in 1957. After that, the steady decline of the total fertility rate has continued until in 1974 it had fallen to the lowest figure ever recorded in American history, and considerably below replacement value. It continued to fall in 1975. (Curve smoothed.)

again be at risk of a temporary rise in fertility rates due to the translation of postponed fertility into released fertility. However, the increasing practice of vasectomy and tubal ligation among individuals in early middle age may prevent the later appearance of released fertility.

The existence of such time lags as have been described in the last two sections, in a human population approaching a stationary phase, is significant enough. In the case of the United States, it presently appears that it may, as noted, carry the total population from about 215 million to somewhere close to 300 million before population growth will be quite halted and zero population growth achieved. In countries presently with the highest rates of growth — such as Morocco, Mexico, Venezuela, and Brazil — delayed response considerations will require that population size will double even if replacement value fertilities can immediately be obtained. It is these kinds of considerations that make exploration of the effects of controlling population increase so very difficult.

Estimating Variations in Fertility and Mortality

Any survey of the possible extent of population control most conveniently starts with the classical analyses of fertility determiners by Kingsley Davis and Judith Blake. They list these determiners as follows:

A. Opportunity for intercourse
   I. Level and duration of sexual unions
      1. Age of entry into union
      2. Extent of permanent celibacy
      3. Duration of fecund periods outside sexual unions
         a. Sexual unions terminated voluntarily
         b. Sexual unions terminated involuntarily
   II. Frequency of intercourse within unions
      4. Voluntary abstinence
      5. Involuntary abstinence
      6. Coital frequency
B. Factors affecting conception
      7. Involuntary fecundity
      8. Use of contraception
      9. Voluntary fecundity (vasectomy, hysterectomy, tubal ligation)
C. Factors affecting gestation and parturition
      10. Involuntary fetal mortality (e.g., miscarriage)
      11. Voluntary fetal mortality (e.g., abortion)

Davis and Blake comment that whereas items 3, 5, 7, and 10 are under environmental control, all the other factors are controlled by human decisions. Thus, while some estimate may be made of the effect of the four environmentally controlled factors on fertility by extrapolating to prevailing public health data, the effect of cultural factors has always been considered more difficult to estimate. Desired and realized fertility are ultimately an expression of individual choices by the male and female coupled in a sexual union. However, it is generally agreed that human societies are usually characterized at any moment of time by a norm of behavior in respect of fertility, as in many other features. In terms of realized fertility, this normative behavior may produce figures for total fertility close to fecundity, which in a society with reasonable medical facilities is usually taken as about 12. Thus, Hutterites in the United States have been recorded as reaching a total fertility of 10.4. At the other end of the scale, East Germany, for example, currently has a total fertility rate of 1.7.

A symbolic representation of this fertility scale was represented in Figure 7−5. Any examination of national fertility statistics shows the national populations of the world mostly transitional between these two extreme positions. It seems that the implicit or explicit costs of having children are being measured against the benefits. There appears, not surprisingly, to be a negative correlation between gross national product and total fertility rates. This economic correlation also holds within national populations. It also — in industrial societies, at any rate — appears to hold for short-term economic variations over time (Table 7−2), as was discussed in the last section.

This phenomenon of realized fertility variation in industrialized societies, with baby booms during periods of prosperity and very low fertility during recessions, seems to occur independently of any changes in desired fertility. Simultaneously, industrialization appears to have been associated in Western societies with a slow but continuous decline in both desired and achieved fertilities. It is generally assumed that there will be parallel declines in underdeveloped countries as these proceed through the industrial revolution, but this does not have to be the case.

> . . . the modernization of India, Taiwan, and other developing nations may have destroyed or greatly modified traditional family structures, or broken the earlier causal link between family structure and fertility. This point takes on added force from the fact that almost all developing nations have experienced a substantial decline in mortality, which strongly influences both family structure and fertility.
>
> *T. K. Burch and Murray Gendell, 1972*

The apparent conflicting effect of economics on fertility in the observations just described was resolved recently by K. O. Mason and his coworkers. They demonstrated that in the least developed nations there was a negative — that is, an inverse — correlation between economic prosperity and fertility. In developed countries, there was, as just described, a positive correlation; whilst in countries with intermediate development, no consistent correlation with fertility was observable. Hence the curve expressing the interrelationship was bimodal.

It seems that voluntary fertility control by one or more of the methods listed by Davis and Blake is established in the cultural traditions of all modern societies. While these traditions persist, the reactions to environmental changes insofar as they are reflected in fertility rate fluctuations are very slow. They can become rapid only when traditions are abruptly abandoned or lost. This conservatism in fertility practices makes the insertion of any rapid fertility change into a system model an especially unrealistic exercise, but it remains one that has to be tested on theoretical grounds when attempting to manipulate a model so as to simulate how to bring the world system into equilibrium.

> The study of fertility confronts us with painful dilemmas. We like people, and children especially, yet we have to admit that in a finite world there can be too many of them. The countries of western Europe and northern North America rose to wealth and power as their populations increased; must we say that developing countries of today have too many people before they even start the process of development?
>
> *Nathan Keyfitz and Wilhelm Flieger, 1971*

The Effects of Various Fertility Requirements

In the Meadows World 3 model the effect of controlling population growth and reaching a stationary population phase was determined, assuming that all the previous input values were kept at the same level, and that effective methods of birth control were immediately made available to the world population, so that effective from 1975 the birth rate could be set to equal the death rate. In this way the world population is held in a stationary mode, while food output per capita, industrial output per capita, and services are able to reach previously quite unattained levels of growth. The flow diagram for this portion of the model shows how the several time lags discussed here were incorporated (Fig. 7-7).

Unfortunately, even when some control of population is attained, extensive continuation of growth in the industrial sectors is associated with severe resource depletion and an accumulation of pollutants, which increases the death rate and decreases per capita food production. These combined effects cause the industrial system to collapse before the end of the run in 2100, and the other systems will actually collapse with it (Fig. 7-8). Although the death rate rises enormously, the population remains stationary, as this is a parameter built into the model. When it is run, this version of the model thus shows an artificial inflation of the birth rate to match the rapidly rising death rate, the only way

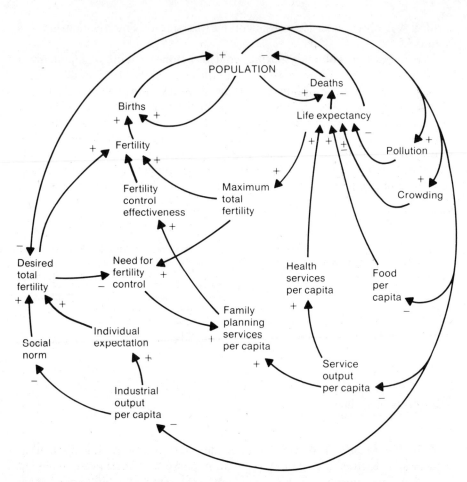

Figure 7−7   The population section of World 3. This portion of the process model of the Meadows World 3 global model shows how the several factors involved in population control are inserted into the model. Reprinted, with permission from, Meadows, Dennis L., William W. Behrens III, Donella H. Meadows, Roger F. Naill, Jørgen Randers, and Erich K. O. Zahn, *Dynamics of Growth in a Finite World,* Copyright © 1974, Wright-Allen Press, Inc., Cambridge MA 02142 USA.

the model can meet the requirement of stationary growth that is built into it. This extreme rise in the birth rate could not occur in the real-world system, which would collapse earlier, because in practice there would be a population decline.

Census taking, a serious business in all countries, is of special significance in a country that relies on economic planning. For the Soviet

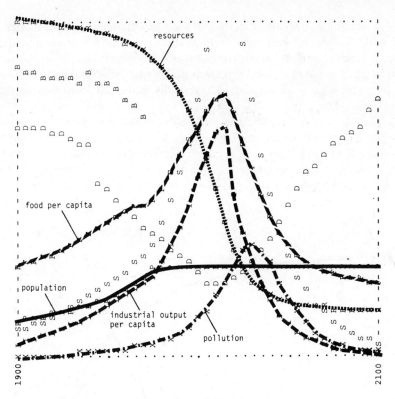

resources

food per capita

population

industrial output
per capita

pollution

1900

2100

Figure 7−8   **World 3 with stabilized population.**   Keeping input values identical with those in the standard run, but providing for perfect birth control, stabilizes the global population. However, industrial production and per capita food production rise excessively, severely depleting the resource base. This eventually causes a crash in both the industrial and the food production sectors, which causes an enormous increase in the death rate. This is not in this particular run reflected by a population crash, because the premise of this run is that the death rate equals the birth rate, so that when the death rate rises so does the birth rate, which it would not do in a real-world situation.

authorities, the 1970 census will establish basic parameters with respect to population characteristics and labor resources that can help in shaping future plans. For outside observers, the census results will be a source of important knowledge about the social and economic conditions prevailing in the Soviet Union.

Murray Feshbach, 1972

When addressing the problem of the effect of various technological fixes, the Meadows group had earlier tested the consequences of applying population

control techniques instead of increasing food production. With the model running with "unlimited" resources and pollution controls, but no increased agricultural yields, "perfect" birth control was introduced. That is, all unwanted
births were eliminated. A food crisis was postponed for several decades because
the population grew slowly, but it eventually collapsed from famine deaths
(Fig. 7–9).

The Mesarovic-Pestel models, to be described more fully in Chapter 9,
also emphasize the influence of time lags in delaying the achievement of a
stationary world population, or *population equilibrium,* as they prefer to call it.
They arrange the regions they recognize into two groups, the developed world
— that is, industrialized nations — and the developing world, which is the

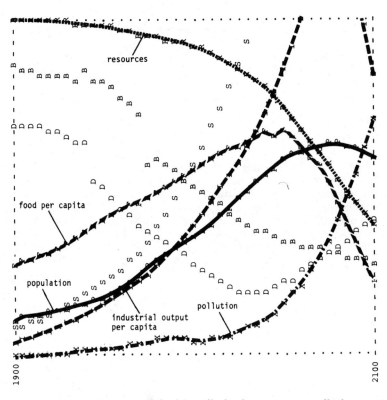

**Figure 7–9   The Meadows model with unlimited resources, pollution controls,
and "perfect birth control."**   This run tries the effect of eliminating unwanted
children by inserting a perfect method of birth control, instead of increasing food
production. This, in effect, is one of the commonly encountered arguments when
the world food situation is discussed. This run shows that the resulting curtailment
of population growth does postpone a food crisis for one or two decades; but per
capita food production eventually starts to decline, soon followed by a population
crash.

Table 7–4   Regional population growth under equilibrium policies.   The regional population figures shown here have been extracted from published predictive runs of the Mesarovic-Pestel models. They represent estimates of regional populations in 2100, if an equilibrium policy is introduced in 1975 and a replacement value fertility rate achieved in 2030. The regional population figures are rounded off and expressed in millions of people.

The population of the developed world under these premises would increase over the present size by approximately one-third, while that of the underdeveloped world would approximately quadruple.

Regional Populations			
Developed World		Underdeveloped World	
North America	375	Latin America	1,750
Western Europe	550	Middle East	530
Japan	130	Tropical Africa	870
USSR and satellites	400	South Asia	5,000
Remainder	200	China	2,000
Total 1,655 millions		*Total* 10,150 millions	

remainder. They run their model with three different dates for the implementation of equilibrium policy: 1975, 1985, and 1995. The results are tabulated in Table 7–4. In all cases, Mesarovic and Pestel have allowed a 35-year transition period after the implementation of equilibrium policy before replacement fertility is achieved.

As Table 7–4 shows, even with a 20-year time lag before introduction of a replacement fertility policy, the *developed* world would rise only from its present approximately 1.25 billion to about 1.65 billion people by 2100. The same timing would see the developing world rise from about 2.5 billion to over *10* billion. Even with the immediate implementation of population equilibrium policy in 1975, the total population of the developing countries would still rise to 6.25 billion people by 2100.

Many different projections now arrive at conclusions very similar to these. A number of them, such as the recent estimates by Tomas Frejka, emphasize that the greatest population increase will take place in countries often the least capable of absorbing such growth (Fig. 7–10). While it is true that the potential half billion increase in developed countries will require a much greater further outlay of the world's nonrenewable resources on a per capita basis than individual additions to the developing world, numerically these additions will reach a total *fifteen times as great.* This will go quite a long way toward equalizing increased resource demands. As Chapter 3 concludes, the world is no longer in a favorable position regarding reserves of nonrenewable resources. *All*

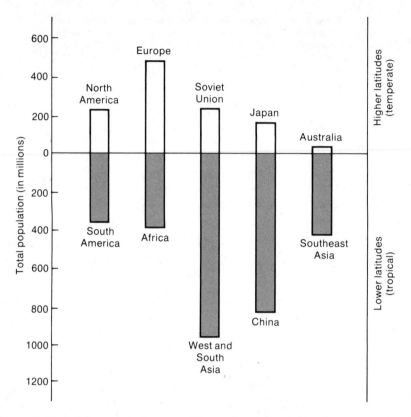

Figure 7–10   Geographical areas of greatest population increase.   In this schematic diagram, it is shown how, because of the high rates of natural increase in tropical areas, most of the population increase during the remainder of this century will be in the equatorial and southern portions of continental land masses. Columns show the total populations projected to 2000. Shaded portion indicates warmer areas, matched against adjoining cooler ones.

further demands on these nonrenewable resource reserves, from whatever source, must be regarded as unwelcome, even though humanitarian considerations require that considerable remaining reserves be devoted to improving conditions in the developing world at its present population levels. The existence of the population control response time lags discussed in this chapter emphasizes that we have no time remaining to squander on continuing international histrionic rhetoric and polemics as to who is to make the first move.

Bibliography and References

Appleman, Philip (ed.) *Thomas Robert Malthus: An Essay on the Principle of Population.* New York: W. W. Norton & Co., Inc., 1976.

Blake, Judith. "Reproductive Motivation and Population Policy," *Bioscience* **21**: 215–220 (1971).

Boughey, A. S. *Man and the Environment.* New York: Macmillan Co., 1971, 2nd ed., 1975.

Boughey, A. S. "World Population Growth — A Global Model," *International Journal of Environmental Studies* **7**:1–13 (1974).

Bumpass, Larry, and Westhoff, C. F. "The 'Perfect Contraceptive' Population," *Science* **169**:1177–1182 (1970).

Burch, T. K., and Gendell, Murray. "Extended Family Structure and Fertility." In *Readings in Population,* edited by William Petersen, pp. 329–341. New York: Macmillan Co., 1972.

Davis, Kingsley. "Biosocial Feedback Mechanisms in Human Populations." Paper delivered to the 140th Annual Meeting of the American Association for the Advancement of Science, San Francisco, February 27, 1974.

Davis, Kingsley, and Blake, Judith. "Social Structure and Fertility: An Analytical Framework," *Economic Development and Cultural Change* **4**:211–235 (1956).

Dumond, D. E. "The Limitation of Human Population," *Science* **187**:713–21 (1975).

Feshbach, Murray. "Observations on the Soviet Census." In *Readings in Population,* edited by William Petersen, pp. 97–107. New York: Macmillan Co., 1972.

Frejka, T. "The Prospects for a Stationary World Population," *Scientific American* **228**(3):15–23 (1973).

Hawley, A. H. "Ecology and Population," *Science* **179**:1196–1201 (1973).

Keyfitz, Nathan, and Flieger, Wilhelm. *Population: Facts and Methods of Demography.* San Francisco: W. H. Freeman and Co., 1971.

Mason, K. O., et al. *Social and Economic Correlates of Family Fertility: A Survey of the Evidence.* Project SU–518. Research Park, N.C.: Research Triangle Institute, 1971.

Odum, E. P. "Optimum Population and Environment: A Georgia Microcosm," *Current History* **58**:355–359 (1970).

Petersen, William (ed). *Readings in Population.* New York: Macmillan Co., 1972.

Rappaport, R. A. *Pigs for the Ancestors.* New Haven: Yale University Press, 1968.

Shantzis, S. B., and Behrens, W. W., III. "Population Control Mechanisms in a Primitive Agricultural Society," in *Toward Global Equilibrium: Collected Papers,* edited by D. L. Meadows and D. H. Meadows, pp. 257–88. Cambridge: Wright-Allen Press, 1973.

Thompson, L. "A Self-Regulating System of Human Population Control," *Transactions of the New York Academy of Sciences* **32**:262–70 (1970).

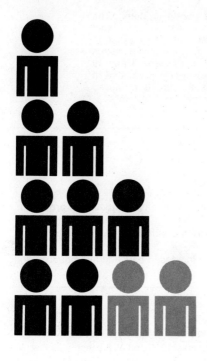

Chapter Eight

Achieving Global Equilibrium

The Meadows group system dynamics computer model World 3 provides the opportunity for the first attempt to assess the extent of technological and social adjustment to our global system that will be needed to bring it into equilibrium in the foreseeable future. From the point of view of the model, this time period was taken to be the next 125 years, that is, to 2100. The procedures followed by the Meadows group in addressing itself to this problem of achieving equilibrium are extremely logical, and they can be followed step by step in an ordered sequence of modifications to various input variables of the global model. This sequence is summarized in Table 8−1. The Meadows group illustrates each step with the printout from a run on the world model, following an appropriate adjustment to a particular input variable. This orderly progression of movement toward the ultimate objective of system equilibrium is initiated by starting with what has already been referred to as the *standard run,* the predictive mode of the model operating to 2100 without adjustment of any input variables from their historic values. In other words, the standard run assumes there will be no change in the *modus operandi* of the global system.

The Standard Run

As discussed earlier, the standard run of the Meadows model simulated the behavior of our global socioeconomic system from 1900 to 1970, and from then on predicts its future behavior through to 2100. From this run the

Table 8−1   Stabilization of the world system. The logical step-by-step sequence of adjustments in input variables followed by the Meadows' group in order to determine how to obtain equilibrium in the global system simulated in their World 3 model. Only steps 9 and 10 produced equilibrium in the global system simulated in their World 3 model. Only steps 9 and 10 produced equilibrium in the model, and so in the world system.

Technological fixes

1. Doubling of resource reserve life (Figure 6−2).
2. Provision of "unlimited" resources (Figure 5−10).
3. "Unlimited" resources and pollution control (Figure 6−8).
4. "Unlimited" resources, pollution control and increased agricultural production (Figure 6−9).
5. "Unlimited" resources, pollution control, and "perfect" birth control (Figure 7−9).
6. "Unlimited" resources, pollution control, increased agricultural production and "perfect" birth control (Figure 6−10).

Social adjustments

7. Population stationary after 1975 (Figure 7−8).
8. Both population and economy stationary after 1975 (Figure 8−1).
9. Both population and economy stationary after 1975 and all the technological fixes listed under 6 introduced (Figure 8−2).
10. As 9 but "natural delays" inserted into the population and economy stabilization instituted in 1975 (Figure 8−3).
11. All controls introduced in 1975 in 8 delayed until 2000 A.D.(Figure 8−4).

Meadows group concluded that the global system with its present historical set of input variables will not reach equilibrium within the stipulated time period, and that it will fail to reach stability in any of the state variables examined. Eventually, and considerably before the end of this model run, there is a catastrophic depletion of nonrenewable resources that leads to a system collapse. The depletion of resources that initiates this collapse occurs so rapidly that it soon begins drastically to reduce the size of the industrial base. However, before the collapse occurs, this industrial base has grown so excessively that it causes an immense increase in pollution levels. The fact that pollution did not begin to increase seriously until there was a turndown in the expansion of the industrial base is due to a built-in time lag in the onset of further pollution resulting from the previous increase in the industrial base.

Every physical quantity growing in a finite space must eventually exhibit one of three basic behavior modes: a smooth transition to a steady state, oscillation around an equilibrium position, or overshoot and decline. The World 3 model was designed to investigate which of the behavior modes is most likely to characterize the evolution of population and capital on this finite earth and to identify the policies that would increase the probability of an orderly transition to global equilibrium.

D. L. Meadows et al., 1974

The combined effects of increasing pollution and the reduction of the industrial base lead to a marked reduction in food production per person. The famines that result from food shortages increase mortality, and deaths come to exceed the number of births. The population then begins to decline seriously, and thus to reinforce the system collapse already initiated by the economic decline.

Social Factors

In the *standard run* of World 3, as just described, system collapse is due not only to uncontrolled expansion of technological processes but, to a lesser degree, also to a lack of social controls on population growth. In the terms of the controversy already discussed several times in these pages, there is both a "boardroom" *and* a "bedroom" effect. One of the procedures followed by the Meadows group was thus to ascertain the effect of modifying several of the social factor input variables that modify population increase.

Replacement Value Reproduction

Whether it takes 10 minutes of atomic warfare or 10 years of overpopulation, overexploitation and overpollution, our world is just as surely going to be destroyed unless each of us is individually willing to take some immediate positive action to avoid this ultimate catastrophe.

A. S. Boughey, 1971

If the system collapse in the standard run is due primarily to lack of population controls, then producing population stability by setting the number of births equal to the number of deaths should remedy this situation. Figure 7–8 shows the effect of requiring in World 3 that the number of births equal the number of deaths from the year 1975. Otherwise, the same input variables derived from our present historical world are entered in the model.

As can be seen from the illustration of the result of this run (Fig. 7−8), there is indeed stability in this model, at least as regards population size, because this is prescribed; but this is the only system state variable that achieves stability. Eventually, in this run, as in the standard model run, there is a depletion of resources that finally causes a reduction in the size of the industrial base. In this instance, it is the reduction in the size of the industrial base that causes the system collapse, because the standard of living is catastrophically reduced. Consequent to this reduction in the industrial base, there is a reduction in per capita food production until starvation deaths begin to occur. However, because in this run births and deaths have been equalized, as the deaths from starvation rise, there is an equivalent increase in births. This increase in the birth rate is a spurious artificial effect, due solely to the prescribed input variables entered into the model.

Replacement Populations and Stabilized Industrial Growth

As the immediate introduction of a replacement value fertility rate does not stabilize the global system, the next model run of World 3 examines the effect of neutralizing the second of the positive feedback loops which cause growth in the global socioeconomic system, and of thus containing capital investment. The amount of further capital investment permitted to be made is set to equal the amount of capital which is depreciated. Other input variables are left as in the standard run of the present world system. As can be seen from Figure 8−1, neutralizing *both* the main positive feedback loops in the world system does achieve at least a temporary stability in some of the principal state variables. For a time, not only are population size and the industrial base stabilized — this has to be so in any case because of the two premises of this model run — but also per capita food and services per capita remain constant. However, as in the previous model run, there is eventually a catastrophic depletion of nonrenewable resources leading to a reduction of the industrial base. This brings about a system collapse, initiated by a reduction in the per capita production of food that leads to an increased number of deaths. Again, the number of deaths cannot become greater than the number of births, because of the premise of the input values entered for these two rate variables.

The argument of "bedroom versus boardroom" thus by itself appears to be largely irrelevant. So, too, are the standard accusations that are currently traded at any international conference on population, food, or technological development. *Neither alone or in combination can control of population levels and stabilization of economies produce equilibrium in the global system.* Stationary populations and stationary economies are not sufficient, at least in the global system as simulated by World 3, by themselves to cure our present troubles. We are forced to consider both these factors in relation to the various technological fixes already explored in a previous chapter.

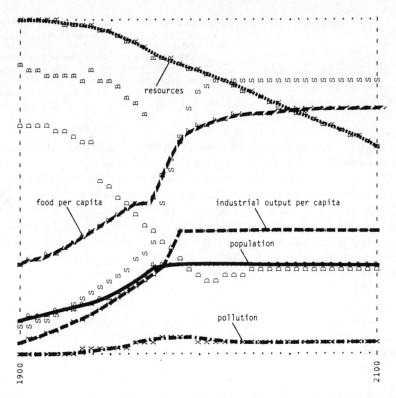

Figure 8−1 The Meadows World 3 model with stabilized population and capital. In this model run, both the principal feedback loops in the world system were neutralized. That is, population growth was stabilized by setting the number of births against the number of deaths, and industrial growth was stabilized by setting the amount of investment capital against the amount depreciated. This modification momentarily stabilizes per capita food production, per capita services available, and population size. However, because no resource conservation technologies have been inserted, the resource base continues rapidly to decline, eventually slowing industrial output. Per capita food production is lowered, as well as output of industrial goods; services deteriorate, and the death rate rises. In this model run the population does not crash because, although the death rate rises, births have been equated to deaths, and so they unrealistically rise with the death rate, stabilizing the population. This would not happen in a real-world situation; it is an artifact from the insertion of equalized births and deaths in the model.

Technological Fixes

The necessity for a stable state is overtly argued (in World 3) not on moral grounds but on the grounds of the physical impossibility of the continuation of economic growth. These physical limits can be attributed on the one hand to pollution effects of growth and on the other to the classical economic variables: land, resources and population. The distinctive feature of the MIT work is this marriage of neo-Malthusian economics with a contemporary stream of ecological environmentalism.

T. C. Sinclair, 1973

As described earlier, on the assumption that technological problems can be overcome by technological advances, the Meadows standard model was modified so as to include four technological adjustments. Nonrenewable resource reserves were set at double the reserves estimated as remaining in 1900. Pollution was controlled so as to develop from 1970 on at a rate of one quarter of its 1970 values. Resource depletion was slowed by recycling and reuse, which returned all but 25 percent of mined material back to industry. A perfect birth control technique was inserted that permitted individual couples to achieve a *desired* fertility; that is, no unwanted children were produced. The effects of these technological fixes introduced individually into the World 3 model on output system variables were displayed and discussed in Chapter 6. When all these modifications to the input variables were simultaneously introduced into the model, the system still did not reach stability, but collapsed because pollution levels were pushed ever higher by an expanding industrial base (Fig. 6−10). The excessively high pollution levels which developed not only had a direct effect on the human population, causing pollution deaths, but also diminished food production per capita through the deleterious effect on crop growth and reinforced increases in deaths through the added factor of starvation. Acting synergistically, pollution and starvation raised the death rate over the birth rate, precipitating a population collapse.

Technological Fixes and Immediate Social Controls

In the next model run of World 3, all the four technological fixes of the model run shown in Figure 6−10 were accordingly inserted into the input state variables, together with the equated births and deaths and investment and depreciation values of the earlier model run (Fig. 8−1). Births were set to equal deaths in 1975, capital investment to equal depreciation by 1990.

The result is the first permanently stable system in which equilibrium is maintained in all system variables, at least for the duration of the model run through to 2100 (Fig. 8−2). As can be seen from this figure, the population, industrial base, pollution levels, food production on a per capita base, and services per capita are all stabilized at an equilibrium value. This equilibrium condition results in a world population about 50 percent higher than the present value (that is, reaching about 5 billion), with an average personal income about

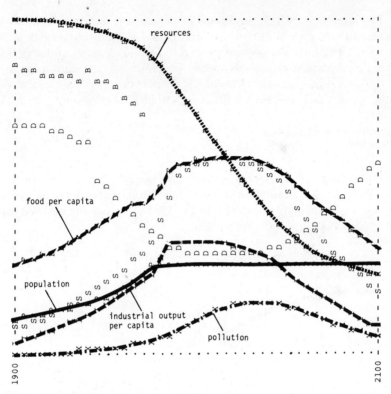

Figure 8-2   The Meadows model World 3 with all technological fixes and immediate social control.   This is the first combination of changes which brings stability to all the system variables in the World 3 model. Industrial output per capita is about three times the 1970 world average, and per capita food production is adequate to prevent starvation.

one half of that of the present average mean income in the United States (that is, about $1,800) and about sufficient food on the average to sustain life without encountering malnutrition.

The needs and the aspirations of the future generations make it our duty to build a sound and operable foundation of national objectives for the management of our resources for our children and their children. The future of succeeding generations in this country is in our hands. It will be shaped by the choices we make. We will not, and they cannot escape the consequences of our choices.

Henry Jackson, U.S. Senator, 1974

The premise on which this model run is based is that there can be an instant cessation of population growth in 1975 and of industrial growth in 1990. That is, by 1990, both the population and the economy are stationary. Unfortunately, as discussed extensively in this text, such instant stationariness is a mere theoretical proposition. Delayed responses in the real-world system would prevent the realization of such a situation within so short a time period.

Equilibrium after Allowance for Time Lags

The next model run, which is shown in Figure 8−3, allows for the operation of time lags for population stabilization and industrial base stabilization, assuming that immediate steps are taken in 1975 to initiate the necessary stabilizing procedures.

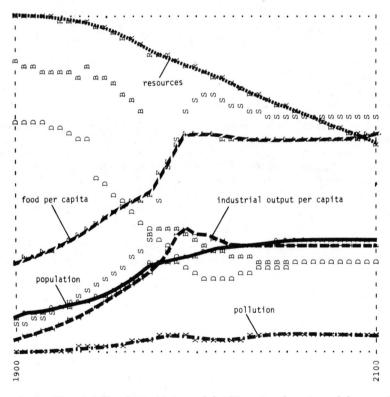

resources

food per capita   industrial output per capita

population

pollution

1900   2100

Figure 8−3   The stabilized World 3 model with natural system delays.   This run provides time for the population and industrial systems to achieve equilibrium following the insertion of the regulatory controls on the previous run. The world population is then higher before the system stabilizes, and the standard of living lower, than in the previous run shown in Figure 8−2.

While this does provide stability, the average standard of living is appreciably less than that which is possible in the previous run, shown in Figure 8–2, because the global population has become substantially larger, without a corresponding increase in basic necessities.

Postponement of Necessary Action

The equilibrium in the world system which is achieved in the last model run is attained by taking steps in 1975 to implement stabilization of the two positive feedback loops into the world system — that is, population and industrial increase — simultaneously arranging for the four technological developments as described. The cost of postponing the immediate implementation of these policies is examined in the final model run shown here (Fig. 8–4). The premise in this instance is that the measures entered in the previous model run are not implemented until the year 2000. As can be seen from this model run, a temporary stability is initially obtained in population size and in the value of food production per capita. Eventually, however, and before 2100, there is a depletion of the resource base which causes a collapse of the system. This is associated with a reduction in the industrial base, followed by a reduction in the food base and deaths from starvation that finally exceed the number of births, bringing about a population crash.

> An equilibrium could permit the development of an unprecedented golden age for humanity. Freedom from ever-increasing numbers of people will make it possible to put substantial effort into the self-realization and development of the individual.
>
> *Jørgen Randers and D. H. Meadows, 1972*

It would appear from this final model run that there is a window open at this moment of time that will soon close, and certainly will not be available by the end of this millennium in 25 years. If this window is utilized now, and all the procedures listed in the run illustrated in Figure 8–3 are enacted, there is a possibility of reaching a lasting equilibrium in the world socioeconomic system. This will not be a very satisfactory equilibrium in terms of average living standards, but at least there will be some general raising of the standard of living for some people (associated with a considerable reduction of the standard of living for the present elitist minority), together with a prevention of deaths from starvation. However, this window will close within a matter of several years from now. After that, some collapse in the system is inevitable.

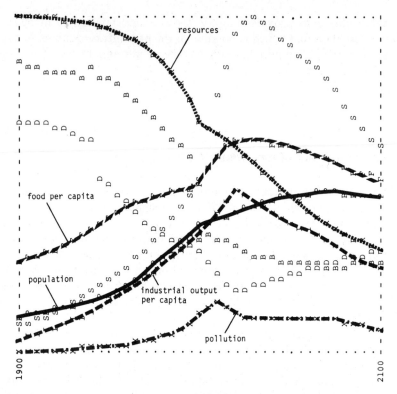

**Figure 8–4   Effect on the Meadows model World 3 of postponement of stabiliz-
ing policies.**   In this run, all the policies instituted in 1975 in the previous runs
were delayed until the year 2000. With this twenty-five-year delay, it is no longer
possible to achieve an equilibrium state in any system variable. Population size
and the per capita amount of industrial output attain such high levels as to create
food and resource shortages before the end of the run in 2100, and the population
has already begun to crash.

As Chapter 7 described, it is an oversimplification to consider the real
world as homogeneous and measure it in terms of per capita averages, for we
are as yet far from being a unified global society. Because of this, all resources
will not be equally shared; some people will retain more than the average, leaving other people with less. There will be local system collapses in developing
areas; but the elitist world will initially be able to protect itself from the worst
consequences of this collapse, although it may immediately begin to suffer a
steadily continuing decline in living standards. The extent of this decline will depend on the degree of voluntary or consequential political involvement that
each nation has with the disaster areas. The nature and extent of such regional
involvement and independence are examined in the next chapter.

Bibliography and References

Beckerman, Wilfred. *In Defence of Economic Growth.* London: Jonathan Cape, 1974.

Jackson, Henry. Statement of Senator Jackson as sponsor of the National Environmental Policy Act of 1969, quoted in "The Origins of a National Environmental Policy" by V. J. Yannacone. In *Energy Crisis,* edited by V. J. Yannacone, p. 385. New York: West Publishing Co., 1974.

Randers, Jørgen, and Meadows, D. H. "The Carrying Capacity of the Globe," *Sloan Management Review* **13**(2):11−27 (1972).

Reischaur, E. *Toward the 21st Century: Education for a Changing World.* New York: Alfred A. Knopf, Inc., 1973.

Salgo, Harvey. "The Obsolescence of Growth: Capitalism and the Environmental Crisis," *Review of Radical Political Economics* **5**(3):26−45 (1973).

Schumacher, E. F. *Small Is Beautiful: A Study of Economics as if People Mattered.* London: Blond and Briggs, 1973.

Sinclair, T. C. "Environmentalism." In *Thinking about the Future,* edited by H. S. D. Cole et al., p. 176. London: Chatto and Windus, 1973.

Special volume. "The No-Growth Society," *Daedalus* **102**(4):1−245 (1973).

Chapter Nine

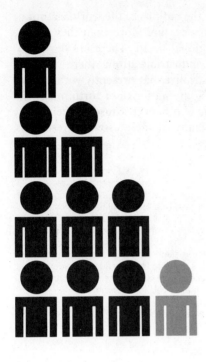

Regional Models

   The examples of system dynamics computer models of real social systems that have been examined extensively so far in this text have been the Forrester World 2 and the Meadows World 3 global models. These two general models constitute the first attempts to model the world socioeconomic system as a holistic entity. Many technical criticisms have been leveled at these models, and some of these were described in the previous pages. However, over and beyond such technical methodological criticisms, there has been a general reluctance to accept the *conclusions* drawn from these two global models as to the changes necessary to attain global system equilibrium. Perhaps the majority of people prefer to dismiss such dynamic models and their conclusions as academic doomsday exercises that engage the fancy of a few pessimistic eccentrics. They prefer to base their policies and their expectations on the regressional linearity of traditional econometric models, despite the fact that these models are feeding back anything but reassuring data.
   In the industrialized world, with its standard of living generally unsurpassed in human history, it is very difficult to conceive of a society courting imminent Malthusian disaster. At the same time, it is very difficult for an entrepreneur, whether bureaucrat or capitalist, in an underdeveloped nation to appreciate why the air cannot stand a little more DDT, the ocean a small increase in mercury, the whale just a little more hunting.
   Such diverse difficulties in the perception of global problems can be partly resolved by an analysis of our socioeconomic systems and their constraints on growth on a regional rather than a global basis. An exercise of this nature still

does not avoid sweeping generalizations, for the nations of the world cannot be neatly categorized as falling into several classes, any more than they can be summed and averaged to provide a single global mean. There are developed nations in various stages of advanced industrialization; there are underdeveloped nations, all struggling to industrialize, but presently with varying and widely divergent degrees of progress. Some nations are fortuitously endowed with natural resources, some have few; others, because of their dense populations, may already have exhausted many of these essential resources, even when some reserves were originally present.

> . . . the human environment — the earth — is finite, the growth of human population and industrialization cannot continue indefinitely. This is a simple and obvious fact, but its consequences pose an unprecedented challenge to mankind. The challenge lies in finding an ethical basis for making the trade-offs that will confront human society in the near future, trade-offs that arise because in a limited world everything cannot be maximized for everyone.
>
> *Jørgen Randers and D. H. Meadows, 1973*

Regional Groupings

With these caveats in mind, it is possible to group nations into five classes on a basis of their present level of industrialization and their possession of essential natural resources. Figure 9–1 shows this basic national division. The first primary group, developed nations, is divided into two categories, A and B. Both have now passed through the demographic transition, and their populations have reached the stationary level, or are approaching it. Category A nations have only moderately dense populations, and can be self-sufficient in food. They also have most of their nonrenewable resource needs. Category B nations, however, have dense populations, and they are accordingly not self-supporting in food; nor do they have a sufficiency of nonrenewable resources within their own territories.

Figure 9–1 Categories of nations. This simple division of nations into five ▶ groups recognizes two categories in the developed world, A and B, and three categories in the underdeveloped world, C, D, and E. In category A are countries like the United States and the Soviet Union, which have extensive resources, including their own fuel supplies, and are able to feed their own populations. Category B is not able to feed its own population completely, and is shorter on natural resources. In category C are the cartel nations, sometimes but not always lacking resources other than the one for which a cartel has been formed, and often unable to feed their populations. Category D nations have adequate resources for their agrarian level of economy. Category E nations do not have adequate resources even for an agrarian economy and their present population levels, and are living with the risk that any natural or economic perturbation will precipitate at least local famine.

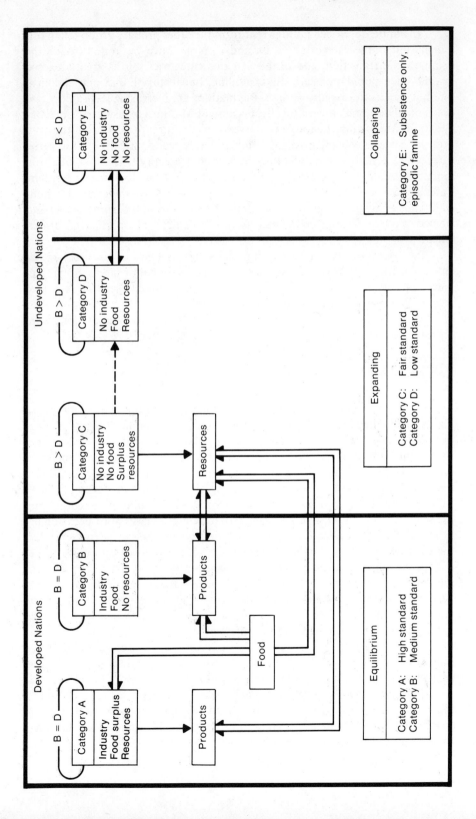

The underdeveloped nations that form the other primary group fall in this scheme into three categories: C, D, and E. None have yet gone through the demographic transition; and in the first two categories, births greatly exceed deaths. Their populations are still exploding. In category E, not only the birth rate but the death rate also is high. Populations are increasing less rapidly and occasionally decline, at least locally, because of Malthusian disasters. Category C nations are fortunate enough to possess some natural resource that they can trade at an extravagant price by joining the appropriate cartel. This cartel category C, usually is not self-sufficient in food. Category D is self-sufficient in food, and requires no nonrenewable resource not located within its borders. Category E is not self-sufficient in food, nor does it have any cartelable mineral deposits. Such nations are sometimes detached from the Third World and labeled Fourth World countries. Their immediate prospects are dismal indeed.

Between these five categories of nations there is a flow of resources, either by way of trade, or in some cases in the form of national or international aid. Each category has a very different socioeconomic system; these five types of systems respond differently to the factors identified in various models presented in this text. Some of these contrasted interactions to environmental limits were identified in the discussion of regional models in Chapter 1.

Category A Nations

These are the most favored nations. They include the two technological giants, the United States and the Soviet Union, and economically smaller countries such as Canada, Australia, Sweden, and Norway. Population densities per square mile are rarely in excess of 55, and their populations are in some cases only just beginning to move from their previous expanding stable mode to a position closer to the stationary one (Fig. 9–2). They are generally self-sufficient in food, even if as in the case of Norway much of it has to come from the sea, and as in the case of Russia external food purchases must occasionally be made. They have adequate sources of energy within their own frontiers when these are developed, in the form of fossil fuels or hydropower, although market conditions may, as in the case of the United States, have resulted in a recent reliance on imported fuels. Many of the 36 raw materials generally considered "critical" for industry are usually located in adequate supply within their national boundaries. The U.S.S.R. is reported to have all but 7 of these; the United States presently needs to import some quantities at least of 26 of these essential materials. In fact, as a consequence of the high rate of natural resource utilization by industry, the United States, like several other nations in this category, may increasingly have to trade food exports for raw material imports.

This first category of developed nations is in the very fortunate position of being able to devote virtually all its surplus production to continuing improvements in the standard of living of its citizens. This capacity is reinforced when imported goods are received in exchange for food exports. Nations in

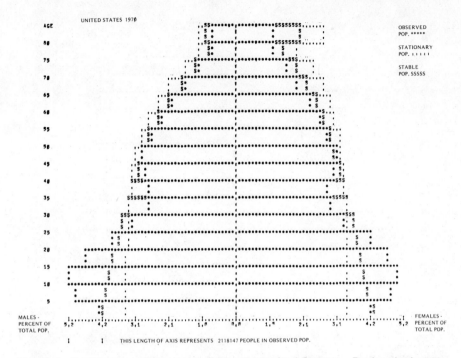

Figure 9−2 The population pyramid for the United States. During the last two decades the United States had a natural increase of approximately 1.0, and its observed population was consequently set in a stable position which was some distance from the stationary. The 1970 census revealed that the stable population was now beginning to approach the stationary population; and the lowering of the net reproduction rate below 1.0 over the past few years, if maintained, will bring this country into a zero-population-growth equilibrium at about 270 million people before the end of this millennium.

category A are thus in one of the two categories that can look forward to a continuing increase in per capita supplies of industrial products. By the same token, it is one of the two categories very favorably placed to devote part of its surplus to less fortunate categories.

Category B Nations

This category includes Japan and the more populous European nations with restricted geographic areas, such as the United Kingdom, the Netherlands, Belgium, Italy, Austria, Switzerland, Portugal, and Denmark. Their populations are stationary, and their population structure is mature, so they are at or close to the zero-population-growth level (Fig. 9−3). Densities per square mile are at about the 3,000 mark. Their agriculture is capital-intensive; despite

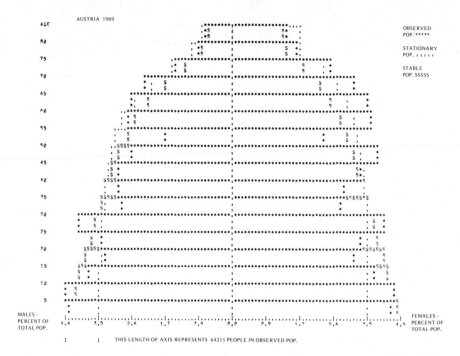

Figure 9–3　The population structure of Austria. The observed stable and stationary positions for the population of Austria are now, as shown in this illustration, beginning to approximate. Some nations in the B category as defined in this text, such as Denmark and the Netherlands, appear now — for the moment, at least — to be set in a pattern in which their observed population in the youngest cohorts lies within the stationary mode line. That is, their populations are now actually in a declining phase.

large expenditures of energy in their agricultural budgets, they are not self-sufficient in food and must import some food by creating a salable surplus of industrial goods. As, with certain exceptions, they generally are also insufficiently endowed with natural resources, including fossil fuels, they must have a further export goods trade to obtain the necessary imports of these raw materials.

The nations in category B are thus in double jeopardy, having to trade manufactured goods for both part of their food and at least some nonrenewable resources. To the extent that they are compelled to trade for these at artificially maintained prices fixed by world cartels, their surplus productivity has largely to be exported. Their standard of living, already below that of the top national class, category A, may slide still further in relative global positioning as their industrial growth is slowed or halted by the inflated cost of imported nonrenewable resources.

Category C Nations

The other category presently with a large surplus is the oil cartel group, featuring some thirteen nations headed by Saudi Arabia and including a minority of non-Arab countries such as Nigeria and Venezuela. Time may see the formation of cartels in other of the "critical" thirty-six mineral commodities, and the consequent addition of other underdeveloped nations to this cartel category.

The populations of these category C nations are characteristically sparse but exploding. Venezuela provides an example of one of the more modest rates of population growth among members of this category (Fig. 9–4). Kuwait, with a reported doubling time of an estimated nine years, illustrates what is perhaps the most extreme population growth in this and indeed any other category.

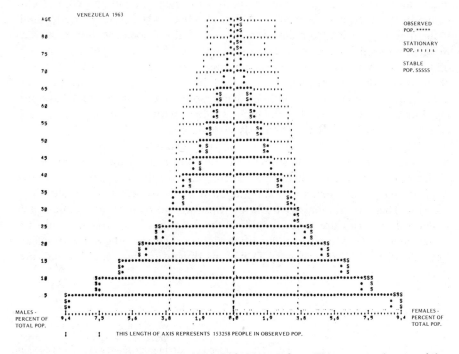

Figure 9–4   The population structure of Venezuela.   This country is one of the oil cartel nations, but it is also one which has other resources and is able to feed itself. Although still set in an expanding mode, as are all the category C nations, it is thus buffered to a large degree from the effects of cartel collapse and the consequent drastic lowering of commodity price.

Some of the OPEC nations could or do already feed themselves, notably the Philippines, Iran, Nigeria, and Venezuela. All, however, presently have too small an industrial base to avoid the importation of industrial goods, even if they so desired. The immense monetary surpluses the OPEC cartel nations accumulate from oil exports actually provide more goods than can be properly utilized by the population, and all the food required. The standard of living for all is set to rise continuously.

There may be a day of reckoning for the nations of this cartel category, but the end is not yet in sight. In none of them is there an effective negative feedback loop presently operating on population growth or on the importation of industrial goods. Only eventual exhaustion of oil reserves, or the discovery by their customers of an alternative energy source, can halt the present bonanza.

Category D Nations

More than half the people of the world live in this category D, which includes the most populous of all nations, China, with an estimated 800 million inhabitants — perhaps now even actually with over one billion people. With China in this category are nearly a hundred other underdeveloped nations, all struggling to progress from agrarian to industrialized societies. Some, such as Mexico, are well on their way. Others, like Burundi, have not yet even made it off first base. What characterizes the nations in this D category is their common ability — for the present, at least — to feed themselves without agricultural imports. Their populations, sometimes dense, sometimes less so, are all expanding. For example, Mexico has the highest rate of natural increase in the world. Others, such as Costa Rica, are nearly as high (Fig. 9–5).

The standard of living in these category D countries is low, and can only be improved to the extent that these nations industrialize, and their industries utilize only domestic raw materials. There is no surplus to trade for resource imports. Any improvement in the standard of living will thus be slow and tedious. There is nothing to trade on the international market unless new mineral discoveries are made, enabling these nations to move over into the cartel category C. Moreover, their often vigorously expanding populations are likely to displace these category D nations downward into the disaster category E.

> Whether we like it or not, the fate of some countries — India, for example — is largely sealed . . . no human agency is likely to prevent the disaster . . . the chain of events leading to the dissolution of India as a viable nation is already in motion.
>
> *P. R. Ehrlich and A. H. Ehrlich, 1974*

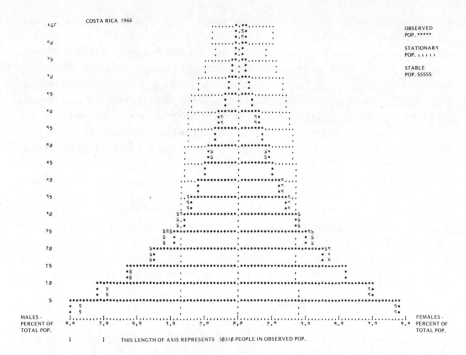

Figure 9-5   The population structure of Costa Rica.   This category D nation is one of several which until recently was recorded as having the highest rate of natural increase, 3.4, among the world's nations. The explosive nature of the population growth in this category D nation is shown in this figure. Fortunately for Costa Rica, this extreme growth phase has not yet reached a point where all its resources have eroded; moreover, it would appear that pressures have already developed, with some government support, for the curtailment of this rate of natural increase. As can be seen, even in 1963 the observed population was considerably less than the stable population in the youngest cohort.

Category E Nations

This is indeed a disaster category, for any realistic appraisal of the immediate future of these nations is grim. They include the second most populous nation, India, with 600 million people; Bangladesh; and smaller nations in Africa and South America — perhaps two dozen in all. Several already have excessive deaths in some of their regions as a result of local famines, as recently reported from Bangladesh, Colombia, Ethiopia, and the seven West African nations including a Sahel savanna region within their national territory.

Reliable census figures for this E category of nations are usually hard to come by, but reported crude rates of natural increase currently range from 2.0 to 3.0, population doubling times, that is, ranging from about 25 to 35 years.

With a continuation of such rates the populations of all the nations in this category must rise so high relative to available food resources that they will suffer major disasters. These are the nations that the Paddock brothers, in 1968, suggested would have to be abandoned when the *triage* system is applied to world famine relief aid. Garrett Hardin, in 1974, in his lifeboat metaphor, suggests much the same treatment, emphasizing that famine supplies merely postpone disaster and make the next incident more difficult to prevent.

This E category of nations is in fact living at the *maximum obtainable population*. As described and illustrated in Chapter 6, this kind of maximum is only momentarily supportable before a negative feedback mechanism operates Malthusian factors that increase the death rate until population size is reduced to the *maximum sustainable population*. A. S. Boughey, in 1974, suggested it would be more appropriate to reinforce fertility control efforts in such nations than send further famine relief supplies, for the sooner their populations are reduced to the maximum sustainable population level, the less suffering there will be. Several years ago, Paul Ehrlich was even more brutal, suggesting fertility control drugs be automatically included in all famine relief supplies to these nations.

The *maximum sustainable population* limit is the level at which nations in category D are presently surviving. Because of their failure to control their rates of natural increase, they are perpetually in jeopardy of slipping into category E by exceeding their maximum sustainable population level. In any case, despite internal pressures for progress, they will never develop the productivity surpluses necessary to move forward toward higher standards of living unless their populations are still further controlled. A graphic model demonstrating this requirement was presented several years ago by Harold Frederiksen (Fig. 9−6).

> Global grain reserves are at their lowest point in nearly two decades, and bad weather, fertilizer shortages, or other unfavorable developments could push some of the perennially hungry nations over the brink into famine within the next few years.
>
> *Edward Groth III, 1975*

Figure 9−6. Economic feedbacks operating on the rate of natural increase. ▶ This process model, prepared a number of years ago by Harold Frederiksen, was designed to show that the economic progress of a nation is greatly enhanced by the demographic transition. Decreasing fertility reinforces the effects of gains made in per capita production. (Reprinted from) Frederiksen, H., "Feedbacks in Economic and Demographic Transition," *Science* **166**:837−847, 14 Nov. 1969. Copyright © 1969 by the American Association for the Advancement of Science.

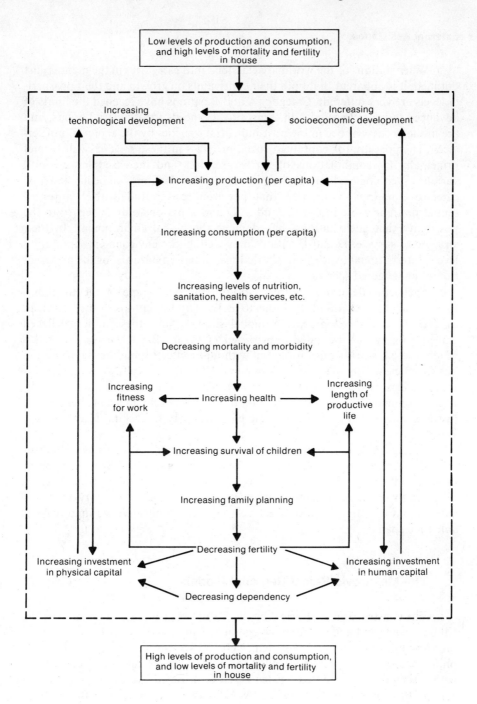

External Assistance

When nations of the world are classified into categories in the manner just outlined, it is apparent that both their constraints on growth and their prosperity levels are very different. Category A and B nations have reached the limits of advanced industrial societies in terms of their needs for industrial goods, and are in the process of becoming post-industrial societies by the expansion of services. The pressure for continued social progress in these societies will be met principally by combinations of further services and increased leisure until various psychological limits are encountered. These nations will be interested in category C nations to the extent that they are forced to trade with them for essential nonrenewable resources, and in D and E nations only in regard to the possibility that such nations may damage the global environment. In their struggle to survive, D and E nations may well ignore environmental pollution levels, international overfishing restrictions, radiation hazards, or the preservation of endangered species.

Such considerations, coupled additionally with some modicum of humanity, may induce A and B nations to assist D and E nations toward survival, or even toward development. A model showing how these underprivileged categories may best be aided is provided in Figure 10–1. The basis for this model is the historic supposition that without an effective middle class a nation has insufficient expertise for development. Without a wealthy ruling class — that is, a class with private money, or with access to the nation's money — lack of developmental capital also inhibits industrial development. Table 9–1 illustrates how either or both of these elements may be lacking in the present world.

Foreign aid, as the model in Figure 10-1 illustrates, can meet either of these deficiencies. Provision of technical experts covers any shortage of expertise in the middle class; financial loans meet the necessary capital costs of development. Both forms of assistance are presently avialable to category D and E nations, but at entirely inadequate levels to be really effective within a reasonable time span.

The Mesarovic-Pestel Regional Models

The construction of World 3 by the Meadows group was sponsored by the Club of Rome and underwritten by several private foundations. The constraints on growth within the *global* system were thus explored and defined. These philanthropic groups next proceeded to sponsor studies on system constraints within socioeconomic systems categorized on a *regional* basis. As mentioned earlier, the work was undertaken by Mihajlo Mesarovic, at Case Western Reserve University, Ohio, and Eduard Pestel, at Hanover University, West Germany. Instead of permitting continuing exponential growth in the world system, and suffering its attendant ills as described in World 3, Mesarovic and

Table 9−1 Relative proportions of middle and upper classes. In order to develop, a country needs the technical knowledge of its middle classes (20−80 percent highest incomes) and the wealth of the upper class (top 5 percent incomes). In these selections from a recent listing prepared by Irma Adelman and C. T. Morris, group A nations are handicapped by an insufficient wealthy class; group B, by too small a middle class. A white supremacy nation like Rhodesia (group C) also has too small a middle class, while South Africa (C likewise) is not too well off either in this respect or in the matter of a wealthy class.

	A			B			C	
	Niger	Mexico	Ceylon	Libya	Gabon	Peru	Rhodesia	South Africa
Wealthy (top 5%)	23.0	28.5	18.4	46.4	47.0	48.3	60.0	39.4
Middle class (21−80%)	46.0	38.3	33.2	10.3	27.0	28.4	31.0	40.6
Poor (20%)	12.0	3.7	4.4	0.1	2.0	4.0	4.0	1.9

Pestel postulate the need for a new form of *organic growth,* or differentiation. This is not actually by any means as new a form as the two authors appear to claim. It is basically merely a development of the service-oriented society forecast in World 3. Several other authors also already have described how societal development is moving into a *postindustrial* phase that will be service-oriented rather than product-oriented.

Be that as it may, the primary objective of Mesarovic and Pestel was to separate the world into regional sections, each displaying a greater homogeneity than is possible when examining the global socioeconomic system as a single unit. Ten regions were distinguished, and 153 countries were allocated to them. Selected countries from each region are listed in Table 9−2. It should be noted that region 3 contains but one country; region 1, only two; and region 5, such apparently oddly assorted economies as the German Democratic Republic and Albania. A few Ruritanian countries listed are best known for their postage stamps (Andorra and San Marino) or their casino (Monaco). Political differences appear to be the only major diagnostics between some regions — separating, for example, North and South Korea, North and South Vietnam, and Taiwan and the People's Republic of China. Few would place Bangladesh in the same socioeconomic category as Taiwan. This kind of ambivalence in the categorization of regions may to some extent dampen the more marked regional socioeconomic differences apparent in the world, such as were described in the first portion of this chapter.

Table 9–2 The grouping of countries adopted for the Mesarovic-Pestel regional model. A few countries have been selected here to illustrate each group.

Region 1. North America (total 2)	Canada United States
Region 2. Western Europe (total 25)	Austria Finland United Kingdom France Netherlands
Region 3. Japan	Japan
Region 4. Rest of the Developed Market Economies (total 6)	Australia Oceania South Africa
Region 5. Eastern Europe (total 8)	Albania Poland German Democratic Republic USSR
Region 6. Latin America (total 27)	Argentina Brazil Cuba Mexico
Region 7. North Africa and the Middle East (total 21)	Bahrain Egypt Iran Morocco
Region 8. Main Africa (total 36)	Burundi Ethiopia Ivory Coast South Africa
Region 9. South and Southeast Asia (total 16)	Bangladesh Laos India Philippines
Region 10. Centrally Planned Asia (total 4)	North Korea People's Republic of China

Description of the Mesarovic-Pestel Model

The systems approach of the Mesarovic-Pestel model is illustrated in Figure 9–7. Describing this as the *total systems approach,* the authors show how economics, agrotechnology, ecology, population, sociopolitical arrangements, and individual values and norms all have to be incorporated in any realistic consideration of the world situation. In the last item, they thus provide for a humanistic decision model which the Meadows group acknowledged they had to omit from World 3. This provision for a reflection of changing moral attitudes permits the inclusion of aid issues such as Garrett Hardin has recently

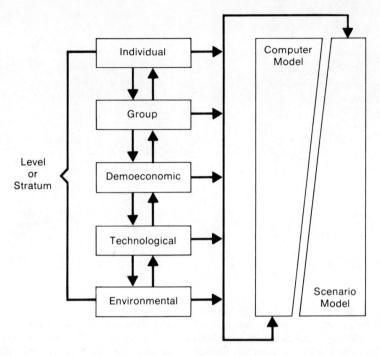

Figure 9–7   The Mesarovic-Pestel regional models.   A scheme showing the breakdown of the behavior of the world system into five levels as recognized in the Mesarovic-Pestel regional-modeling exercise. Each level provides representation of the world system as recorded in existing data. The complete model incorporates all five strata in an interrelated system dynamics computer model based on cause-effect linkages. Adapted from *Mankind at the Turning Point,* M. Mesarovic and E. Pestel, E. P. Dutton (1974).

raised in his lifeboat analogy. By providing for such social changes, the Mesarovic-Pestel model can include what the authors term *subjective* aspects, as well as the *objective* descriptors of World 3.

A diagram of the Mesarovic-Pestel model and a map of the regions demarcated are shown in Figures 9–8 and 9–9. This model is much more complicated than World 3; the authors state that it contains about 100,000 system interactions as against the several hundred of World 3. This does not imply that bigger or more complicated models are better, nor do Mesarovic and Pestel claim this. The obvious danger of larger models is that they will further complicate and enlarge any inadvertently introduced error. The results of the various runs are presented as *scenarios,* and it is hoped in this way to minimize the forecasting aspects which, despite the authors' repeated warning against such extrapolations, tended to become attached to the output of World 3. Runs were made over 50 years, because there was often a time lag in the models of up to twenty-five years in accommodating to changes in particular input variables.

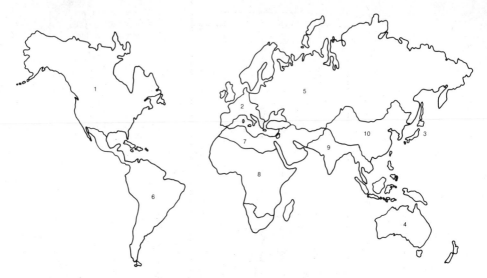

Figure 9-8   Regional subdivision of the world.   This map shows the geo-graphical regions associated in the regional grouping of the world for the pur-poses of the preparation of the Mesarovic-Pestel model. The regions are usually but not invariably contiguous. Region 4, for example, stretches across the Indian Ocean from Australia to southern Africa.

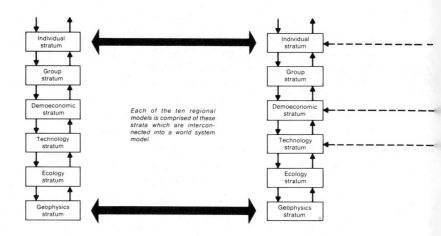

Each of the ten regional models is comprised of these strata which are intercon-nected into a world system model.

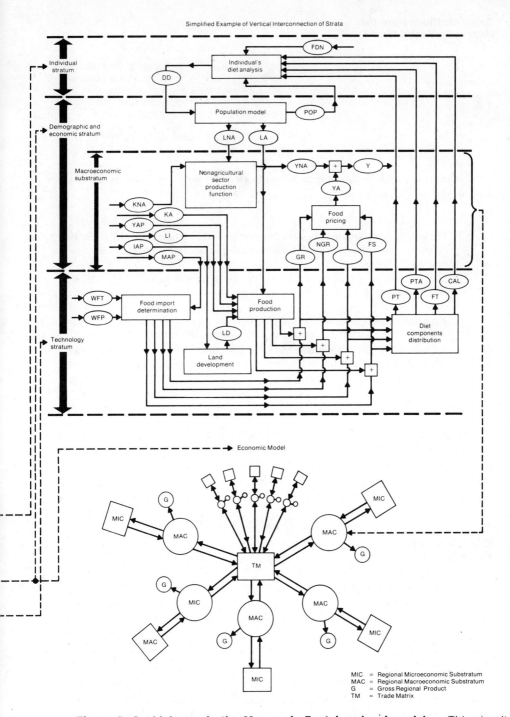

Simplified Example of Vertical Interconnection of Strata

MIC = Regional Microeconomic Substratum
MAC = Regional Macroeconomic Substratum
G = Gross Regional Product
TM = Trade Matrix

Figure 9-9   Linkages in the Mesarovic-Pestel regional models.   This simplified chart shows how the various sectors and levels of the Mesarovic-Pestel
regional models are linked into the complete system dynamics model.

**Generalizations from the
Mesarovic-Pestel Model**

> The economic prosperity of the U.S. is in-
> extricably interwoven with that of the world, and
> thus Americans, along with everyone else, will
> suffer if the world trade system and international
> monetary managements collapse.
>
> *P. R. Ehrlich and A. H. Ehrlich, 1974*

Mesarovic and Pestel summarize the deductions they have made from their model as follows:

1. The world socioeconomic system must be viewed in reference to the prevailing differences in culture, tradition, and economic development exhibited by its interacting regions.
2. System collapse of particular regions could occur well before 2050, although at different times and for different reasons. These regional collapses will affect other regions.
3. Regional catastrophes can be avoided only by adjustments in the total world system. Without global adjustment, each region will in turn be affected.
4. Adjustments must achieve differentiated growth analogous to organic growth, rather than undifferentiated (exponential) growth, which is ultimately fatal.
5. Delays in devising and implementing a suitable strategy for survival are not only costly but actually deadly.

Conclusions from this Mesarovic-Pestel regional analysis thus extend and confirm those from the Meadows World 3 model, and emphasize that exponential growth in socioeconomic systems must be terminated forthwith. They substantiate from the regional analysis all the arguments that have already been presented on a global basis as a result of runs on the Meadows World 3 model.

**World Crises at the
Regional Level**

In the first place, the Mesarovic-Pestel model depicts the widening gap between have and have-not nations (Fig. 9—10). This inevitable outcome of the continuation unchanged of the present global socioeconomic system has been expressed intuitively for many years, as well as demonstrated more recently by system dynamics models. It has now been further quantified, as Figure 9—10 shows. Fifty years from now, industrialized countries will have increased their per capita income to such an extent that the mean income is twenty times as high as that in South Asia. A large element of this increased disparity arises from unchecked population growth in this already impoverished region.

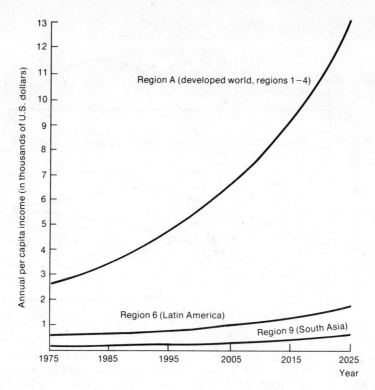

Figure 9-10 The gap between the developed and the underdeveloped world. The curves shown here represent projections of the Mesarovic-Pestel regional model in regard to regional development. Region 6 (Latin America) and region 9 (South Asia), already with a major disparity in their per capita economic standards as compared with the developed world, here indicated by a grouping of regions 1-4, do not show any lessening of this gap over the next fifty years. At best, the gap remains proportionately the same; but in some instances, it widens.

The distressing consequences of failure to check this population growth are dramatically illustrated by Figure 9-11, which provides a scenario relating protein levels to child deaths. The Mesarovic-Pestel model emphasizes what may already be seen in any television news feature on an underprivileged population — that food shortages more especially kill the young children. In South Asia and elsewhere the population structure that has developed from unchecked growth has resulted in children being in a large majority, so that even if there were no differential mortality, more children than adults would die. Food exports to South Asia from the rest of the world would not check the expected rise in child deaths entirely, but would hold the peak total to about one half of what will occur if the present situation continues unmodified.

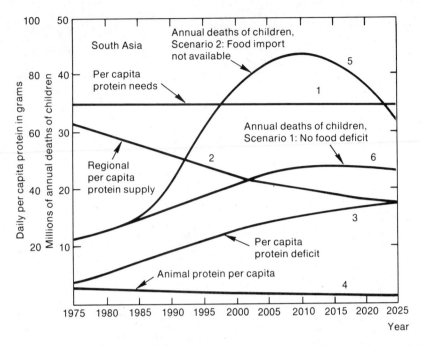

Figure 9-11   Starvation and malnutrition. The horizontal lines show the daily protein needs, and the declining curve 2 indicates the daily per capita supply in South Asia. Curve 5 shows the number of deaths among infants and juveniles to be expected over the next fifty years if population growth continues in this region and there is no provision of food imports.

> . . . a state like Massachusetts is one and a half times the population density of India. And a state like Massachusetts is no better able to support that population from inside its own borders than is India. We have probably more of a population problem in the developed countries than we have in the underdeveloped countries, if you cast the measure in terms of whether or not the developed countries could sustain their present population at their present standards of living within their own borders.
>
> *J. W. Forrester, 1975*

  The dangers to individual regions arising from unchecked population growth are well illustrated in the Mesarovic-Pestel graph shown in Figure 9-12. In the more populous regions, population density will progressively limit increases in food production not only by necessitating a greater production, but also by encroaching on cultivated land. Foreign aid to bring about changes in socioeconomic practices in these underdeveloped populous areas cannot be provided too early. The Mesarovic-Pestel scenarios presented in Figure 9-13 clearly demonstrate that delays in providing this aid enormously increase the total cost of the assistance that eventually must be sent.

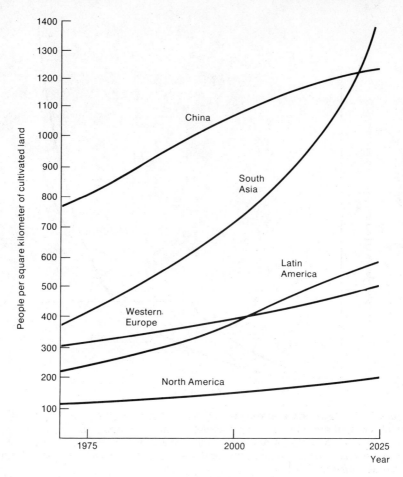

Figure 9−12 Population densities and potential agricultural areas. These projections from the Mesarovic-Pestel model show how, if present population increases continue in China and in South Asia, enormous pressures will be placed on all potential agricultural land in those regions within fifty years. Much of the land which is potentially cultivable in these regions has in any case already been developed.

How much of this assistance might come from the OPEC cartel the Mesarovic-Pestel model does not specify, but an assistance factor was used to calculate an optimum world price for petroleum. As can be seen from Figure 9−14, increasing oil prices beyond an optimum price does not increase either the gross national product of the Middle East oil nations or their total monetary wealth received in payment for oil exports. The effect of varying the oil price on developed regions has been shown in Table 1−3. Unfortunately, world oil prices already have exceeded what Mesarovic and Pestel consider the optimum oil prices.

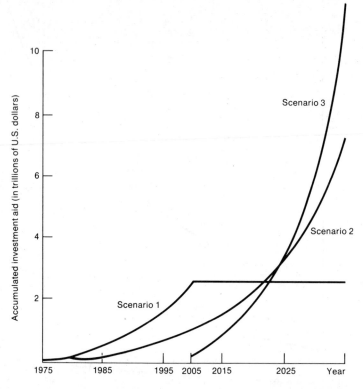

Figure 9−13   Foreign assistance.   These three scenarios from the Mesarovic-Pestel regional model show that if economic aid is supplied by the developed to the undeveloped world immediately, the cost will be far less than if aid is started now but given in too small amounts, or if aid should be delayed altogether until the turn of the millennium.

> An ever present danger will be that Washington will extend America's commitments to feed the hungry nations beyond the limit of our resources. . . . Not only are the food stocks limited . . . but also all the rest of the range of resources.
>
> *William Paddock and Paul Paddock, 1967*

Perhaps the most spectacularly dramatic scenario series of the whole Mesarovic-Pestel investigation is contained in Figure 9−15. This depicts the rise in regional urban populations during the next 50 years. It is estimated that nearly *one billion* urban jobs will have to be created to absorb the new urban residents, about half of these jobs being required in region 9 alone, that is,

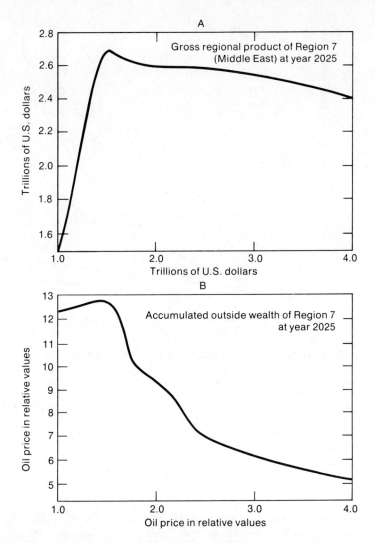

Figure 9-14 Oil prices and accumulated wealth. These two graphs from the Mesarovic-Pestel model show that if OPEC pushes oil prices too high (example B), the total wealth of the Mideast region will be less than if the oil price is kept to what is called an "optimum" price (example A). It is believed the optimum price has already been exceeded.

South Asia. To achieve such a feat within the lifetime of nearly one half of the people who are already alive on this planet is a most formidable and intimidating challenge. Even with an immediate and dramatic lowering of the natural increase rates of underdeveloped populous regions, the task will remain of herculean dimensions; without such a reduction in the rate of natural increase, it will simply be impossible.

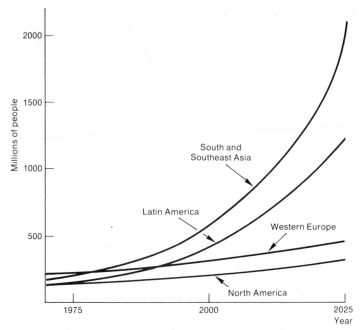

Figure 9–15   Growth of urban populations in towns and cities over 20,000 population.   Urbanization is now proceeding apace in underdeveloped regions. These graphs from the Mesarovic-Pestel regional model show the enormous increase which is expected in South and Southeast Asia, and in Latin America, in the number of urban inhabitants in these regions. Urbanization in Western Europe and in North America has, by contrast, virtually come to a halt.

The Club of Rome met again in April 1976 to determine what course to follow now that (as described in the first chapter) it had successfully stimulated the production of the World 2 and World 3 models, as well as dissemination of the conclusions from their outputs. It decided the next attempt would be to close the gap between the developed and the developing world by a policy of *selected growth.* Such a policy requires developed nations to assist voluntarily in speeding up the development of the rest of the world while curtailing their own further growth. The various actions necessary to implement this policy have already been outlined by a Dutch economist, Jan Tinbergen, and a number of collaborators in a report entitled "Reshaping the International Order." The Club of Rome hopes the Mesarovic-Pestel regional model can be used to prepare scenarios — and thus to test the effects of particular economic policies aimed at this egalitarian objective — before they are implemented. The Club appears to be counting on a generally favorable reaction to its proposals as a result of an exploration over the last few years, by Ervin Laszlo, of social reactions to the implications of the Forrester-Meadows global models.

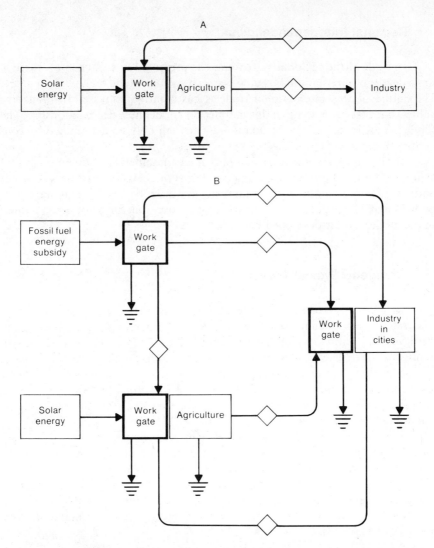

Figure 9–16 Energetics models for developed and underdeveloped countries. In example A is shown the Odum energetics model for a developed country in category A, and in example B the energetics model for an underdeveloped country in category D or E. The manner in which Odum models the basic energetic systems of these two contrasting types of economy is fundamentally the same approach as that used for the preparation of the energetics model developed in Figure 6–11. Diagrams developed from Odum, H. T., 1971.

> Cities accumulate the poor and disadvantaged who find themselves isolated in the central city. Problems of crowding, housing, health care delivery, and antisocial behavior, for example, are intensified in the urban core and are determined or influenced by population processes.
>
> *F. W. Stearns and Tom Montag, 1974*

Regional Interdependencies

In both of the regional system models presented in this chapter, there is some degree of international trading between various of the regions recognized. The nature of this international trade is customarily expressed in monetary values, but costs quantified in this manner do not define a real relationship. The fundamental nature of such trading practices can only be determined by converting these monetary values to energy costs.

H. T. Odum several years ago presented a number of system models that simulated regional international trade in terms of energetic processes. Considerations of energy models of this kind suggest that obstacles to regional development may be partially overcome by compromises that have not been featured in the models so far developed here.

Energetic System Models

In Figure 9—16 the basic energetic systems of two kinds of nations are illustrated by the Odum procedure. Fig. 9—16A presents the system of an underdeveloped nation; it could be in either category D or category E, as described in the first section of this chapter. This nation can produce its own food, provided that its population does not outstrip the amount of available agricultural land. Should it do so, the amount of photosynthetic energy input into the energetic system will be too low (see Fig. 3—7). Malthusian disasters will follow as a consequence.

Figure 9—16B models the energetics of a developed country. If its fossil fuel needs can be met within its own borders, it will represent the situation in a category A nation; otherwise, it will fall into category B.

As modeled on this energy basis, both a category D or E nation and a category A one could theoretically exist as self-contained systems. In practice, this is unlikely; the extent to which they may engage in international trade is explored in Chapter 10.

A California Model

There have been a number of attempts to model single and smaller individual regions. One of the more comprehensive of these is the SPECULATER model of California prepared by a group headed by K. E. F. Watt at the University of California at Davis. The process model for SPECULATER is illustrated in Figure 9—17, and the basic model flow diagram is reproduced in Figure 9—18. As may be seen from these illustrations, SPECULATER relates the rural-urban socioeconomic system of California to that of the rest of the United States. A typical output for a run on this model was shown in Figure 4—13. As was noted in presenting this illustration, SPECULATER can be validated by running it in a simulation mode for the years from 1950 to 1970. In

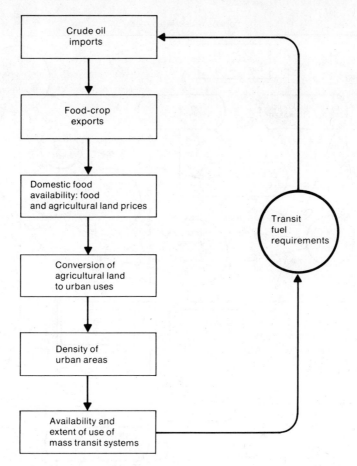

Figure 9–17   The SPECULATER model for California. This regional model, prepared by K. E. F. Watt and his group at the University of California at Davis, is represented by the simplified process model shown in this illustration.

this mode, its output can be checked against historic data points. As the model performed well on these validation tests, it was used in its predictive mode to project behavior of the system through to the end of this millennium. Table 9–3 presents some of the predictive output from this model, selected so as to simplify its examination. The SPECULATER output actually presents a high, medium, and low set of figures. The output entered in Table 9–3 in this specific example records only the run at the medium level.

From Table 9–3, it may be observed that SPECULATER predicts that during this present millennium, California wheat yields will double, as will the price of wheat, and also that of agricultural land. Crude oil demand will double, per capita gasoline demand will increase slightly (Figure 4–13 shows a run of the low value; hence the discrepancy with this medium expectation), and the total population of the United States will rise from 204 to 278 million.

COMPOSITE URBANIZED AREA (CUA)

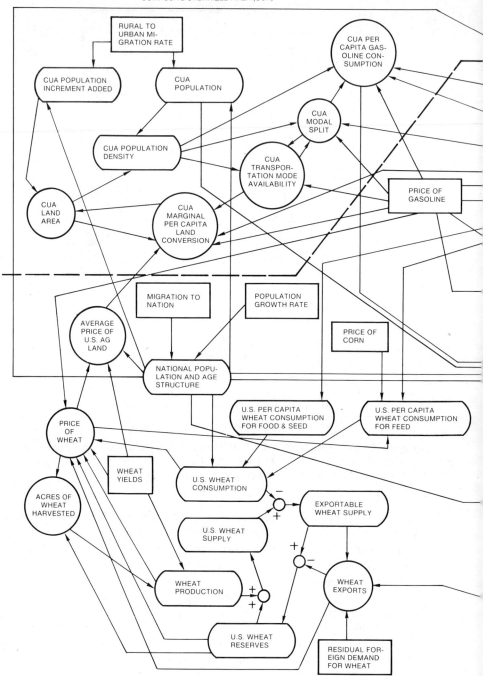

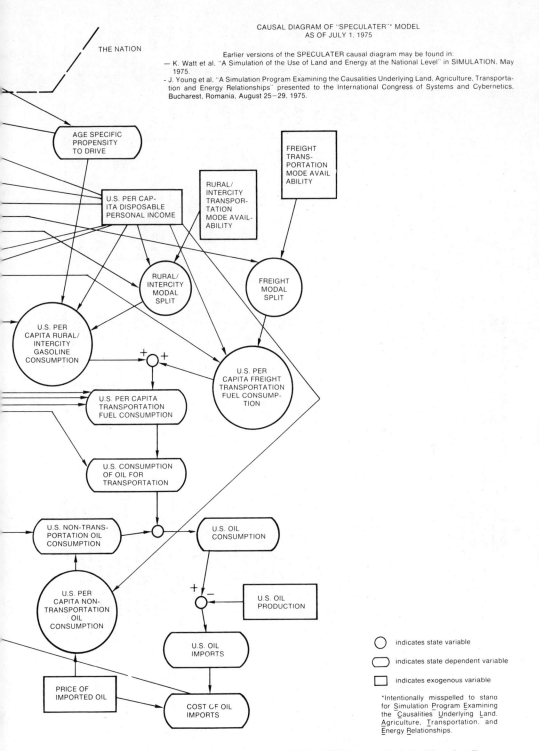

Figure 9–18 Flow diagram for the SPECULATER model of California. Reprinted by permission of K. E. F. Watt and Associates.

Table 9–3   Output from the SPECULATER model for California. The three separate runs for 1975, 1985, and 2000 may be simplistically stated as representing high, low, and median estimates, respectively. All prices shown in the table are in 1967 dollars. Reprinted with the permission of K. E. F. Watt and associates.

	1970	1975			1985			2000		
	All Runs	Run 1	Run 2	Run 3	Run 1	Run 2	Run 3	Run 1	Run 2	Run 3
Conversion rate of agricultural land to urban (acres per person added)	.21	.18	.18	.18	.13	.14	.133	.095	.104	.102
Modal split (percent of trips using public transit)	15.8	15.9	13.3	15.9	19.1	12.3	24.7	20.4	12.6	27.0
Transportation mode availability ratio	.20	.16	.15	.16	.24	.13	.34	.29	.14	.43
Per capita gasoline demand (gallons per capita per year)	300	292	373	292	231	419	163	210	390	145
Acres of wheat harvested (millions of acres)	50.9	75.8	67.3	75.8	78.2	75.1	52.8	84.9	85.2	82.9
Price of agricultural land (dollars per acre)	190	266	206	266	264	234	241	813	431	469
Wheat exports (millions of bushels)	1,093	1,850	1,554	1,850	2,452	2,322	1,263	3,457	3,475	3,353
Population density of C.U.A. (people per square mile)	3,762	3,717	3,717	3,717	3,752	3,740	3,751	4,029	3,980	4,010
Crude oil demand for gasoline (millions of barrels per year)	2,167	2,171	2,776	2,171	1,833	3,324	1,291	2,069	3,840	1,433
Total crude oil demand (millions of barrels per year)	5,461	6,162	6,909	6,162	6,096	8,973	5,553	7,354	13,143	6,718
Crude oil imports (millions of barrels per year)	1,207	2,039	2,786	2,039	699	3,576	156	1,852	7,641	1,216
Cost of crude imports (in billions of 1967 dollars)	2.16	16.84	5.71	16.84	5.77	7.33	1.29	15.30	15.66	10.05
Wheat production (billions of bushels)	1.58	2.62	2.32	2.62	3.27	3.14	2.21	4.47	4.49	4.37
Wheat reserves (millions of bushels)	500	100	100	100	100	100	883	100	100	100
Price of wheat (1967 dollars per bushel)	1.41	5.21	1.53	5.21	2.25	1.49	1.78	4.98	2.97	3.36
Total U.S. population (millions of people)	204	210	210	210	224	224	224	278	278	278

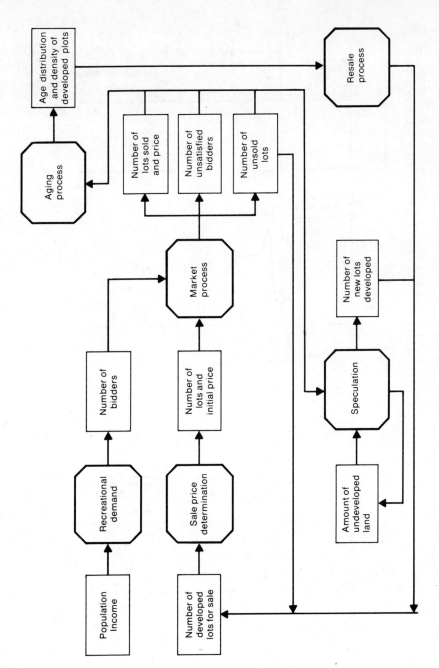

Figure 9–19   Flow diagram for the Holling land resources model. Developed from Holling, C. S., 1969.

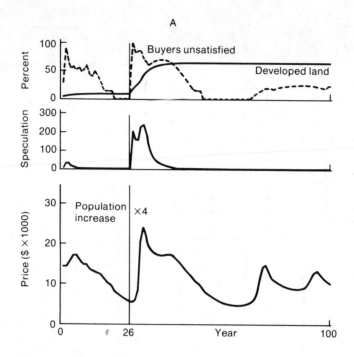

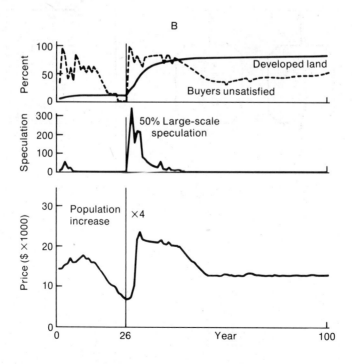

Cost of Recreational Land
in Western Canada

One of the earlier attempts at regional system modeling was an investigation by a group of ecologists, economists, foresters, and planners at the University of British Columbia headed by C. S. Holling to simulate recreational land price fluctuation in the Queen Charlotte group of islands off the Canadian Pacific Coast. These islands are of prime recreational value as increasing demand for such land arises from the expanding urban populations of Seattle, Vancouver, and Victoria.

The process model for this simulation is given in Figure 9–19. A submodel generates annual regional populations by income and family size. These are converted into a population of bidders of varying capacities, representing demands. The supply of recreational land and the demand for it are then incorporated into another submodel that simulates the real estate market process. The output enters a further market submodel that simulates the effects of intensity and duration of use.

The model was operated with stable inputs for 25 years in order to let it settle down; then the system was perturbed to test its stability. The effect of increasing the population fourfold in the 26th year is shown in Figure 9–20A. Land prices rise initially, but soon fall away again as the number of unsatisfied buyers diminishes. Periodically, demand may again approach supply, and prices may again rise for a time, but to a lower peak and for a lesser time.

On the other hand, when the model is run with a sixfold increase in population at the 26th year, the system is unable to recover (Fig. 9–20B). Land prices reach the highest level permitted in the model, and remain at that level for the rest of the run. Insufficient available land remains to return prices to lower values. The same result obtains when large-scale speculators enter the market operation. Land is then only placed on the market when price appreciation provides a certain profit margin.

Other System Models

Reference has already been made to other system models. One referring more specifically to water use in the Central Valley of California was described in the opening chapter. A continuation and expansion of this work by J. W. Skiles will enable more specific answers to be provided as to the nature of further development in the five counties that lie in the lower basin of the Central Valley (Fig. 9–21).

◄ **Figure 9–20 The Holling land resource model.** In example A, this model simulates the effects of a fourfold increase of population in the 26th year of the model run on the dynamics of land acquisition over a 100-year run. Free play of the market still provides for a fall in prices once demand slackens as buyers are satisfied. In example B, there is large-scale speculation in land, and the free play of the market is prevented by releasing land for sale only when prices are high. From *Diversity and Stability in Ecological Systems,* accession number BNL–50175, available from the United States Department of Commerce.

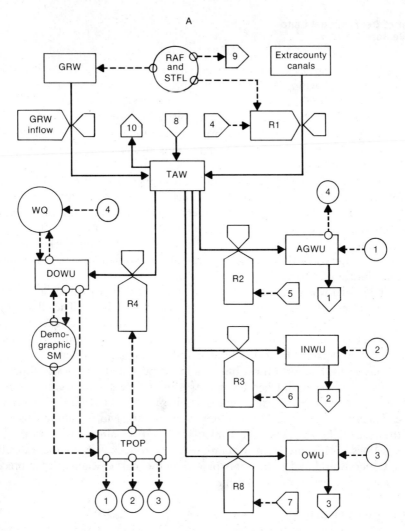

A

Figure 9-21   Skiles model for water use in the lower basin of the San Joaquin Valley. In this flow diagram is charted the relationship between water demand and water use in five counties of the lower basin of the San Joaquin Valley in California. From J. W. Skiles, unpublished work.

The International Biological Program biome models have also been mentioned. Two of these — for the grasslands and the deserts, respectively — have become massive models that require considerable expenditure of funds when they are run. Whether these ecological models are called system dynamics com-

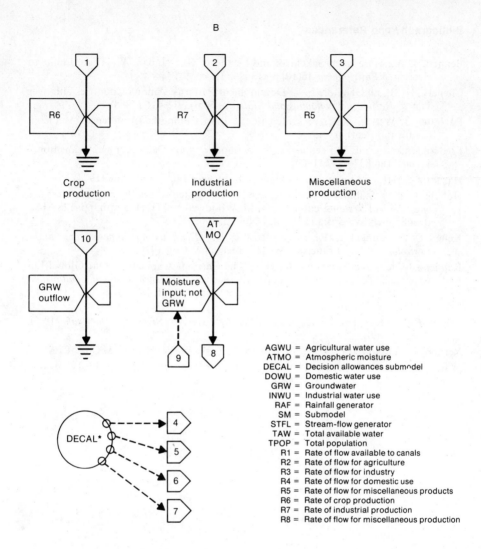

B

Crop production

Industrial production

Miscellaneous production

GRW outflow

AT MO

Moisture input; not GRW

DECAL*

AGWU = Agricultural water use
ATMO = Atmospheric moisture
DECAL = Decision allowances submodel
DOWU = Domestic water use
GRW = Groundwater
INWU = Industrial water use
RAF = Rainfall generator
SM = Submodel
STFL = Stream-flow generator
TAW = Total available water
TPOP = Total population
R1 = Rate of flow available to canals
R2 = Rate of flow for agriculture
R3 = Rate of flow for industry
R4 = Rate of flow for domestic use
R5 = Rate of flow for miscellaneous products
R6 = Rate of crop production
R7 = Rate of industrial production
R8 = Rate of flow for miscellaneous production

*DECAL submodal run separately for each level.

puter models, following Forrester's terminology, or not, this is what they are. Basically, all the regional system models described in this chapter have been prepared by the same methodology which developed World 2 and World 3, and which was described step by step in Chapter 4.

Bibliography and References

Bennett, J. W.; Hasegawa, Sukehiro; and Levine, S. B.   "Japan: Are There Limits to Growth?" *Environment* **15**(10):6−13 (1973).

Chenery, H. B., and Taylor, L.   "Development Patterns: Among Countries and over Time." *Review of Economics and Statistics* **50**(4)391−416 (1968).

Forrester, J. W.   In paper presented to the Joint Computer Conference, Anaheim, California, February 1975.

Frederiksen, Harold.   "Feedbacks in Economic and Demographic Transition." *Science* **166**:837−847 (1969).

Hardin, Garrett.   "Living on a Lifeboat," *Bioscience* **24**(10):561−568 (1974).

Holling, C. S.   "Stability in Ecological and Social Systems." In *Diversity and Stability in Ecological Systems,* edited by G. M. Woodwell and H. H. Smith, pp. 128−141. Brookhaven Symposia in Biology No. 22, 1969.

Kelley, D. R., Stunkel, K. R., and Wescott, R. R.   *The Economic Superpowers and the Environment.* San Francisco: W. H. Freeman & Co., 1976.

Randers, Jørgen, and Meadows, D. H.   "The Carrying Capacity of Our Global Environment: A Look at the Ethical Alternatives." In *Toward Global Equilibrium: Collected Papers,* edited by D. L. Meadows and D. H. Meadows, pp. 315−335, Cambridge: Wright-Allen Press, 1973.

Simpson, David.   "The Dimensions of World Poverty." *Scientific American* **219**(5): 27−35 (1968).

Vernon, Raymond (ed.)   *The Oil Crisis.* New York: W. W. Norton & Co., 1976.

Ward, Barbara.   "An Urban Planet?" *Architectural Forum* **137**(5):30−39 (1972).

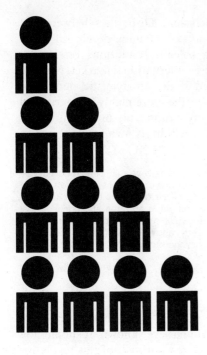

Chapter Ten

Future Socio-economic Systems

The World 2 and World 3 Forrester-Meadows global models were constructed with the declared primary objectives of obtaining an insight into possible limits to growth in the global socioeconomic system, and of studying any identifiable constraints on increase in human populations and their cultural activities. Secondary objectives were the identification and investigation of major influences on the behavior of such human systems, and the nature of the interactions that occurred within them. With these declared objectives, it was considered that it would be possible to observe any specific major trends in current economic and social systems, and to provide an opportunity to change these by political action, if desired, so as to avoid future disequilibrium.

Despite extensive criticism, the chief elements of which have been presented in these pages, there can be no doubt that these Forrester-Meadows models have succeeded in their declared objectives. They have emphasized that exponential growth of human populations and their industries never was more than episodic, and will soon in this latest and twentieth-century episode have to level off at a new asymptote if major disasters are to be avoided. The Forrester-Meadows models have exposed the limits placed by available resources and waste product accumulation on the current exponential growth processes of the world socioeconomic system. They have, however, done far more than this, for they have established system dynamics computer modeling as the best available instrument for the exploration of socioeconomic systems. The authors themselves, moreover, identify one further unplanned result from their models; they emphasize that unless appropriate political action is taken, gaps and inequalities in our heterogeneous world system will continue to increase. The

Mesarovic-Pestel models reinforce this conclusion. Disparities between the haves of the developed nations and the have-nots of the underdeveloped world cannot right themselves simply by passing solemn resolutions on human freedoms and encouraging the interplay of a free international market. Nor can global environmental balance be maintained if the chauvinistic pursuit of isolationist policies becomes the general rule for the more highly industrialized segments of world society. Nor, indeed, can any nation truly prosper if it continues largely to ignore economic heterogeneity within its own borders.

> Either you believe that people collectively are wise and brave and decent enough to take command of their destiny and shape it to their ends, or you shrug and grin and concede that the forces which apportion to us our enjoyment of life, liberty, and the pursuit of happiness have passed beyond our control.
>
> *W. A. Caldwell, 1973*

The opening sentence of the Preface to this text stated that we are in the midst of the greatest social revolution the world has ever known. It should now be apparent that one end result, if not the declared purpose, of this revolution might well be the establishment throughout the world of globally planned socioeconomic systems in balance with the total environment. The various systems-modeling studies described here, and the new methodologies which they have inspired, have revealed both the constraints and the limits upon further socioeconomic growth, and the urgent need to restore the global system and its component parts to a steady-state or dynamic equilibrium condition. This does not mean instant socialism or instant capitalism. The same balanced system can be achieved by several different methods of political control. Nor can it mean an instantly achieved equality between rich and poor, either within a nation or between nations. The second Club of Rome exercise described in Chapter 9 — construction of the Mesarovic-Pestel regional models — presented scenarios of the behavior of regional socioeconomic systems, patently now still at different evolutionary levels, as these adjusted slowly but relentlessly, each to achieve its own environmental equilibrium.

During the present century the world has become more formally divided into two socioeconomic camps. As was described in Chapter 9, one camp, usually considered to contain 31 nations, comprises the elitist world of so-called Western industrialized nations and includes Russia and Japan. The remaining nations, somewhere in the region of 140, depending on how the several political arrangements are reckoned, still languish in a more or less underdeveloped state. During the first part of the century, the elite nations actually governed or — in some less tangible political arrangement — manipulated many of the nations in the other camp, influencing more especially their political and economic development. The international trade system that emerged at this time was basically an exchange of industrial products, produced by the burgeoning industries of the developed world, for basic nonrenewable resources extracted from the mineral reserves of the underdeveloped trading partners.

Historians of the future may well judge the international social revolution that the second half of this century is witnessing to have been the most significant event ever to occur in the evolution of our global social systems. This radical change goes far beyond the political consequences of the end of colonialism and paternalism that heralded the appearance of over 70 newly independent nations. On the economic front, there was a realization by the newly emerging independent nations that they could radically readjust the commercial arrangements between themselves and their highly industrialized trading partners. The first group to organize into a resource cartel were the 13 oil-producing nations forming OPEC (Organization of Petroleum Exporting Countries). As Table 1−3 showed, the monetary results of this new cartel were both immediate and startling. The effects on international trade were modeled in Figure 9−14. The instant and demonstrable success of the OPEC oil cartel in radically improving the terms of one side of this international trade in oil encouraged the formation of cartels in other commodities. In rapid succession, underdeveloped nations having iron ore, bauxite, nickel, tin, copper, and other increasingly scarce mineral resources are starting to group together to form cartels to raise the price of their products in the international market to levels that they consider more appropriate.

> . . . foreign energy, foreign resources, and foreign markets. . . . these are all beginning to change, because the Western economies have been based on a particular economic balance in which they have been taking in very low priced energy and commodities and resources produced in areas where the resources were excess and the labor to extract them was excess, and in the exchange they have sold a monopoly product, namely high technology, beginning with textiles in the 1800's and on through other forms of high technology. . . . and that whole picture now is changing.
>
> *J. W. Forrester, 1975*

The huge monetary balances rapidly accruing to the member nations of these several cartels had two effects, one of which was not immediately grasped by the citizens of the industrialized nations involved in contributing the immense payments to cartel nations. These industrialized nations had so long enjoyed an elitist position in the trading world, which they regarded as the just reward of their own honest endeavors, that it was only slowly and with difficulty that they adjusted to the realization that the international trading balance of power had radically changed. There are now some 1.25 billion world citizens in this elitist industrialized category. Of the 4 billion people in the world in 1974, there remain a further 2 ¾ billion people increasingly aware of the way of life of this elitist minority, and anxious to divert any newly discovered monetary wealth they can lay their hands on toward industrialization and urbanization processes that would bring them at least somewhat closer to receiving the material rewards paralleling those of the elite nations. This underprivileged majority segment of the world's population is, moreover, the one presently showing the largest population increase, both in absolute and in percentage terms, so that its size is likely over the next few decades at least to double. This poses an enormously important question. Can the world system support the rapid conversion of these largely agrarian societies into industrialized, urbanized ones without sustaining irreversible environmental disequilibrium?

A partial answer to this vital question can be derived from a scrutiny of the regional models discussed in Chapter 9. If the underdeveloped world were to remain content — for the present, at least — with labor-intensive rather than capital-intensive agriculture and industries, then a slow socioeconomic evolution might proceed without risk of consequential perturbation exceeding the recovery threshold of the global system.

A bioenergetic plan showing how international trade can assist in this process has been modeled by H. T. Odum.

International Trade and Energetic Systems

Odum modeled national energetic systems, as has already been described (Fig. 1−5). He considers that when the energetic systems of two nations are quite similar — for example, those of two category A nations as defined in Chapter 9, such as Canada and the United States — trade between these countries is not likely to cause domestic disequilibrium. However, should a category A nation such as the United States, say, establish an export food trade with a category D nation, the latter might suffer distress among its peasant food producers, whose labor-intensive mixed farming system cannot compete economically with the capital-intensive monocultures of the developed nation. As Odum states, the cheaper food becomes anywhere in the world, the more the peasant farmer loses ground.

How this situation may be avoided is shown by the Odum energetics system diagram in Figure 10−1. The underdeveloped national system produces a cash crop for export, and with the foreign currency it receives on such sales, it purchases cheap food products from a developed nation for its own consumption. In effect, this means that what has been called here a category D or E nation can, by labor-intensive methods, produce an agricultural commodity it can trade for food from a capital-intensive category A nation. It can do the same with an industrial product produced by labor-intensive methods so long as its labor remains cheap. Politically, the D or E class nation thereby falls into a satellite relationship with its A class trading partner. Moreover, under its labor-

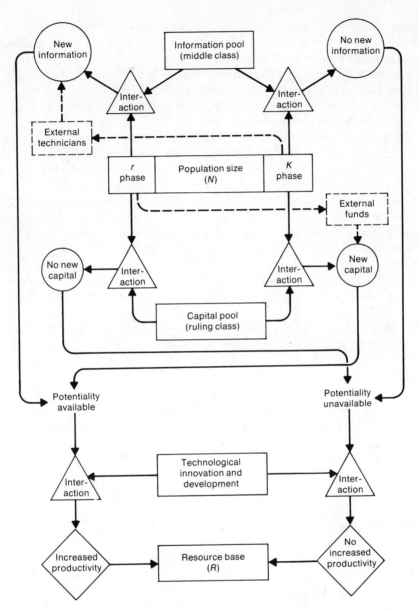

Figure 10–1 Cultural feedback mechanisms and development. A society cannot advance its technology unless it has a middle class with the necessary inventive expertise and a wealthy class to provide the required capital funds. As this diagram illustrates, in the presence of both of these population features, feedback loops then utilize known inventions and innovations to improve technological production capacities and enlarge the resource base. Foreign aid by way of technicians and development capital will adequately supplement indigenous deficiencies in the middle and wealthy classes, respectively. (Reprinted from) Boughey, 1974, with the permission of Gordon and Breach, Science Publishers Ltd.

intensive system, its citizens must work more arduously than those of its capital-intensive system trading partner. This is the price the D or E nation has to pay for development and the steady advancement of the standard of living of its citizens. Odum quotes as an example the trading relationship between the United States (as a category A nation) and Puerto Rico (as a category D nation). Sugar and rum are produced by labor-intensive methods in Puerto Rico, and traded for capital-intensive food products from the United States. As Odum remarks, this was the energetics system patterning colonialism, but political relationships make no difference to the energetics relationship.

Odum proceeds to diagram the energetics relationship when a category A nation (he cites the United States), instead of trading, proffers food aid to a category E nation (he cites India). The energetics of this situation are shown in Figure 10−2. As may be seen, this is not a closed-loop system, and so lacks any positive feedback loop stimulating production in the class E nation such as was contained in the energetics model diagramed in Figure 10−1. Lacking this reinforcement, as Odum remarks, the category E nation develops larger and larger populations with little or no direction of their activities. This is precisely the argument that Garrett Hardin has developed in his lifeboat metaphor, as discussed in Chapter 3.

Odum suggests an alternative energetic system to this and to the satellite capital-intensive/labor-intensive one. It is shown in Figure 10−3. In this relationship a category A nation provides as foreign aid not food but fossil fuel, industrial equipment, and technical know-how. This sets up a category D or E nation in its own independent closed-loop energetic system. The system has already been described by the process model illustrated in Figure 9−16. Odum notes that this kind of aid was supplied by a category A nation (the United States) to Japan after World War II, although Japan even then has to be categorized as a class B nation, not a D or an E. It is the last two categories of nations that normally qualify for this kind of international aid; other categories only fall temporarily into this group after sustaining major disasters.

Energy Supplies

In view of the major role that energy supplies play as a constraint on the development of any national system, it is important to examine the present

Figure 10−2   The bioenergetics of foreign food aid. This process model shows ▶ how H. T. Odum graphically describes a foreign-aid food program. A category A nation provides free or subsidized food for a category E nation, which otherwise would lapse into a famine situation. The bioenergetic system of the food-receiving nation remains open; there is no development such as is inserted, for example, in the system depicted in Figure 10−1. The United States several years ago abandoned this approach to the solution of famine problems in India after writing off a $0.5 billion expenditure on this humanitarian effort. Diagrams developed from Odum, H. T., 1971.

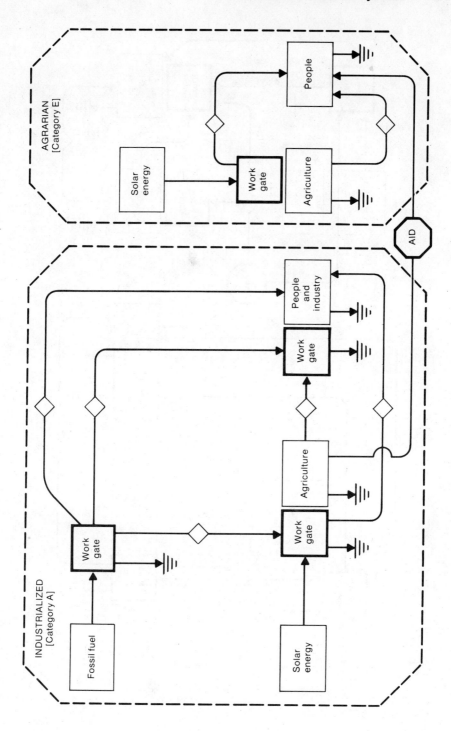

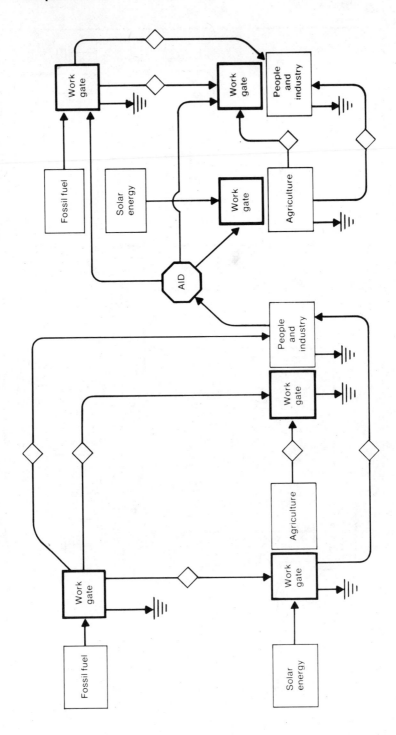

◀ **Figure 10–3 The bioenergetics of foreign technical assistance.** In this process model, H. T. Odum showed how the open system of the recipient society represented in Figure 10–2 could be converted into a closed system with appropriate feedback stimulation. Fossil fuels and technology are supplied from a category A to a category D or E nation. This permits the underdeveloped nation to start its own feedback loop operating between its population needs and the level of its resource base. Diagrams developed from Odum, H. T., 1971.

global sources of energy. Despite current concerns, new energy sources have not yet received major attention. The greatest adventure of our time has been space exploration. Future generations will judge as to the wisdom of our choice and as to the consequences of the preoccupation of the two greatest industrial powers of the twentieth century with this extraterrestrial enterprise. Before this century is over, there is time for one more great adventure. History will rate our present generation very poorly if we fail now to take the initiative. This last supreme challenge is the search for a means of providing a cheap, universal, abundant, and pollution-free form of energy. The favored candidate with realistic research and development prospects within our strictly limited time frame is nuclear fusion power from the deuterium and tritium in seawater. With this plentiful supply of energy for fixed engines, seawater can be electrolyzed to provide hydrogen to power our mobile machines.

The Federal Energy Research and Development Administration (ERDA) has now stated that even under optimal circumstances the United States cannot expect appreciable assistance from new energy sources within the next twenty-five years. Until such assistance is available, the traditional natural gas, petroleum, and coal resources must provide the greater part of the energy the nation requires for its industrial, commercial, and domestic purposes.

Despite increasing costs and various efforts to curtail consumption, by mid-1975 gasoline consumption had exceeded 7 million barrels per day. ERDA estimates that by the year 2,000 the United States may be consuming 165 quadrillion British thermal units of energy, approximately double the 1975 rate. Only crash development of existing sources of petroleum, natural gas, coal, and nuclear power will stave off the socioeconomic breakdown that would result from a general energy shortage during this period.

ERDA has separated the solution of the U.S. energy problem into proximate (the next ten years), mid-term (from there to the end of the millennium), and ultimate (the new millennium and beyond). For the near term it considers increased coal production essential, coupled with the greater residual oil recovery that would result from the stimulus of higher petroleum prices. Also, environmental objections to further development of nuclear power will have to be met in order immediately to restore impetus to this supplementary program.

For the mid-term, the greatest emphasis will be on the gasification and liquefaction of coal, and the extraction of petroleum products from oil shale. Again there are both economic and environmental strictures presently delaying the full-scale realization of plans to increase energy supply in this way.

Present ideas on the ultimate solution for the U.S. energy problem reside especially in the development of fusion power and of solar energy. The hope once placed in fast-breeder fission reactors is diminishing, because of the critical environmental situation presented by the main fuel that is generated, plutonium. In any case, it will be many years before the first effective fast-breeder reactor can be in full production.

As yet ERDA is not proposing anything like the Apollo program, which in ten years, with an expenditure of 25 billion dollars, placed men on the moon. At present, the ultimate plans of ERDA forecast that with the start of the new millennium the United States will have 450 nuclear generating plants, as opposed to the present 55, and 200 solar energy plants. Energy use will be mostly all-electric, 10 to 15 million homes will be solar heated, and 50 million vehicles will be electric powered.

The laser implosion techniques for utilization of fusion power technology are known. Recently, both the laser trigger developments and microballoon implosion processes have been declassified and are open for civilian development. Thanks to fallout from space exploration, so is the utilization of hydrogen as a fuel in vehicles. A rival process to the laser implosion fusion technique, involving the magnetic control of plasma in which fusion of deuterium to helium is induced, has been developed as far as a prototype production unit, Tokamak (Toroidal Kamera Magnetic), by the Russians. A $215 million test reactor of this type is presently under construction at Princeton University. It seems a very small price to pay for the eventual solution of the global energy problem. If all goes well, this test reactor will go into operation early in the 1980 decade, a 500-megawatt demonstration power plant will be constructed in the 1990s, and working fusion power plants will be functioning by the end of the century.

The role of energy as a limiting factor has already been discussed in this chapter and elsewhere in this text. The provision of a universally available, abundant, cheap supply of energy within a generation from now would be the greatest single step forward ever undertaken by industrialized societies. It would improve still further the already enhanced lot of the A and B nations; but if they would provide technical assistance and financial aid to category D and E nations, as the model in Figure 10-1 indicates, thus enabling them to break out of their present restrictive energy cycle, the underdeveloped nations would be enabled to leap forward in one bound into the industrialized mode that they so obviously desire. The energy source cartels in category C would not fare so well, and many would have to replan their economies, but mineral ore cartels might continue for a while. It has been suggested that those energy cartel nations occupying desert areas might change to offering supplies of power obtained from direct solar energy, for they have quite suitable open space over which to spread solar panels.

Abundant cheap energy would permit category A and B nations to recycle and reuse nonrenewable resources as never before, thus freeing remaining unmined reserves about the world for the use of developing nations. Already, category A and B nations have amassed as industrial junk and trash piles more than enough resources to supply their industrial machines for many years on this basis alone. Category D and E nations, however, will have to improvise to build up their stocks by substitution, by extraction of lower grade sources, and by importation. It is the need for these critical resources that will prolong the life of some raw material cartels for some time after the oil cartel has been disbanded.

Even beyond these immediate and immense benefits from the development of a new energy technology, fusion power will finally dispense with the need heavily to pollute the environment in the name of progress. Industrialization can proceed apace without the inevitable cost to the global environment of more irreversible land degradation, more air pollution, more water pollution, and more deaths and sickness imposed on the millions of patient, long-suffering human inhabitants of this planet.

It should be emphasized that the significance of nuclear fusion energy lies in its present uniqueness as an abundant, cheap, nonpolluting energy source. Any other source meeting these requirements would be equally beneficial. The direct entrapment of solar radiation, other than in the photosynthetic process, is a very obvious alternative, but one whose technological development seems more remote than the prospects for the utilization of nuclear fusion power from lighter atomic elements. On a small scale, entrapment of solar radiation is widely favored. The necessary technologies are already known, and their capital cost is not prohibitive. Solar energy use is contained, not energy-producing, and quite pollution free. Perhaps theoretical physics will so expand our understanding of nuclear particles and of plasma behavior that as yet undreamed-of new sources of energy may soon be revealed.

National Heterogeneity

> The slums of San Juan have been built through the efforts of individuals and their families in search of a niche where they may meet the necessities of life and death. . . . the incoming tide brings debris from the harbor (untreated sewage from the city as well as the accumulation of sewage from the slums) into the network of house piles and walkways. To this accumulation is added the garbage of the slum homes.
>
> *A. B. Hollingshead and L. H. Rogler, 1963*

Our world presently constitutes a mosaic of heterogeneous national systems. Modeling of the global system and of the national systems, as has been outlined in this text, identifies some tendencies or constraints that are moving these several systems toward stability, others which move them toward disequilibrium. As has just been described, the nature of the constraints or limits on growth at the national level are beginning to be understood. There remains, however, one major type of socioeconomic heterogeneity that to date has received totally inadequate attention. This is the kind of heterogeneity that exists not between nations but *within* them. No nation, whatever its particular political ideology, is without rich and poor, privileged and underprivileged, haves and have-nots. Just as on an international basis there are category D and E nations living always close to catastrophe, so also in every nation there are deprived citizens struggling to exist but unable to move far from the brink of disaster. The process of urbanization now proceeding apace in category D and E nations is vastly increasing the proportion of deprived citizens in this kind of nation. The term *pueblos jovenes* refers to the slums these newly urbanized poor inhabit; other commonly used names are *bidonvilles, bustees, ranchos, barriadas,* and *favelas.* Class A and B nations have not yet completely eliminated the disparities of living standards that were accentuated when they themselves earlier passed through this phase of intensive urbanization. In their cities, however, the slums are not outlying shanty towns, the *pueblos jovenes,* so much as decaying residential properties in the inner city long abandoned by their prosperous owners, who moved on according to the escalator process of the Burgess zonal hypothesis.

> All too often the movement of migrants from rural to urban areas causes an excessive accumulation of the labour force in marginal service activities, and of families and households in substandard or hastily improvised housing. Nevertheless, judging from the unbroken momentum of urbanization during several decades of the past, even inferior economic and social conditions are rarely a deterrent in this seemingly irreversible movement.
>
> *United Nations, 1972*

The process model shown in Figure 10–4 illustrates this internal heterogeneity within a theoretical national population. It assumes a universal compulsory period of education for all citizens, modified to a greater or lesser extent according to whether the recipient is a member of the elitist or nonelitist class. Social mobility rates between the citizen classes may vary from one national system to another; the social filter may relate to actual ability, as in a meritocracy, or depend on inherited privilege, as in the former caste system in India; but political scientists have failed as yet to identify any national system, or even to construct one in practical terms, that involves no separation of an elitist class from the nonelite masses of the population.

> It is clear that if there were no difficulties or costs of movement of any kind between occupations or locations, that the population would tend to distribute itself in such a way as to make

the total advantages of all occupations and
situations equal. This is the principle which has
been christened the "principle of equal advantage.". . . Potential differences tend to be
eliminated by movement, but if the movement is
impeded by resistances then the potential
differences can persist for long periods or even
indefinitely.

K. E. Boulding, 1968

In this theoretical system model, outlined in Figure 10−4, five categories
of citizens can be identified. Classes 1 and 2 are elitist groups. They are the
wealthy and the professionals who are salaried, self-employed, or just simply
leisured. Groups 3, 4, and 5 are the nonelitist majority, wage earners when
employed, welfare recipients when not. These five classes are similar in many
ways, as already observed, to the national categories defined in Chapter 9 (see
Fig. 9−1). Class 3 citizens are the equivalent of the cartel group; they have a
scarce commodity with which to barter — their occupational services. These are
the garbage collectors, bus drivers, maintenance electricians, coal miners — any
group that can by collective withholding of its labor bring the whole national
economic system or some part of it rapidly to a halt. Class 3 citizens can obtain
high wages and accumulate considerable savings by employing suitable tactics,
but can never make it over to the elitist classes and establish substantial credit
because of their insecurity of job tenure.

. . . in the winter of 1973−74, coal miners
showed a willingness to bring the British
economy to its knees rather than remain near the
bottom of the economic heap. As inflation continues (driven up by the rising cost of raw
materials), pressures from the lower end of the
economic scale seem bound to increase.

P. R. Ehrlich and A. H. Ehrlich, 1974

Category 4 citizens are the main bulk of the working class. They can
negotiate almost continuously for modest adjustments toward a higher living
standard; but lacking the threat capacity of category 3, their monetary rewards
are inevitably lower, insufficient in amount to develop a surplus to transfer to
savings; again, workers in this category are in too insecure a position to obtain
substantial credit. If displaced by technological innovations or disabled, class 4
citizens fall very quickly into class 5. This is the disaster category with no work,
no savings, no possibility of credit. At best, class 5 citizens are almost inevitably
sentenced to an indefinite existence on welfare. There are presently believed to
be about 8 percent of U.S. citizens in this class. Age, misfortune, or a combination of these two can propel individuals from any other group into class 5. So
can sustained periods of inflation such as have recently been experienced in the
United States and in many other nations.

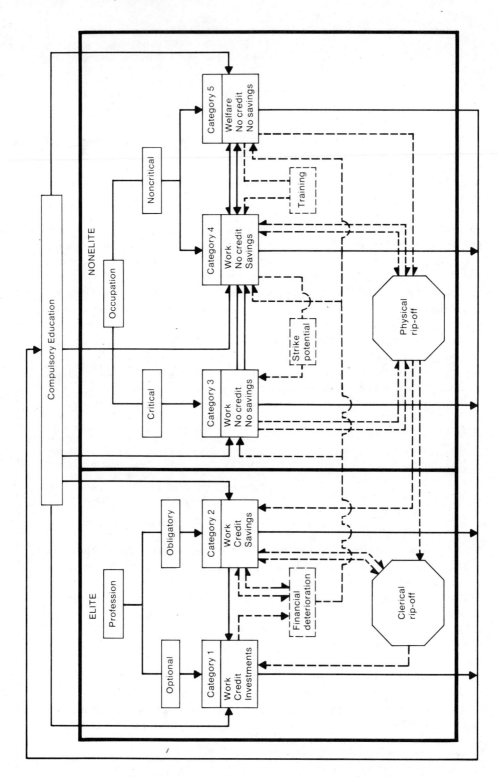

◄**Figure 10-4   Societal heterogeneity.** A diagrammatic representation of the basic and balanced heterogeneity within all existing societies, irrespective of their political nature. The societal categories in this diagram correspond approximately with the national categories represented in Figure 9-1. Social mobility is possible in all of these systems, but may be so slow as to constitute in many instances a social trap. Although juveniles may be forced into the same educational system, they are returned as young adults into the category in which they were born.

Deterrents of various levels of intensity invariably develop to prevent individuals from breaking out of such social traps and thereby threatening system equilibrium. Unlawful procedures thus represent the easiest and quickest way out of this social trap. Categories 3-5 resort to strong-arm measures like robbery, burglary, extortion, and kidnapping; categories 1 and 2 favor fiscal manipulations like embezzlement, forgery, bribery, and fraud.

The main difference between citizen categories 1 and 2 lies in the amount of savings. These can either be inherited or earned. If they are inherited savings, class 1 citizens will not need to learn and to practice a profession. Their savings level as represented by their investments will be sufficiently high to provide them with very extensive credit facilities. Their wealth will exceed the threshold necessary for entry into many profitable enterprises. The savings of category 2 citizens are too small in amount for credit to be based solely on this; their credit derives primarily from their professional standing and the guarantee of continuity of earnings that it implies.

Despite the theoretical absence of constraints on social mobility in the United States, it is very difficult or even impossible for category 3, 4, and 5 citizens to move into the 1 or 2 category if they operate within the conventional constraints of the system. Nor is it very easy for 2s to move over to 1s except by waiting for the accumulation of savings within the collective family holdings of three or four generations. The socioeconomic system modeled here, in fact, operates on the assumption that conventional constraints will *discourage* social mobility. System maintenance is dependent on the general observance of these constraints; that is, without "law and order," stability of the system would be destroyed.

Listen to the younger generation: they don't want equality and regimentation. Listen to working families the length and breadth of Britain: they don't want growing state direction of their lives. Listen to the men and women at work: they don't want to be propped up by subsidies. . . . The charm of Britain has always been the ease with which one can move into the middle class. It has never been simply a matter of income, but of a whole attitude to life. . . .

Margaret Thatcher, 1975

There are two points where deterrents react with these constraints to reinforce law and order and maintain the system. Among the elitist section, the system-maintaining deterrents prevent class 2 citizens from acquiring savings to the point of becoming wealthy and entering class 1 by what may be called antisocial financial methods, that is, by embezzlement and fraud. In U.S. society, for example, class 1 citizens have taken such a poor view of other citizens who attempt to join their privileged ranks in this way that the legal penalties for financial chicanery are quite severe. To have too many people successful at playing the game would soon destroy the elitist social system.

Class 4 citizens can organize in an attempt to move themselves over into category 3, where withholding their services can hold society to ransom. In the United States, some civil servant groups appear to be presently attempting this maneuver by introducing what is known as *collective bargaining* procedures. Local police forces have tried it without too much obvious success; so have schoolteachers. Alternatively, individual class 4 citizens may resort to strong-arm tactics, that is, to attempt acts of robbery, burglary, and theft of all kinds that will increase savings. For category 5 citizens, this is indeed the only way in which they can get off the ground. Deterrents against this kind of system disturbance by class 4 and 5 citizens are thus again severe constraints operating through punishment, as was the case with system-disturbance action on the part of class 1 and 2 citizens.

> The youngsters are privileged, satisfied, content, smug. There's no adventure, rebellion, dissatisfaction in them. They think having a nice personality and good looks is more important than being a good student. They want the diploma but not the learning. They cheat to get good grades. . . . They are regimented and insulated by their parents against war, death and poverty.
>
> *T.V. documentary on a prosperous Middle West suburb*
> — *William Paddock and Paul Paddock, 1967*

There is, however, one way in which class 5 people can be moved into class 4 within the maintenance operational rules of the system, and that is by further training. The cost of such training, unfortunately, can be met only by taxing categories 1, 2, and 3. All resist this taxation. Class 3 citizens do not want to part with any of the higher wages that their unique bargaining power has brought them. Category 2 citizens do not want to give away any of the savings their thrift has accumulated. Category 1 does not want to deplete its wealth and risk falling back into category 2. The usual treatment of category 5 citizens by category 1, 2, and 3 citizens is thus to relegate them to the status of "non-persons" and to try to forget all about them. This is made somewhat easier by the self-effacing attitude usually induced in underprivileged members of any society by *operant conditioning*.

Few people seem to understand that the pattern of tomorrow's city is being formed by today's rapid population growth. Will the city . . . degenerate into a socioeconomic sinkhole for mankind?

Can sprawling shantytowns which make up the cities of Asia, Africa and Latin America evolve into habitable places which provide adequate services so necessary to urban life?

Annabelle Desmond, 1960

Operant Conditioning and Cybernetic Processes

Systems models and operant conditioning have several similarities. Both appear to be logical philosophical approaches to the solution of many socioeconomic problems, and both encounter practical difficulties in application arising from a general apprehension that their adoption implies some measure of authoritarian control of human behavior. This fear of possible infringement upon human freedom is very deep-seated and perhaps more emotional than rational in content. As B. F. Skinner emphasizes, human behavior is never absolutely free; it is the product of interaction between environmental factors and the innate behavior directed by the individual gene bank that every person inherits from the past.

Operant conditioning as conceived by Skinner supposes that if what we do has a desirable outcome, we tend to do it again. We have in fact received *positive reinforcement* for a particular choice of behavioral action. On the other hand, if what we do has an undesirable outcome, we tend not to repeat that behavior. In this second instance we have received *negative reinforcement,* that is, we have been subjected to aversive control of behavior. Natural selection can be thought of as offering the most extreme positive reinforcement in that it permits a system to *survive.* It expresses negative reinforcement by causing a system to go to extinction. Natural selection will lead to the survival of systems whose positive feedback mechanisms permit growth when resource availability is favorable to growth, and whose negative feedback mechanisms produce a steady state when resource limitations demand stability as the price for survival.

As Skinner remarks, we do not like an aversive world which forces people to take actions they do not wish to take because of the penalties involved in not taking the necessary action. Moreover, this kind of aversive coercion produces aggression. In the same way, people do not like a world controlled by the negative feedback of Malthusian disaster. Control by Malthusian disaster likewise tends to produce aggression. If we are to accept Skinner's alternative of behavior modification through positive reinforcement control, then logically we also have to accept a socioeconomic world where system modification is obtained by manipulation of positive feedback mechanisms. There is no alternative to this acceptance other than the painful aversive world of natural selection for survival, with extinction as the ultimate fate of the unsuccessful.

From these last two chapters it will have become apparent that too long an adherence to a doctrine demanding unfettered positive feedback mechanisms may now have carried some societies and some groups within societies beyond the threshold where a change of policy can even at this late hour enable them to avoid aversive punishment.

There is growing evidence from the study of what J. L. M. Dawson has called *biosocial psychology* that human social behavior patterns are very persistent. The growth ethic may be expected to linger for many years in those societies which only recently colonized the territories they now occupy — recently, that is, in historical terms. The present civilizations of the Americas, Australia, and most parts of Africa are recent in this sense. Their societies have been selected for genomes and cultures which interacted to provide for pioneering, establishment, and growth in new environments. While operant conditioning may well quickly modify their cultures to accommodate the dynamic equilibrium of a steady-state economy, patently many millennia must elapse before the effects of the selection for adventurous genomes can be overridden by chance variation and direct negative selection against such exploratory activity.

Until this high enterprise level in both cultures and genomes has been reduced, deterrents to social mobility will continuously produce social stress, and the environmental ethic will never completely be accepted. Older societies, by contrast, suffer less stress from restrictions on social mobility and generally already possess paradigms which conform to an environmental ethic. The older civilizations of Western Europe have occupied their territory for at least several millennia. Without an environmental ethic they would have long since destroyed their home base. If they had not accepted social stratification, their societies would finally have exploded into terminal anarchy.

Unfortunately, the process of urbanization sets off a new round of adventurism in this biosocial psychological sense. The urban environment is new territory for the Third World. Genomes and cultures which interact to maximize enterprise and initiative within this new territory are highly selected. The result is likely to eventuate in the appearance of so different a biosocial animal that A. S. Boughey in 1971 suggested it would merit taxonomic recognition as a new species, *Homo innovatus*. In terms of the social values approved by *H. sapiens*, it would not be a very nice animal. Indeed, the transition period before *H. sapiens* finally becomes extinct may show all the horrid features of an Orwellian world. But in terms of its biosocial adaptation to the urban environment, *H. innovatus* would be *successful;* in a biosocial world successful survival is all that counts. Ideological philosophies are irrelevant unless they have survival values.

The theoretical national socioeconomic system as it is modeled in a very basic way in Figure 10−4 is thus in balance only when constraints on social mobility are operated by one sector of the population against another. Universal education does not automatically generate an egalitarian society. Nor, indeed, does it appear that, given the individual variation in performance and achievement that clearly exists within national populations, any truly egalitarian system can ever be devised. In order to operate any form of social system, constraints have to be imposed in order to prevent the system from rapidly encountering disequilibrium. As numerous specific human societies are known to have survived — in some instances for many centuries — the constraints and feedback mechanisms conventionally recognized by them, together with efficient deterrents discouraging system-disturbing behavior, must often have proved effective. We need now urgently to analyze our own current national systems in dynamic modeling terms, to identify the operative feedback loops, the constraints on growth, and the nature of our conventional behavior. While it presently is impossible to conceive how a completely egalitarian society could be constructed, at least we can attempt to design a system that reduces the privilege gap, that better provides for social mobility without system disequilibrium, and that thus constitutes a true meritocracy with a minimum of temptation to engage in antisocial system-disruptive behavior.

Conclusion

In the Preface it was noted that computer technology has provided an immensely powerful new tool for systems research. This text has described and discussed many aspects of the current applications of this new tool to the exploration of environmental, economic, and social systems. The realization of the full power of computer technology in the *analysis,* and even more importantly in the *manipulation* of systems, has yet to be extensively appreciated. A glance through the current literature will be sufficient to confirm that the application of computer technology to system simulation has been for the most part a theoretical exercise undertaken in and by university groups. Only predictive models have been extensively used to date by industry and commerce, and systems models have scarcely penetrated into the political field. Before they do so it is vital that socioeconomic simulation be recognized as *presenting choices,* not *deciding* them. It would be easy to slip into the error of assuming that Forrester's World 2, or the Meadows' group World 3, models demand a specific course of action. Rather they point up the need for *decisions* as to some appropriate action.

The possible misapplication of systems dynamic and other simulation models of social systems is not so immediately apparent as the misuse, say, of nuclear fission or fusion. Nevertheless the results of such misapplication would be just as real. It is quite clear that in the dynamic equilibrium or steady-state phase into which our global society is now moving, at least in the developed and industrialized world, society will have to conform to various planned restrictions. Some of these have been mentioned in the text, and the implementation of certain of these is extremely urgent. For example, the state of Hawaii has for several years been developing a state plan. It is fortunate in a way that its island situation will facilitate the operation of such a plan if it ever is approved. Hawaii is almost out of further sources of fresh water. Its remaining open space is rapidly being consumed; its food supplies may be jeopardized by the concentration of local agriculture on such export cash crops as pineapple and sugar cane. Vehicles may soon clog its limited highway system and pollute to intolerable limits the air of its major cities.

In the American West, California is attempting to pass a bill through its state senate to prohibit further conversion to other uses of any of its remaining twelve and one-half million acres of prime agricultural land. There is already a law severely restricting further commercial exploitation of coastal lands. Many states are likewise attempting to limit further encroachment upon fertile land or on the recreational and wilderness space within their boundaries.

These are problems of industrialized nations; the majority of the world's population, those who reside in the over one hundred underdeveloped nations, face different problems. As they look to the industrialized nations of the West, they see what they tend to lump together as the Americo-Russian model of centralized, capital-intensive agricultural and industrial production. They look also to the East and see what they call the Chinese model of decentralized, labor-intensive production. They look at their own circumstances and the manner in which they may expect to develop their own nations to provide something better for their own citizens. They realize that they lack the resources to aspire, at least in the near future, to the Americo-Russian model. At the same time they hope for something better for their people than condemning 80 percent of them to serve for all time as laborers in the fields.

It is apparent that it was never the intention of the Forrester-Meadows group to have its global models used as authoritarian instruments to decide the fate of nations. The purpose of the World 3 model, and others like it, is to describe a general global situation and to provide a systems model that will permit the prediction of various scenarios of the future when input variables are changed in specific ways. Such models do not make political decisions for us, as is made clear in this text and in all the literature to which reference is made. Predictive models, whether on a global or a regional basis, merely predict with various degrees of versimilitude the possible outcomes of particular actions. Once cause and effect have been identified, decision-making falls back squarely on to the collective responsibilities of individual decision makers. The Meadows' group considers it unlikely, on the basis of present information — some of which has been presented here — that the current growth phase of the world system can continue for another century. They warn that action must be taken to impose constraints on the system, and that postponement of decisions is in itself a strong action, for every delay brings the world ever closer to its ultimate limits. Earlier in this text reference was made to Kenneth Boulding and the term he coined — *cowboy economics.* This same theme has been continued in the work of Herman Daly, who deplores *growthmania,* an economic policy he considers to embody the philosophy that there is no such thing as enough.

American society over the last two centuries has been characterized by economic growth and social change. There is an increasing feeling in various sectors of American public opinion that growthmania really has gone far enough. It is time for a halt in further material demands upon the environment, and for emphasis instead on what is described in the Meadows World 3 model as service activities, and for some measure of decentralization.

Many people are beginning to decide for themselves that so much is enough. This kind of reaction, which goes far beyond a general and continuing fall in the fertility rate, is registered in numerous and at first seemingly unconnected ways. For example, there is, somewhat surprisingly perhaps, a generally widespread acceptance throughout the United States of a 55 mile per hour highway speed limit. If the people were not generally prepared to conform to this recently lowered limit most of the time, it would be totally unenforceable. There is a widespread lack of enthusiasm for the proferred opportunity for airplanes to travel at Mach 2 or 3, and a willingness to rest content with a mere 600 knots. Concorde and Concordsky are not generally welcome in these United States. There is no immense public demand for reintroduction of the American supersonic aircraft program that was halted several years ago. One of the most remarkable phenomena of recent years has been the extraordinary approval of what can be termed the 'small is beautiful' philosophy that was presented by E. F. Schumacher in his book of this title. In the 200 years of American history there have always been some feelings against excessive centralization of power. Certainly now there is an increasing reaction both against centralized government control and against multinational commercial dictatorships. The present corporate complexity seems to foster indifference to issues of environmental costs and limitations. Patterns of urbanization, with the opportunities they offer for both social and geographical mobility, tend to reinforce this indifference. The same feeling of the need for decentralization is expressed in the book by Catherine Lerza and Michael Jacobson on global food corporations and agribusiness, and in the work cited earlier by Frances Lappé. Because of the existence of these giant food processing corporations, we are forced to consume more preservatives and additives, and less and less actual nourishment. In order to be centrally processed and widely distributed, food has to be mistreated in many ways. It must be held for so long between the farm and the table that it has to be full of preservatives of one kind or another. In order to retain its color, it has to be made redder, yellower, or greener, or somehow dressed up so that it does not appear to be the colorless and lifeless thing it has become. It has to be artificially stiffened and strengthened so that on its many and long journeys it does not totally disintegrate. We even have to be subjected to televised advertisements demonstrating the satisfactory noise that can be made when crunching these artificially colored, flavored, preserved, and stiffened new food substances. There is now in the United States not only an increased favoring of decentralization in agricultural production, but also a decided move towards household and community based urban food production. Such localized production promises better yields and quality, lower food costs and less pollution.

If this current trend towards decentralization continues, and if we return to more local organizations and a greater self-sufficiency, much use can be made of regional systems models. They will provide data as to planning options on which political decisions can be taken. They will also illuminate the extent of interdependence that may be contemplated between one region and another. The world has suddenly become much smaller, and no region can ever be totally independent. Moreover, there will still always be a need for global systems models. It would not otherwise be possible to handle such matters as the urgent need for an international cereal grain reserve. We have an international forum, the United Nations, that can make the necessary political decisions based on predictions made by validated global food production systems models. We may also have to provide, through the United Nations, for a worldwide distribution of some natural resources on a basis of such global systems models. They would encompass not only the utilization of critical elements like tin, copper, iron, and aluminum, but also the legal crop quotas for whales, tuna, herring, and other hunted species. What we must avoid is the use of such global systems models for self-seeking economic purposes. For example, it would be easy for the select multinational car manufacturers to prepare a global model for automobile production, to determine the strategy that would best optimize auto sales, and to harness all the undoubted power of Madison Avenue to influence personal choices so that the variables of the model were manipulated to achieve the desired commercial end. Such an economic maneuver would entirely ignore externalized costs, the increased pollution, the further depletion of fuel and mineral reserves, the choking of transport systems, uncontrollable pressures on recreational facilities, disruption of urban functions, encroachment on agricultural land, and increased pressures on medical facilities. The list extends far beyond these few items that immediately come to mind. This is the real threat of system dynamics and other socioeconomic simulation computer models. They go much further than the econometric models on which commercial development previously relied. The opportunity for manipulation of the behavior of an unsuspecting population is very much greater, as will be apparent after due reflection on the possibilities.

Such matters are of special concern as the system dynamics and other simulation methodologies find increasing application in narrower social domains. Frequently such analyses are commissioned by a client; this narrows their scope, sharpens their objectives, and constantly raises important ethical issues. Some professional modelers may feel that clients may regard them as technocrats, as mere technicians to fashion the procedures for management manipulations. Indeed, in their attitude towards user-client relations in the application of system simulation computer modeling techniques to the solution of specific social problems, some professional modelers may have the attitudes of technocrats.

We live in a world of ever-increasing social complexity and interaction. We are subjected continuously to social pressures that are finally coming to be better understood, but by this very circumstance we are increasingly susceptible to direction by self-seeking manipulators. System simulation models provide a new and immensely powerful tool for the estimation of the action that will achieve specific objectives. The choice of objectives, however, still remains entirely ours unless we permit it to be taken away. It is up to us to decide how we are to use these new instruments, for better or for worse.

There is one other consideration that has emerged from the several global system models as a result of their demonstration of the limits to material growth. This is the circumstance that growth is still acceptable providing it is concentrated in the service sector of the economy. The Meadows World 3 model includes projections of such noncommodity service activities. The United States is the only nation to date to pass the point where a majority of its labor force is engaged in this kind of service activities. These include health service personnel, such as doctors, nurses, home-helps, and paramedics. They include the whole field of entertainment, actors, dancers, musicians, artists, writers, producers, directors, and athletes, an ever-increasing spectator service area. They cover the total spread of educators — the teachers, publishing houses, educational networks, and administrators. The communication industry itself is a service activity, capable of absorbing enormous growth without a vast parallel waste of material reserves or degradation of the environment. An expansion of all such services can lead to what some will regard and accept as great improvements in the standard of living. No longer must this be measured solely in the material criteria registered by the GNP. What form each society elects for its own life-style improvements must be left to its own decision, after it has had appropriate opportunity to examine the estimated consequences of the several available options. For historic reasons alone, apart from any other contributory factors, this choice will always have to vary.

Bibliography and References

Adelman, Irma, and Morris, C. T. "An Anatomy of Income Distribution Patterns in Developing Countries," *Development Digest,* October, 1971.

Boulding, K. E. "An Economist's View of the Manpower Concept." In *Beyond Economics,* by K. E. Boulding, pp. 16—17. Ann Arbor: University of Michigan Press, 1968.

Caldwell, W. A. (ed.). *How to Save Urban America,* p. 1. New York: New American Library, 1973.

Cook, Earl, "Energy Sources for the Future." *The Futurist* 6(4):142—150 (1972).

Daly, H. E. "Toward a Stationary-State Economy," in *The Patient Earth,* edited by John Harte and Robert Socolow. New York: Holt, Rinehart and Winston, 1971, pp. 236—237.

Dawson, J. L. M. "Research and Theoretical Bases of Bio-Social Psychology." Inaugural Lecture from the Chair of Psychology, University of Hong Kong, 1969.

Denman, C. C. "The Function of Rural Small Towns," Paper presented to the Annual Meeting of the American Association for the Advancement of Science, February 20, 1976.*

Desmond, Annabelle. *Population Bulletin* **16**:109—131 (1960).

Frejka, Tomas, *The Future of Population Growth: Alternative Paths to Equilbrium.* New York: John Wiley & Sons, Inc., 1973.

Frey, W. P. "Criminal Justice Systems," Paper presented to the Annual Meeting of the American Association for the Advancement of Science, February 23, 1976.*

Hirsch, G. "Human Services Delivery Systems," Paper presented to the Annual Meeting of the American Association for the Advancement of Science, February 23, 1976.*

Holling, C. S., and Goldbert, M. A. "Ecology and Planning," *Journal of the American Institute of Planners* 37(4):221–30 (1971).

Hollingshead, A. B., and Rogler, L. H. "Attitudes towards Slums and Public Housing in Puerto Rico," in *The Urban Condition,* edited by L. J. Duhl, p. 236. New York: Simon and Schuster, 1963.

Klausner, S. Z. "Thinking Social-Scientifically about Environmental Quality," *Annual of American Academy* 389:1–10 (1970).

Liederman, S. M. "Feasibility and Impact of Urban Food Production—Evidence and Proposals," Paper presented to the Annual Meeting of the American Association for the Advancement of Science, February 18, 1976.*

Lerza, C. and Jacobson, M. (ed.). *Food for People, Not for Profit.* New York: Ballantine Books, 1975.

McGinnis, Robert. "A Stochastic Model of Social Mobility," *American Sociological Review* 33:712–722 (1968).

Paddock, William, and Paddock, Paul. *Famine—1975.* Boston: Little, Brown and Co., 1967.

Picardi, A. "The West African Sahel," Paper presented to the Annual Meeting of the American Association for the Advancement of Science, February 23, 1976.*

Terlecky, N. E. "Measuring Progress toward Social Goals: Some Possibilities at National and Local Levels," *Management Science* 16(12):765–778 (1970).

Thatcher, Margaret. Interview reported in *Time,* February 24, 1975, pp. 30–31.

United Nations. "U.N. Department of Economic and Social Affairs," *Statistical Yearbook, 1971.* New York, 1972.

Van Arsdol, M. D., and Schuerman, L. A. "Redistribution and Assimilation of Ethnic Populations: The Los Angeles Case," *Demography* 8(4):459–480 (1971).

* Official tapes of these lectures are available for purchase; for details write to the American Association for the Advancement of Science.

Glossary

Arithmetic growth. A process of growth in which incremental additions relate solely to the original quantity or number.

Asymptote. The leveling-off value of a logistic curve.

Binary fission. Reproduction in a single-celled organism by the splitting of the mother cell into two identical daughter cells.

Biocides. Chemical substances that inhibit the growth of living organisms.

Bioenergetics. Energy links in living systems.

Biosphere. That portion of the earth in which living systems are located.

Birth rate (crude). The annual number of births occurring in a population per thousand individuals.

Carrying capacity. The total population that can be carried in a particular environment that contains a stated value of a factor limiting the further growth of this population.

Celibacy. Complete abstention from sexual intercourse.

Cohort. Used as a demographic term: a group of individuals of the same age.

Coitus. Culmination of a sexual union by the ejaculation of sperm into the vagina.

Counterintuitive. An eventuality that is radically different than would be deductible from a mental model.

Cybernetic. Applied to an interaction whose direction and rate of progress are governed internally by a feedback loop.

DDT. The first pesticide of the form that is known as a chlorinated hydrocarbon to be produced commercially. Because of its long persistence and detrimental effects on biological systems, its use has now generally been restricted in industrialized societies.

Death rate (crude). The annual number of deaths occurring in a population per thousand individuals.

Deuterium. A radioactive form (isotope) of the element hydrogen of approximately double the atomic weight of the most common hydrogen isotope; widely distributed at low levels in all natural hydrogen compounds, notably in fresh and salt water.

Dynamic equilibrium. A situation where counterbalancing factors controlling the level of a particular entity hold it steady at a given value.

Ecosphere. The portion of the earth that includes the biosphere and all the ecological factors that operate on the living organisms it contains.

Environmental resistance. The factor or factors that operate to reduce the rate of growth in a logistic type of natural increase.

Eutrophication. A successional process in the aquatic populations and communities of natural waters, in which the amount of living matter and of mineral salts slowly increases. In *cultural eutrophication,* man-induced additions accelerate and often divert the successional processes.

Exponential growth. A process in which the total growth process allows for incremental increases on increments, as well as on the original amount or value.

FAO. The Food and Agricultural Organization of the United Nations.

Fecund. Potentially capable of reproduction.

Fecundity. In its demographic meaning, a theoretical statistic representing the total potential human reproduction when cultural factors otherwise limiting this biological quantity are inoperative.

Fertility.   The total quantity of actual human reproduction.

    Cohort fertility.   The individual total fertility of one group (cohort) of women that have passed completely through their fecund life.

    Period fertility.   The summed fertility at any one time of each cohort of women into which the total fecund life has been distributed.

    Postponed fertility.   Potential reproductive capacity whose expression as released fertility has been delayed through the operation of some environmental feedback.

    Replacement fertility.   The figure for the total fertility rate that is necessary to maintain a population at a given level: about 2.1 in industrialized societies.

    Total fertility.   The sum of all the age-specific birthrates for each fecund cohort.

Geometric growth.   A process of growth in which incremental additions relate not only to the original quantity or number, but also to all previous increments.

GNP.   Gross national product, the total value of all the goods and services produced by a nation expressed on a per capita annual basis.

Hysterectomy.   Surgical removal of the uterus or womb.

Inflection point.   The point in a growth curve where a continuous trend is reversed in direction.

Infanticide.   The killing of infants; in this text, as a population control measure.

Iteration.   The process of sequential calculation of a mathematical expression with the insertion of new values derived from the iteration immediately preceding the one being computed.

Laterization.   A soil process as a result of which once workable soil hardens to form a solid, impenetrable pan.

Linear relationship.   A relationship between two variables that when plotted with the value of the one variable on one axis, and of the other on the second axis of a chart, produces a straight line.

Logistic.   In terms of growth, a form of increase that is gradually reduced and finally halted as it approaches some environmental limit.

Model.   A mental, verbal, graphic, or computer program construct that represents the critical features of a real system.

Mortality.   Used as a demographic term: the incidence of death in a given population.

Natality.   Used as a demographic term: the incidence of births in a given population.

Net reproduction rate.   A demographic measure of the mean number of *female* births per female aged 15−44 in a given population adjusted to allow for mortality; a population with a net reproduction rate of 1.0 is *stationary*.

Normative.   A type of process or behavior that represents the norm for a given society.

Nonlinear relationship.   The relationship between two variables such that when the different values of the one variable are plotted on a chart against the corresponding values of the second variable, the line produced is always something other than a straight line.

OPEC.   Organization of Petroleum Exporting Countries. A consortium of sixteen nations including the Arab block, the Middle East, Venezuela, and Indonesia, which have banded together into a monopoly structure to control the world price of petroleum.

Operant conditioning.   The modification of behavior as a result of reward or penalty feedbacks.

Paradigm.   A verbal model accounting for a social behavioral process.

Parturition.   The process of birth.

Pesticide.   A chemical substance inhibiting the growth of a pest.

Petroleum.   A more precise word for crude oil, the natural deposit that contains a mixture of various combustible hydrocarbons including gasoline, kerosene, diesel oil, tar, asphalt, and so forth.

Regression. The mathematical relation expressing the effect of one variable on the numerical value of one or more other variables.

Replacement fertility. The total fertility value that will produce a stationary situation; varies with the mortality rates in a given population. In an industrial population that normally has good medical facilities, replacement fertility is about 2.1. That is, on average, each female in the population needs to produce 2.1 children for that population to maintain a constant size.

Sigmoid curve. A mathematical form of increase that initially is slow, becomes greater, then finally levels off.

Socioeconomic. Applied to social factors affecting populations and economics.

Stable population. A smoothed-out theoretical and calculated population structure derived by projecting the observed population far into the future until all random variations have disappeared.

Stationary population. A population that maintains a given value for its size.

Steady state. An equilibrium condition in a system in which negative and positive feedback is balanced.

System dynamics. A methodology requiring the construction of a mental or written plan of a system incorporating the feedback loops that determine the level of the various rate variables.

Third World. A loose political epithet originally applied to the 120 or so uncommitted underdeveloped nations that did not belong politically either to the capitalist industrialized group of nations or to the Communist planned-economy consortium.

Tritium. A radioactive form (isotope) of the element hydrogen of approximately three times the atomic weight of the most common hydrogen isotope; widely distributed at low levels in all natural hydrogen compounds, notably in fresh and salt water.

Tubal ligation. Prevention of egg release into the uterus, and sperm penetration to the egg, by tying or severance of the Fallopian tubes; thus an effective method of birth control.

Urbanization. The process whereby an urban population very rapidly increases in size, more especially by in-migration from surrounding rural areas.

Vasectomy. Sterilization of males by surgical interruption of the flow of semen along the paired *vas deferens*.

Appendix

```
C*****************************************************************
C
C                                        WRITTEN BY JAY SKILES
C                                                   12-APR-75
C                                        LAST REVISED
C                                                   27-JUL-75
C
C
C   A. S. BOUGHEY
C   J. W. SKILES
C
C
C       ASSIGN DEVICE 6 TO KEYBOARD
C       ASSIGN DISK TO DEVICE 7 (HARD COPY OF OUTPUT)
C
C
C
C
      DIMENSION OUTMIG(51),IYEAR(51),PERMIG(51),UNEMPR(51)
      REAL NETMIG(51),NTOT(51),N(51),NN(51),NJOBS(51),NHOUSE(51),
     CINMIG(51)
      INTEGER REPLY
C
C   INITIALIZE ARRAYS
C
   25 DO 5 I=1,51
      IYEAR(I)=0
      PERMIG(I)=0.
      NETMIG(I)=0.
      N(I)=0.
      NN(I)=0.
      NTOT(I)=0.
      NHOUSE(I)=0.
      NJOBS(I)=0.
      UNEMPR(I)=0.
    5 CONTINUE
C
C   ASK FOR AND ACCEPT INPUT FROM KEYBOARD
C
      WRITE(6,200)
  200 FORMAT(/1X,'ENTER ALL THE FOLLOWING QUANTITIES',
     C/1X,'FOLLOW THE ORDER AND SPACING EXACTLY',/1X,
     C'RIGFHT JUSTIFY',//1X,
     C'BIRTH RATE, DEATH RATE, POPULATION, NO. LEAVING, NO. ENTERING')
      WRITE(6,201)
  201 FORMAT(///1X,'-- -- ------- ----- -----')
      ACCEPT 100,B,D,N(1),TOTOUT,TOTIN
  100 FORMAT(F2.0,2X,F2.0,2X,F7.0,2X,F5.0,2X,F5.0)
      WRITE(6,205)B,D,N(1),TOTOUT,TOTIN
  205 FORMAT(/1X,'INPUTS ARE:',/13X,5F10.0)
      WRITE(6,240)
  240 FORMAT(/1X,'ENTER JOB CONSTANT AND NUMBER OF PEOPLE PER HOUSE',
     C//1X,'-.-- -.--')
      ACCEPT 120,ECON,FOLKS
  120 FORMAT(F4.2,2X,F4.2)
      WRITE(6,245)ECON,FOLKS
  245 FORMAT(/1X,'INPUTS ARE:',/13X,2F10.2)
      WRITE(6,220)
  220 FORMAT(/1X,'ENTER YEARS SIMULATION BEGINS AND ENDS',//1X,
     C '---- ----')
```

```
       ACCEPT 105,IYEAR(1),IENDYR
       WRITE(6,225)IYEAR(1),IENDYR
   225 FORMAT(/1X,'BEGINNING YEAR IS ',I4,' AND THE ENDING YEAR IS  ',
      C I4)
       WRITE(7,300)ECON,FOLKS
   105 FORMAT(I4,2X,I4)
       WRITE(7,225)IYEAR(1),IENDYR
       I=1
C
C   CALCULATE TABLE
C
    10 R=(B-D)/1000.
       NN(I)=N(I)+(N(I)*R)
       OUTMIG(I)=TOTOUT
       INMIG(I)=TOTIN
       NETMIG(I)=TOTIN-TOTOUT
       NJOBS(I)=NETMIG(I)/ECON
       NHOUSE(I)=NETMIG(I)/FOLKS
       NTOT(I)=NN(I)+NETMIG(I)
       PERMIG(I)=(NETMIG(I)/NN(I))*100.
       N(I+1)=NTOT(I)
       HOLD=(NTOT(I)-OUTMIG(I))/ECON
       OUT=NTOT(I)/ECON
       ARATE=HOLD/OUT
       UNEMPR(I+1)=(1-ARATE)*100.
       I=I+1
       IYEAR(I)=IYEAR(1)+(I-1)
       IF(IYEAR(I) .EQ. IENDYR+1)GO TO 15
       IF(IYEAR(I) .LT. 1960)GO TO 400
       IF(IYEAR(I) .LT. 1970)GO TO 500
       B=B*0.95
       TOTIN=TOTIN-3750.
       GO TO 10
   400 B=B*1.15
       D=D-0.1
       TOTOUT=TOTOUT+500.
       TOTIN=TOTIN+5500.
       GO TO 10
   500 TOTIN=TOTIN-2500.
       GO TO 10
C
C   PRINT TABLE HEADINGS
C
    15 WRITE(6,250)
       WRITE(7,250)
       WRITE(6,210)
       WRITE(7,210)
   210 FORMAT(1X,'YEAR',2X,'POPULATION',2X,'+NAT. INC.',2X,'POPULATION',
      C2X,'MIGRANTS',2X,'MIGRANTS',2X,'MIGRANTS',2X,'UNEMPLOYED',2X,
      C 'REQUIRED',2X,'REQUIRED',8X,'YEAR')
C
C   PRINT TABLE
C
       ISPAN=IENDYR-IYEAR(1)+1
       DO 20 I=1,ISPAN
       WRITE(6,215)IYEAR(I),N(I),NN(I),NTOT(I),OUTMIG(I),INMIG(I),
      CPERMIG(I),UNEMPR(I),NJOBS(I),NHOUSE(I),IYEAR(I)
       WRITE(7,215)IYEAR(I),N(I),NN(I),NTOT(I),OUTMIG(I),INMIG(I),
      CPERMIG(I),UNEMPR(I),NJOBS(I),NHOUSE(I),IYEAR(I)
    20 CONTINUE
```

```
  215 FORMAT(1X,I4,3(2X,F10.0),4X,F6.0,4X,F6.0,6X,F4.1,8X,F4.1,
     C 4X,F6.0,4X,F6.0,8X,I4)
C
C   QUIT OR RECYCLE?
C
      WRITE(6,230)
  230 FORMAT(///1X,'ENTER ''1'' TO RESTART PROGRAM',/1X,
     C'HIT RETURN TO TERMINATE EXECUTION',//1X,'-')
      ACCEPT 110,REPLY
  110 FORMAT(A1)
      IF(REPLY .EQ. 1H1)GO TO 25
  250 FORMAT(///1X,18X,'POPULATION',2X,'TOTAL',7X,'OUT',7X,'IN',
     C 8X,'%NET',6X,'PERCENT',5X,'NEW JOBS',2X,'HOUSING STARTS')
  300 FORMAT(/1X,'PEOPLE SUPPORTED BY EACH JOB HOLDER (INCLUSIVE)',
     C' = ',F4.2,/1X,
     C 'NUMBER OF PEOPLE PER DWELLING = ',F4.2)
      CALL EXIT
      END
```

Author Index

(Italicized page numbers indicate the full citation of references.)

Subject Index

Agrarian societies, 143–145, 151, 174–195, 210–219
Agricultural production, 42–45, 125–127
Arable land, 43–45
Arithmetic growth, 3, 21–23
Auxiliary energy, 47–50, 133

Bedroom versus boardroom, 1–2, 163–164
Bioenergetics, 47, 133, 212, 214–217
Births, 25–30
Birth control, 131
Birth rates, 139
Burgess' zonal hypothesis, 6
Business cycles, 102–104

Capital intensive systems, 133, 214
Carrying capacity, 11–13, 38–39, 107–112
Catastrophe theory, 85
Categories of nations, 174–195
Categories of social subgroups, 219–224
Chromium, 56, 59–60
City decline, 138
Club of Rome, 210
Compound interactions, 89–91
Computer models, 69, 77–86, 92–95, 237–239
Cowboy economics, 40
Cultural controls, 110
Cybernetic processes, 225

DDT, 61–64
Deaths, 25–30, 191–192
Death rates, 108, 121, 142
Delayed responses. See Time lags
Demographic transition, 174
Desertification, 111
Desired fertility, 131, 142
Deterministic models, 69, 81, 85
Detritus ecosystems, 15
Deuterium, 218
Differentiation, 185
Doubling times, 24
Dynamo, 77

Economic growth, 39–41
Ecological models, 15
Energetics relationships, 16–17, 47–49, 197, 212–219
Energy resources, 47–52
Environmental degradation, 2–3, 34, 111–112
Environmental resistance, 39

ERDA (Federal Energy Research and Development Administration), 217–218
Exponential growth, 17–18, 21–35
Exponential reserve life index, 54

Feedback loops, 25–26, 61, 74–75, 163–164, 182–183, 213–214, 225–226
Fertility, 139–151
  cohort, 141, 146–147, 182–183
  period, 141, 146
  postponed, 145–151
  realized (released), 146, 151
  total, 150
Fission processes, 218–219
Flow charts, 11, 77
Flow diagrams, 17, 73–76, 206–207, 213
Food production, 42–45, 121
Foreign aid, 184, 194, 217
Fourth World, 176
Fusion processes, 218–219
Future socioeconomic systems, 209–230

Geometric growth, 3, 22
Global equilibrium, 161–170
Global models, 7
Grain reserves, 182
Grain yields, 129
Graphic models, 69–70, 97–102
Green Revolution, 44
GNP (Gross National Product), 31–34, 39–41, 47, 191, 231

Industrial growth, 30–34, 132
Industrialization, 47–52, 174
Industrialized societies, 145–147, 151, 174, 210–219
Infanticide, 143
Input variables, 76, 84, 166
Intrinsic rate of natural increase, 28
Invention and innovation, 117–134

Kern County, 9–13
Kondratieff cycle, 102, 104
Kuznets cycle, 102, 104

Labor intensive systems, 133, 214
Land degradation, 132
Land use planning, 1–2, 228
Lead, 56, 60
Lifeboat metaphor, 182, 186–187
Life expectancy, 139
Linear interactions, 68–72